IMMIGRANTS AND THE INFORMAL ECONOMY IN SOUTHERN EUROPE

Books of Related Interest

The Politics of Immigration in Western Europe
Martin Baldwin-Edwards and Martin A Schain (eds.)

Southern European Welfare States
Between Crisis and Reform
Martin Rhodes (ed.)

Crisis and Transition in Italian Politics
Martin Rhodes and Martin Bull (eds.)

The Euro-Mediterranean Partnership
Political and Economic Perspectives
Richard Gillespie (ed.)

The State in Western Europe
Retreat or Redefinition
Wolfgang C. Müller and Vincent Wright

Immigrants and the Informal Economy in Southern Europe

Editors

Martin Baldwin-Edwards
Joaquin Arango

FRANK CASS
LONDON • PORTLAND, OR

First published in 1999 in Great Britain by
FRANK CASS PUBLISHERS
Newbury House, 900 Eastern Avenue, London IG2 7HH

and in the United States of America by
FRANK CASS PUBLISHERS
c/o ISBS
5804 N.E. Hassalo Street
Portland, OR 97213-3644

Website www.frankcass.com

British Library Cataloguing in Publication Data

Immigrants and the Informal economy in Southern Europe
1. Europe, Southern – Emigration and immigration 2. Europe, Southern – Economic conditions
I. Baldwin-Edwards, Martin II. Arango, Joaquin
304.8'4

ISBN 0 7146 4925 2 (cloth)
ISBN 0 7146 4484 6 (paper)

Library of Congress Cataloging-in-Publication Data:

Immigrants and the informal economy in Southern Europe / editors, Martin Baldwin-Edwards, Joaquin Arango.
p. cm.
ISBN 0-7146-4925-2 (alk. paper). – ISBN 0-7146-4484-6 (pbk. : alk. paper)
1. Europe, Southern–Emigration and immigration–Economic aspects.
2. Europe, Southern–Emigration and immigration–Government policy.
3. Immigrants–Europe, Southern. 4. Alien labor–Europe, Southern.
5. Illegal aliens–Europe, Southern. 6. Informal sector (Economics)–Europe, Southern. I. Baldwin-Edwards, Martin, 1956- II. Arango, Joaquin.
Jv7590.I463 1999
331.6'2'094–dc21 99-30821
CIP

This group of studies first appeared in a Special Issue on 'Immigrants and the Informal Economy in Southern Europe' of *South European Society & Politics,* 3/3 (Winter 1998) ISSN 1360-8746, published by Frank Cass.

Printed in Great Britain by
Antony Rowe Ltd., Chippenham, Wilts.

Contents

Where Free Markets Reign: Aliens in the Twilight Zone

MARTIN BALDWIN-EDWARDS

It is now more than a decade since Gildas Simon pointed out, in the first major study of immigration into southern Europe, that there were an estimated 2 million aliens in the region – predominantly clandestine, with a wide range of nationalities and explicitly connected with the growing underground economy (Simon 1987:287). He also noted the paucity of national policies to deal with these matters. A year later, a major study was commissioned by the EC and undertaken by ISOPLAN. Their study considered the figure for 1988 to be more like 3 million immigrants across southern Europe, and in its wealth of detail it provided much-needed data necessary for even the beginnings of analysis. In their concluding section (CEC 1991:113-129) they construct several scenarios, making a forecast (based on extrapolation from the late 1980s) that by 2000 there would be 2 million legal and an equal number of clandestine extra-EU immigrants resident in southern Europe.

Much has happened since these early writings. The collapse of the East European regimes has led to migratory flows – most notably from Albania into Greece and Italy. The flow of Kurds from Turkey and Iraq continues in fits and starts, whilst regional conflicts in Africa and elsewhere have provided other unwilling migrants. We have not even mentioned Yugoslavia... . Yet, even with these unexpected sources of emigration, it appears that the total number of non-EU immigrants across southern Europe is under 3 million and unlikely to increase significantly in the near future.

It is our aim in this volume to make an interim assessment of the evolution of the immigration phenomenon, along with a comparative analysis of how southern European governments have so far responded, and the results of such responses.

I should like to thank Russell King for providing access to unpublished information, much needed in this still under-researched area.

TOWARDS A MODEL OF SOUTHERN EUROPEAN INTEGRATION

A casual observer might expect that the immigration phenomenon in southern Europe would be broadly analogous to that previously observed in the North. One could hardly be more wrong! In fact, the case can be made that adoption of restrictive immigration practices via the EU and Schengen (see Baldwin-Edwards 1997) has been a major cause of 'wrong' policy in southern Europe – at odds with domestic economic needs and socio-political tendencies. Worse, as we shall see, that such imported policies may have been counter-productive by substituting illegal immigration for legally controlled flows. Of course, none of the countries under study had any immigration infrastructure at the start of mass immigration flows; thus we are faced with a counterfactual problem of what each country *might* have done in the absence of European integration.

Turning to the specificities of immigration patterns into southern Europe, we can identify several characteristics, as shown in Table 1.

TABLE 1

COMPARISON OF IMMIGRATION CHARACTERISTICS IN SOUTHERN AND NORTHERN EUROPE

SOUTHERN EUROPE	**NORTHERN EUROPE**
numerous diverse nationalities	specific [few] nationalities
diverse educational levels	predominantly lower educational levels
general illegality [of entry, residence and/or work]	general legality [except in France]
employment recruitment by private illegal 'brokers'	employment recruitment by state agencies
illegal trafficking by private agents	little trafficking
high absorption by the informal economy	incorporation into formal economy
bi/multi-lateral treaty for expulsion arrangements	bilateral treaty gives legal protection
often no social and few legal rights	equality with nationals or specific legal base

Thus we can see that there is little obvious comparison between the new immigration and the traditional *Gastarbeiter* recruitment or post-colonial flows.[1] Whereas the migrants to northern Europe were either recruited or condoned by the state, and entered regular employment with substantial legal protection, this is far from the case in southern Europe. Despite the lack of official recruitment, immigrants into southern European countries seem to occupy jobs which would not otherwise be filled by natives (Malheiros, Veiga, Reyneri (this volume); Iosifides

1997). This is despite high or even very high unemployment rates in all but Portugal. The range of nationalities is extraordinarily wide, especially in Italy (see Zincone, this volume), as is the level of education. Vastly different levels of education are observed, with some national groups such as Filipina with a rate of around 50 per cent university-educated (Iosifides 1997:34) whilst others, such as Albanians, are predominantly unskilled or semi-skilled. Gender specialization too is evident, although relatively understudied (Chell 1997; Baldwin-Edwards and Safilios-Rothschild 1999).

Why should this have occurred? To some extent, we can advance a simple geographical explanation (supplemented by southern countries' relatively weak immigration controls, at least in the 1980s): thus Albanians choose Greece and Italy as destinations, partly through proximity and partly for ease of return (**pendle** migration). Other factors suggested (e.g. King 1998) include the diversion effect of closed northern European borders; colonial links; and demographic 'push', from North Africa, for example.

Whereas these explanations seem at least plausible, the most important factor without doubt is the attraction of large underground economies capable of supporting – even requiring – the employment of immigrant labour. A convincing explanatory model is provided by King *et al.* (1997:10) who identify three preconditions more or less specific to southern Europe.

These three preconditions are: the co-existence of high and low-productivity sectors, partially corresponding with the urban-rural division; the rapid transfer of indigenous workers from high to low productivity sectors, often through internal migration; and a rapid decline in the rural population in the 1970s and later. Following on from these, a three stage model is developed. In the first phase (1950s to 1970s), excess labour supply and weak unions allowed low wages and high capital accumulation; in phase 2 (1970s to 1980s), a reduced labour supply and a massive shift to high productivity sectors led to higher wages and lower capital accumulation. In the final phase (1980s to date), unemployment increases as reduced investment coincides with recession. However, the indigenous population prefers unemployment (or more time spent in education) to low wages, leaving excess demand for labour in the low-productivity sectors. These economic sectors cannot raise wages, or they will become internationally uncompetitive, therefore their very survival depends on the work of (often illegal) immigrant labour.

Finally, we should not ignore the role of increased globalization of markets. International transport and communication have lower costs, the flows of goods, services and capital have vastly increased with correspondingly more open borders. Except, supposedly, for people. In reality, all four countries are heavily dependent on tourism: this alone is sufficient to create a problem for the implementation of a tight immigration policy. In addition, the coastal and mountainous borders are quite impossible to police effectively for Spain, Italy and Greece: thus spontaneous illegal entrants, along with 'trafficked' migrants, are numerous. A new problem observed in the 1990s is trafficking (Salt and Stein 1997) and related forced prostitution (IOM 1995). Although not confined to southern Europe, it is nevertheless significant for the region; Campani (this volume) examines its European evolution and specifically the Italian case, concluding that the trafficking of women for prostitution has arisen directly from the globalization phenomenon.

FORMS OF ILLEGALITY

Illegality is always defined with reference to legality, which may or may not be appropriate in certain circumstances. Owing to policy deficit in all four countries, illegal immigration and employment themselves became almost a norm in the 1980s. As Jahn and Straubhaar (this volume) comment, southern European countries do not so much need immigration policies as policies to deal with illegal immigration.

As shown by Jahn and Straubhaar (Figure 1, their article), there are three routes by which immigrants can arrive in the clandestine economy. The first is simply through illegal entry to national territory – a straightforward illegal immigrant. The second is by means of legal entry (e.g. with a tourist visa, or applying for political asylum) and subsequent illegal residence; the third, which seems to be more common in southern European countries than in northern, is illegal working whilst technically legally resident. For all three forms, however, work is necessarily in the underground economy. Given the large extent, and strong traditions, of the informal sector in these countries (see below), immigrants have found it relatively easy to find work. The work is almost always badly paid, unskilled and precarious – characteristics of the secondary labour market (Veiga, this volume).

The Informal Economy

The underground economy (encompassing the whole range of illegal activities, therefore wider than just the informal sector: see Feige 1990) has, it seems, been expanding in almost all European countries. A European Commission Report of 1990 concluded that in most northern European countries (except France and Belgium) the 'black economy' was about 5 per cent of declared work, compared with 10–20 per cent in southern countries (CEC 1991). A more recent survey by Censis in Italy produced the following data, shown in Table 2.

TABLE 2

ESTIMATED UNDERGROUND ECONOMY AS PERCENTAGE OF GDP

Greece	29.0
Italy	27.3
Spain	23.1
Belgium	22.4
Switzerland	19.8
Denmark	17.6
Ireland	16.1
Germany	15.0
France	14.3
Netherlands	13.6
UK	13.0
Austria	8.9
Finland	2.0

Source: *Corriere della Sera*, 17 June 1998

These figures are roughly in accord with almost all estimates for the southern European countries, but higher than might be expected for others – such as Switzerland, Denmark and Germany. However (with the usual caveat of doubting macroeconomic estimates), there is no reason to assume identical causal patterns or comparable consequences of informal activities in different settings.

Three forms of informality have been identified by Portes *et al.* (1989): labelled *survival, dependent exploitation,* and *growth*. 'Survival' is a subsistence strategy of the individual or household through direct production or market sale of goods or services. 'Dependent exploitation' identifies the strategy of increasing managerial flexibility and decreasing labour costs through informal hiring and subcontracting. 'Growth' is explicitly a strategy for capital accumulation by small firms, using connections, greater flexibility and lower costs.

As Portes (1994) points out, these three types are not mutually exclusive. Thus the survival strategy of illegal immigrants is utilized as flexibility by the firm which hires them; or a small firm may be successful enough to launch into a new path of increased growth and legality. The 'survival' strategy is known to us from the Third World; however, these latter two are specific to capitalism – whether derived from classical forms or a new form of exploitation in advanced capitalism.

Williams and Windebank (1995) in an innovative article, propose a fourfold typology of 'black economy' activity along two axes of high and low activity, and 'exploitative' versus 'autonomous'. They identify most areas in southern Europe as being of Type 1 – exploitative and high level activity. The characteristics associated with this type are:

- a relatively deprived population,
- a preponderance of small firms with cost-cutting strategy for survival,
- high tax and social insurance contribution levels,
- social norms conducive to acceptance of illegal work,
- dense social networks,
- a broad socio-economic mix,
- relatively low education levels,
- poor access to permanent state benefits,
- lax enforcement of regulations.

Specifically, they point to north-eastern and southern Italy (Mingione 1991); Andalucia, Sabadell, Valdencia and Alicante (Lobo 1990; Benton 1990); and all of Greece (e.g. Leontidou 1993) as examples.

Type 2, consisting of high illegal activity but of a more autonomous kind, is distinct from Type 1 in that it is associated with an industrial structure using technological innovation, relatively affluent with low unemployment, and sometimes lax enforcement of laws. They identify the North-west of Italy (Mingione 1991) and the area around Madrid (Benton 1990) as good examples of this type.

Thus Williams and Windebank make the point that the black economy has a hierarchy of its own, as segmented perhaps as the formal economy. There exists a 'core' workforce of skilled workers who benefit from weak regulation as much as their employers, alongside a 'peripheral' workforce who accept their employers' terms. Furthermore, they suggest that any assessment of the claim of exploitative work in peripheral regions (e.g. southern Europe) can be made only on the basis of empirical work - which until now has been almost entirely absent.

Finally, we should note the distinction made by Portes (1994:433), citing Lomnitz, between a sociological approach to informal activity and the neo-classical:

> The degree of formality and the inability of the formal system to satisfy societal needs gives rise to informal solutions. If the formal system is able to produce and distribute the goods and services required by all members of society, informal solutions would be less needed and thus less pervasive.

This he contrasts with the neo-classical view, where interference with free markets will automatically give rise to alternative solutions – allegedly contradicted by north-eastern European economies.[2] Thus, according to Portes, the marketization of the state does not so much represent the triumph of the informal sector as the elimination of the distinction between the two sectors. In the absence of regulation, capitalist development cannot occur because long-term productive investment becomes a near-impossibility (Portes 1994:432). Nevertheless, we might observe that to all intents and purposes, the underground economy (our 'twilight zone') obeys the crude laws of supply and demand – in the short run, at least, it is a free market zone.

Immigrants in the Informal Economy

Across southern Europe, there is a common pattern – with some national and regional variations – of immigrant insertion in the labour market. The sectors occupied by immigrants are predominantly construction, agriculture, domestic service, tourism and catering, factory work and street-hawking. Other opportunities do exist, but are numerically unimportant.

Construction. This sector has taken off dramatically over the last decade. As Malheiros (this volume, Table 2) shows, the increase in Portugal of employment of immigrants in the sector has been large, but starting from a low base. By 1996, construction represented just under 50 per cent of legal employment of aliens, with an additional estimated comparable number in clandestine employment. Veiga (this volume) notes the massive increased employment of illegal immigrants in Spain, owing to restructuring of the industry into effectively primary and secondary sectors. The workers are always male, and with certain nationalities dominant: in Portugal, Cape Verdeans; in Greece, Albanians; in Italy and Spain, several nationalities from North Africa and eastern Europe – particularly Moroccans and Poles.

Agriculture. This sector needs seasonal labour, for heavy and demanding work over a brief period. Owing to its low productivity level, wages are not high and the indigenous population is not sufficiently interested to satisfy labour demand at harvest time. In the case of Spain, Veiga suggests that this is the employment in which most nationalities – but not most immigrants – are engaged. This is the only sector where immigrants are found consistently to be working alongside natives, although the temporary nature of such employment seems to label the sector as secondary and unlikely to be attractive to indigenous labour.

The work is almost exclusively carried out by male immigrants; again there is concentration of certain nationalities – Albanians in Greece, Moroccans, Ghanaians and Gambians in Italy, and a diverse range in Spain including Moroccans, Algerians, Portuguese, some African, Latin American and East Europeans. The important point is that immigrants constitute a reserve army of labour, and may well be un- or under-employed for the rest of the year: some policy considerations may flow from that fact.

Domestic service. This is almost exclusively female employment and a large amount of it is 'live-in', which employment is no longer attractive to any southern European country's native women. The number of women employed is very large; the women tend to be from the Philippines, with a large presence of South Americans in Portugal, Spain and Italy (King 1998). The work is secure – unlike almost all other forms of employment for immigrants – but carries its own set of problems, such as unlimited working hours. The 'live-out' form of employment is still attractive to native workers, and there is considerable competition between immigrants and natives for these jobs (for Greece, see Markova and Sarris 1997).

Tourism and catering. These are illegal, unskilled and low pay jobs in such activities as washing-up, cleaning and unskilled maintenance; relatively little research has been done on this sector, probably because of its diverse and often specific nature.

Factory work. This is relatively rare, but some heavy industry in industrialized Spain or northern Italy does employ immigrants – more commonly as legal employees. In Greece, some specific industries, such as fish-farming and flower-growing, have noted their absolute reliance on immigrant workers (Baldwin-Edwards and Safilios-Rothschild 1999). Such work seems to be complementary to that of the indigenous workforce, enabling the latter to advance into cleaner and better-paid jobs.

Street-hawking and self-employment. A wide range of activities is included under this heading (including prostitution), but it seems to be dominated by specific nationalities – Egyptians in Athens (Iosifides 1997), Maghrebi and Senegalese in Spanish and Italian cities (King *et al.* 1997), Bangladeshi in Rome (Knights 1997). 'Ethnic entrepreneurship' appears to have had some successful in Italy and Spain, where King *et al.* cite the rise of Latin American shopkeepers in Madrid, or Iranian carpet-sellers in Italy. In general, it seems more to be a subsistence level occupation for the vast majority of immigrants engaged in it.

POLICY RESPONSES

Until the 1980s, in the cases of Spain and Italy, and the 1990s for Greece and Portugal, the immigration controls in all four countries dated back to before the Second World War. The first policy initiatives in the region – in Spain and Italy – were focused on dealing with the large and growing illegal immigrant populations. Thus regularization programmes (i.e. legalization of illegal immigrants) were established in 1986 in both Italy and Spain. Table 3 gives a comparative schema of the framework laws passed in the region.

TABLE 3

EVOLUTION OF FRAMEWORK IMMIGRATION LAWS IN SOUTHERN EUROPE

	1984	1985	1986	1987	1988	1989	1990	1991	1992	1993	1994	1995	1996	1997	1998
ES	A	I	R					R			A		R		
I			I/R				I/R/A					R			I
GR								I		A			A	R	
P									R	I/A			R		

Key
A = Asylum Law
R = Regularization Law
I = Immigration Law

As can be seen from Table 3, a large amount of the activity has been the enactment of regularization programmes. These initiatives vary from one country to another, but always with the intention of pushing illegal immigrants into legal residence and employment. Until recently, Greece had failed to implement such a programme, with an attendant very high number of illegal immigrants (Baldwin-Edwards and Fakiolas, this volume). There are many problems attached to regularization programmes: the most serious are that a large proportion drop back into clandestinity; that it encourages more illegal immigration which will at some point in the future be legalized; and that employers are disinclined to support it, as it adds to their fiscal costs. Reyneri (this volume) shows through a detailed study of the 1995/6 Regularization in Italy that the problem is not so much with the illegal immigrants as with the Italian labour market: legalization is not a cure for serious structural factors which perpetuate, encourage or even require the illegal employment of workers. In the case of Spain, a special 1996 programme was set up solely to draw back into legality those whose work permits had expired from the previous legalization of 1991. The Greek case is still in progress, but looks unlikely to fare any better than its counterparts.

Naturally, immigration and border controls are an important and new part of the immigration infrastructures of southern Europe. Other policy instruments used are deportations and summary expulsions; carrier sanctions on airlines; readmission agreements to facilitate expulsions. All of these areas are covered in some detail by European agreements on measure to combat illegal migration and employment (see Baldwin-Edwards 1997). Yet, these measures sit uneasily alongside the institutionalized underground economies of southern Europe: to combat these, employer sanctions are the only real policy instrument available (Jahn and Straubhaar, this volume). Another uneasy relationship is that concerning length of work/residence permits. Prior to the immigration reforms across the region 1985–93, only one-year work permits had been available. It made no difference if immigrants had been resident for twenty years, annual renewal was still required. Although this has been changed, with longer duration permits now available, their granting has been minimal in all countries. As Watts (this volume) points out, this is 'institutionalized precariousness', which also leads inevitably to periods of illegality through bureaucratic problems in renewal and perhaps for reasons of employment.

In summary, there is serious inconsistency between the severity of immigration control and the laxity of labour market regulation. This, combined with high social insurance and tax obligations for both employers and workers, seems to have created not so much opportunity for illegality but even its very necessity for economic survival. As Reyneri notes, if only politicians would devote as much care and resources to their own labour markets as they do to the borders of the so-called European 'fortress'.

The Shaping of Policy

Still, little research has been done on policy-making in southern Europe. Recent research on Italy (Radaelli 1998; Zincone, this volume) suggests a significant role for expert committees; it seems doubtful that this is so significant in the three other southern countries, though.

More general recent debates on immigration policy have tended to focus on two issues: the allegedly increasing 'gap' between policy goals and policy outcomes (Cornelius *et al.* 1995:3; Joppke 1998) and the supposed tension between the 'client politics' of proponents of expansionary immigration policies and anti-immigration voter preferences (Freeman 1995). There is, of course, a lot of common ground between these two positions; however, the 'gap hypothesists' are positing a primarily technical problem – how to control migration flows effectively – whereas the 'client politicists' are suggesting that organized interest groups have shaped expansionary immigration policies outside of democratic discourse.

Turning specifically to southern Europe, no country has yet openly exploited immigration as a political issue (see Zincone, this volume, for more detail in the case of Italy). There is no evidence even to suggest that employers' needs have been paramount in the shaping of policy: indeed, limited evidence from Spain[3] shows that employers have been slow to recruit labour from outside the territory. The precise reason for that is unknown, but clearly labour demand has been satisfied by existing domestic or foreign (illegal) workers. Recent research (Baldwin-Edwards and Safilios-Rothschild 1999) shows that in Greece anti-immigrant sentiment is directed not at immigration *per se*, but rather at illegal immigration and criminality of immigrants. Similar observations seem to have been made across southern Europe. Thus the control of illegal immigration and illegal immigrants, along with their perceived criminality, is a potential electoral issue.

The 'gap hypothesis' is more convincing, however. If it has been the intention of legislators to control immigration – legal or otherwise – they have dismally failed to do so. The utter dependency on regularization initiatives has seemingly institutionalized the route for legitimate employment. Thus Reyneri (1997) notes that half of the Third World legal residents in Italy had obtained their status through the 1990 regularization, and that almost all had obtained their work permits this way. Similarly, RIMET (1997:70) notes a doubling of the number of work permits in Spain simply through the 1991 regularization. Thus any comparison with the formal procedures of northern European countries or the USA in labour recruitment are completely misplaced. Southern European countries have established their own pattern of immigration and policy which requires specific analysis.

One policy imput, though, has been membership of the EU and lately of Schengen. Opinion is divided on how much the EU and Schengen have set the agenda for immigration policies across southern Europe. Freeman (1995:895) is quite clear that the chief factor driving Italian and Spanish policy is European policy; Corkill and Eaton (this volume) suggest the same for Portugal. Perlmutter (1996:381) is doubtful of this. Elsewhere (Baldwin-Edwards 1997), I have tried to put forward a more sophisticated account of the relationship. In the case of at least two countries – Greece and Italy – it is evident that an emergency response to mass exodus from Albania was an important explanatory factor of policy. Thus tighter border controls can be domestically inspired, as well as fitting the Schengen/EU requirements. Other policy requirements – such as resolutions on controlling illegal employment of third country nationals – have been accepted by all four countries. The implementation of them is still awaited.

The major actors shaping policy across southern Europe appear not to have been employers. Trades unions have been important in all four countries, and have consistently promoted the legalization and acceptance of immigrants (Watts; Zincone; Baldwin-Edwards and Fakiolas, this volume). For Italy, as noted above, Zincone stresses the role of expert committees, along with pro-immigrant pressure groups. Generally, the most important role in shaping policy appears to have been played by civil servants – with a resultant over-emphasis on legal formality rather than outcomes. One consequence of this, revealed clearly in the case if Greece, is that the different interests and approaches of various ministries have had to be reconciled. One obvious interest, which has not appeared with such clarity in the other countries, is official connivance in the trafficking of migrants, forced prostitution, and the sale of residence permits. Campani (this volume) notes some ambiguity on the part of the state in tackling the problem of trafficked prostitutes in Italy; although no suggestion is made of complicity, that possibility should never be forgotten.

SOME TENTATIVE CONCLUSIONS

Despite the mass migratory movements into southern European countries, despite the inadequate and overly reactive policies, despite serious failures and even official complicity in the trafficking of migrants, it seems that the immigration phenomenon is not out of control. Tighter border controls and restrictive granting of permits have to some extent kept out legal immigrants, but at the same time opened up a market for trafficking of migrants. Illegal immigration and work have become structural features in all of the southern economies, although to different extents. *Ad hoc* measures like regularizations and annual quotas have contained the situation, without addressing some important longer-term issues.

Thus the real problem – the apparently insatiable underground economy – is still healthy and still attracting migrants from across the globe. Essentially, the onerous bureaucratic and fiscal demands of the state in all four countries have pushed the private sector into taking matters into its own hands. In the underground economy, free markets reign: labour costs are minimized and production, which might otherwise be internationally unviable, continues. This 'free market' allocation of supply and demand is hardly optimal however. There is a social cost – both for the immigrant and perhaps for society, with an increased risk of criminality for survival; there is an opportunity cost, in that many immigrants are highly educated but given low-level work; there is also a cost for the state in implementing periodic regularization programmes – only for many of its beneficiaries to lapse into irregularity whilst yet more illegal immigrants are attracted by the prospect of future amnesties.

For both Jahn and Straubhaar and also Reyneri (this volume) the proximal cause of the large and burgeoning informal sector is the inefficient labour market, with its unnecessary rigidities and problems. Clearly this is true; however, it is doubtful that employer sanctions could ever be implemented. Not only would they be open to corruption and inefficient implementation, the very great extent of small and family businesses in southern Europe would make the cost of policing too high. Rather, the solution seems to lie in addressing the efficiency and *raison d'être* of the state itself. We might note a strong negative correlation between the size of the underground economy and state efficiency across the region – see Table 2 above. Fundamental behavioural patterns of the bureaucracy, along with over-protected employment and sometimes pension rights, have led to these labour market problems. Thus a reconsideration of the role of the state looks like the only solution: given the extensive economic restructuring which has begun across the EU, perhaps that cannot be ruled out.

Meanwhile, what of the immigrants themselves? Although many consider themselves *Gastarbeiter* of the 'twilight zone', and expect one day to return home, they may not. Others have no intention of returning. Already immigrants have started to redefine the social space of Mediterranean cities (Iosifides and King, this volume); male immigrants take the strain of unpleasant and heavy work, whilst women are occupied in cleaning or provide social support in child care and nursing the elderly. Their own future welfare needs are scarcely considered, yet they will occur. Increasingly, family reunion and family migration are happening: what of their role in the host society? The responses so far have been 'ostrich-like', with national citizenship requirements increased in an openly exclusionary manner (Baldwin-Edwards 1997:512–13): yet this can only be a phase in southern European development. As Zincone (this volume) shows, there is a distinct southern European pattern of 'enlightened' forces, which could shape the future. Perhaps that road holds out more promise than the gloomy view of immigrants and immigration portrayed by some of our northern European partners.

NOTES

1. A partial exception exists in the case of Portugal and her former African colonies, as shown by Corkill and Eaton, and Malheiros (this volume).
2. However, we might note that Portes forgets his own third paradox (p.443) – that the more credible the state enforcement apparatus, the more likely its mechanisms will miss the actual extent of informal activities. It may be that perceptions, rather than realities, are changing in the northern European economies.
3. The 1993 quota allocation received only 6,415 applications – compared with over 25,000 accepted in the following year when it was extended to illegal residents as well (Mendoza 1998)

REFERENCES

Baldwin-Edwards, M. (1997): 'The Emerging European Immigration Regime: Some Reflections on Implications for Southern Europe', *Journal of Common Market Studies* 35/4, pp.497–519.

Baldwin-Edwards, M. and K. Safilios-Rothschild (1999): 'Immigration and Unemployment in Greece: Perceptions and Realities', *South European Society & Politics* 4/3 (forthcoming).

Benton, L. (1990): *Invisible Factories: The Informal Economy and Industrial Development in Spain*, New York: State University of New York Press.

CEC (1991): *Immigration into the Countries of Southern Europe*, supplement of *Social Europe*, Luxembourg: CEC.

Chell, V. (1997): 'Gender-Selective Migration', in R. King and R. Black (eds): *Southern Europe and the New Migrations*, Brighton: Sussex Academic Press, pp.75–92.

Cornelius, W. *et al.* (1995)(eds): *Controlling Immigration: A Global Perspective*, Stanford: Stanford University Press.

Feige, E. (1990): 'Defining and Estimating Underground and Informal Economies: The New Institutional Economics Approach', *World Development* 18/7, pp.989–1002.

Freeman, G. (1995): 'Modes of Immigration Politics in Liberal Democratic Societies', *International Migration Review* 29/4, pp.881–902.

IOM (1995): *Trafficking and Prostitution: The Growing Exploitation of Migrant Women from Central and Eastern Europe*, Budapest: International Organization for Migration.

Iosifides, Th. (1997): 'Immigrants in the Athens Labour Market', in R. King and R. Black (eds): *Southern Europe and the New Migrations*, Brighton: Sussex Academic Press, pp.26–50.

Joppke, C. (ed) (1998): *Challenge to the Nation State*, Oxford: Oxford University Press.

King, R. (1998): 'Towards a Pattern of Immigration into Southern Europe', in M. Anderson and E. Bort (eds): *Schengen and the Southern Frontier of the European Union*, Edinburgh: International Social Sciences Institute, University of Edinburgh.

King, R., A. Fielding and R. Black (1997): 'The International Migration Turnaround in Southern Europe', in R. King and R. Black (eds): *Southern Europe and the New Migrations*, Brighton: Sussex Academic Press, pp.1–25.

Knights, M. (1997): 'Migrants as Networkers', in R. King and R. Black (eds): *Southern Europe and the New Migrations*, Brighton: Sussex Academic Press, pp.113–37.

Leontidou, L. (1993): 'Informal Strategies of Unemployment Relief in Greek Cities', *European Planning Studies* 1/1, pp.43–68.

Lobo, F. (1990): 'Irregular Work in Spain', in *Underground Economy and Irregular Forms of Employment, Final Synthesis Report*, Brussels: Commission of the EC.

Markova, E. and A. Sarris (1997): 'The Performance of Bulgarian Illegal Immigrants in the Greek Labour Market', *South European Society & Politics* 2/2, pp.57–79.

Mendoza, C. (1998): 'New Labour Inflows in Southern Europe: African Employment in Iberian Labour Markets', unpublished PhD, Dept. of Geography, Kings College London.

Mingione, (1991): *Fragmented Societies*, Oxford: Blackwell.

Perlmutter, T. (1996): 'Bringing Parties Back In', *International Migration Review* 30/1, pp.375–88.

Portes, A., M. Castells and L. Benton (eds) (1989): *The Informal Economy: Studies in Advanced and Less Developed Countries*, Baltimore: Johns Hopkins University Press.

Portes, A. (1994): 'The Informal Economy and its Paradoxes', in N. Smelser and R. Swedberg (eds): *Handbook of Economic Sociology*, London: Sage.

Radaelli, C. (1998): 'Networks of Expertise and Policy Change in Italy', *South European Society & Politics* 3/2, pp.1–22.

Reyneri, E. (1997): 'The Informalisation of Migrant Labour: An Oversupply of Illegal Migrants or a Pull Effect by the Underground Receiving Economy?', mimeo.

RIMET (1997): *The Member States of the EU and Immigration in 1994*, Luxembourg: CEE.

Salt, J. and J. Stein (1997): 'Migration as a Business: The Case of Trafficking', *International Migration* XXXV/3, pp.467–91.

Simon, G. (1987): 'Migration in Southern Europe: An Overview', in OECD: *The Future of Migration*, Paris: OECD, pp.258–91.

Williams, C. and J. Windebank (1995): 'Black Market Work in the European Community: Peripheral Work for Peripheral Localities?', *International Journal of Urban and Regional Research* 19/1, pp.23–39.

A Survey of the Economics of Illegal Migration

ANDREAS JAHN and THOMAS STRAUBHAAR

1. INTRODUCTION

A quick glance at international newspapers shows that the topic of illegal immigration has been receiving more and more interest all over the world. It has become a heated public debate in the USA, it is a major topic of right-wing parties in Western Europe such as the *Front National* in France or the *Freiheitlichen* in Austria, and it is also discussed in Japan and other countries of the Far East. Illegal migrants break laws and rules and clearly challenge the credibility of judicial systems and confidence in constitutionally derived power and authority. Their presence also conflicts with public transfer systems. Illegal foreign workers do not pay direct income taxes, but on the other hand use public goods or publicly subsidized services like schooling or medical treatment for their children. 'Illegals' compete with 'legals' for job opportunities but have the possibility avoiding certain obligations, costs, taxes and fees compulsory for legal workers. These legal, economic and social provocations make it easily understandable that politicians and voters are not willing to accept the phenomenon of illegal migration.

Regardless of these negative impacts on the host society, illegal migration exists and is growing throughout the world. And this is not only due to the vehement and irreversible will of hopeless and desperate people from poor regions to enter the 'Holy Land' of wealth and glory. There is also a need and demand for illegal immigrants. Some people (e.g. house owners needing some help in cleaning and maintenance) and

---

Earlier versions of this paper have been presented at the CEPR workshops in Halkidiki (1995) and Athens (1997) and at the HWWA-Institut für Wirtschaftsforschung workshop in Hamburg (1997). The authors acknowledge the very helpful comments from the participants and the financial support of the CEPR research programme on *European Migration from Economic Analysis to Policy Response* led by Klaus F. Zimmermann (Munich).

economic groups (such as restaurant owners or farmers) benefit from illegal migrants. They try to avoid direct labour costs, indirect social payments and costly regulations. The supply of, and demand for, illegal foreign workers create an economic market for illegal migration and a political market for the supply and demand of border controls and labour market regulations. Consequently, the phenomenon of illegal migration has to be analyzed within an economic framework but also with an understanding of the political economy behind the setting of laws and rules. It is the aim of this article to give a general survey of these two views of illegal migration. Furthermore, we will present some economic and politico-economic insights into the political action that has been taken to control and regulate illegal immigration. We summarize some experiences with different political instruments (i.e. border controls, internal controls, employer sanctions and amnesty programmes).

Our paper has to be seen in the context of some recent efforts to analyze causes and consequences of illegal migration. This topic has gained tremendous academic interest recently. In *political science* the question of whether democratic states could and should control unwanted immigration has been debated controversially (see e.g. Freeman 1994, 1995, 1995a, 1996; Brubaker 1995; Perlmutter 1996; Joppke 1996). Other research has evaluated the effectiveness and the efficiency of different migration policies. Kubat (1993) has looked for 'The Politics of Migration Policies'. He sees migration policies as 'a matter of waiting to see what will happen next while issuing *ad hoc* regulations' (Kubat 1993:xxiv). This largely reactive, defensive and short-term 'muddling through' migration policy was also confirmed by Collinson (1993:ch.3) for north-western Europe. In almost all major industrialized democracies there is a wide and growing gap between the *goals* of national immigration policy and the actual *outcomes* (Cornelius, Martin and Hollifield 1994).

Political economists have looked at the powerplay and interaction of different vested interest groups. They have analyzed the domestic demand and supply pattern for illegal migrants (Jahn and Straubhaar 1995, Hillman and Weiss 1995). They are interested in the mechanisms that create illegal migration (Epstein, Hillman and Weiss 1998). Labour market economists have concentrated on the question of whether, and for whom, illegal migrants are a substitute or a complement, and whether native skilled or unskilled workers and capital might benefit from illegal migration.[1]

The remainder of the article is organized as follows. In section 2 we briefly present the difference between legal and illegal migration; section 3 gives some data on the magnitude of this phenomenon. Section 4 analyzes the effects of illegal migration, section 5 the determinants. Sections 6 and 7 discuss some policy instruments used to combat illegal migration. The paper ends with some more general concluding remarks.

2. WHAT MAKES MIGRATION ILLEGAL?

The formal distinction between legal and illegal migration is obvious: the former is within the laws and rules of a mostly nationwide valid migration policy, the latter remains outside. While the right to *exit* is a fundamental human right protected by international law – and more or less respected all over the world since the collapse of the Iron Curtain – the right to *enter* a country remains a matter of national sovereignty. It is an undisputed basic principle of international law that national governments have the sovereign right to decide whom and how many non-nationals or non-citizens they allow to enter, stay and work in their territory. Nation states would lose one of their most fundamental constitutive powers if they abrogated the right to set rules defining what aliens are *allowed* to do (rights), what they are *required* to do (duties) or what they *should* do (orders). Consequently politicians all over the world are very anxious to keep control over the entrance, residence and economic behaviour of non-nationals. They know that their voters would just not accept an uncontrolled free immigration policy.

Consequently, it is the immigration law of the receiving country that defines whether foreigners enter, stay or work legally or illegally in a society. If we had no legal barriers to the entry, residence or employment of persons – as within national boundaries or, for EU nationals, within the European Union – illegal migration would be a non-issue. A look at contemporary migration laws around the globe shows very clearly that there is no such thing as illegal migration *per se*, but a large spectrum of different opinions about the circumstances in which the entry, stay and work of foreigners is legally allowed and those in which the activities of people are defined as 'illegal'.

The illegality of foreign people can stem from several causes (Figure 1):

1. Foreigners can *enter* a country illegally. They can cross the border, either by avoiding border controls (sometimes with the help of smugglers and labour traffickers) or by using false documents.

2. Foreigners might have entered the country legally but they *stay*

illegally. Either they entered with a tourist visa but did not leave and overstayed, or they entered as asylum seekers and stay even if their application has been rejected.

3. Foreigners might have entered legally, they might live under regular conditions but they could lose their legal status as a consequence of administrative or political changes in granting residence permits. If they do not leave, they become irregular residents. It might be that because of worse conditions in the labour market, foreigners are no longer wanted or needed by natives and are excluded from access to the labour market for purely economic reasons. Thus, they become irregular by an administrative act. The same might happen to refugees once they lose their status because their country of origin has moved back to more peaceful conditions with no danger to life for minorities. They are no longer granted a permit to stay and they become illegal if they do stay.
4. Foreigners could enter legally, stay legally, but they might *work* illegally. Illegal work does not concern foreigners only. Similarly, citizens are active in the shadow economy and work illegally without declaring it in order to avoid social security contributions and income taxes. Here, the issue of illegal migration is combined with the existence of a shadow economy in general.

Immigration laws also need to be enforced. Enforcement can take place at the border – choosing the people who are allowed to pass (external controls), and within the country – checking the permit to reside or to work (internal controls). Both types can capture only a fraction of illegal immigrants. Border controls cannot catch those who enter legally but overstay or work illegally, and internal controls usually rely on labour market checks and therefore fail to capture those who stay illegally but do not work.

Enforcement, too, varies between countries. It also varies within the same country. Some ports might control entry more intensively than others; some agencies might apply national law more severely than others. In some unattractive activities with a very low supply of legal workers (e.g. domestic work, tomato picking) rules and laws might be much less strictly enforced than in other more 'sensitive' branches or areas. In certain districts with a high surplus demand for unqualified work, there is also a strong incentive not to check too carefully the legality of people fulfilling activities which no natives want to do.

FIGURE 1

WHAT IS AN ILLEGAL IMMIGRANT?

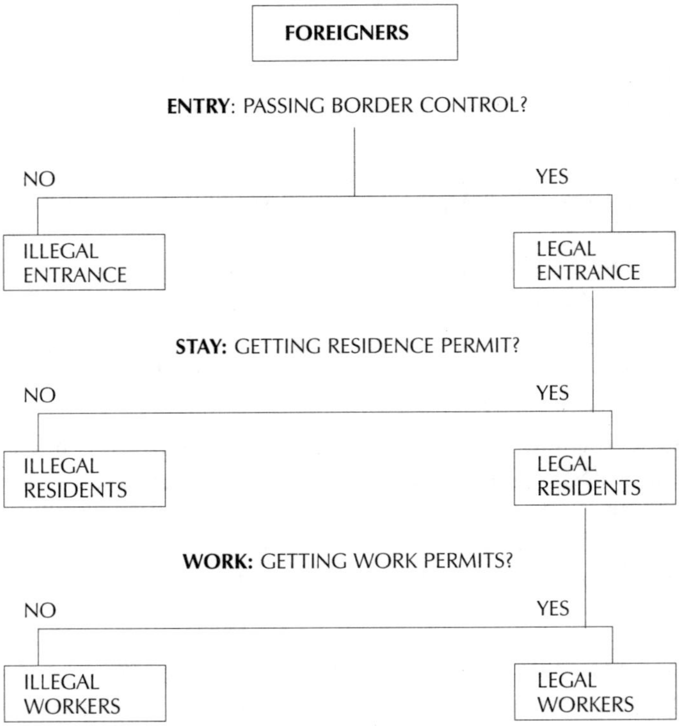

Finally, there is also a *time dimension* that makes migration more (or less) illegal. Owing to the absence of immigration law in some countries, immigrants have no special legal status of residence and sometimes are even allowed to work. If these countries with almost no historical tradition for migration restrictions – like southern European countries – suddenly start regulating immigration they also produce illegal migrants. Other countries with historically a very pragmatic attitude towards illegal immigrants – like the USA – might change quite unexpectedly the rules of the game. This case also shows very clearly how closely legal and illegal immigration are linked. Sometimes legal migration is the precursor to illegal immigration which occurs as soon as legal migrants have become established. This network migration or the legalized family reunification of formerly illegal migrants is extremely difficult administratively. Or to turn it the other way around, social and economic networks of legal migrants are one of the most important conditions for the existence of illegal migrants. Illegals need the support of these networks to survive in their illegality.

3. HOW MANY ARE THERE?

One of the most challenging and controversial issues in the discussion of illegal immigration is the estimation of the size and growth rate of illegal immigrant populations within a country. By definition, illegal immigrants are not registered in official records. They avoid contact with governmental and formal sectors. Therefore reliable numbers are almost impossible to obtain. On the other hand, there is a huge demand for numbers and estimations among policy-makers. Not surprisingly, many estimations are floating around with doubtful theoretical background. Most of the data on illegal migration are politically biased and misused. All we know for sure is that the number of illegal migrants has strongly increased over the last decade.

The extent of illegal immigration depends on the ability and willingness of a country to enact its immigration laws. Among other things, this includes permanent control of entry, exit, residence and working permits. Moreover, some countries tolerate illegal migrants more easily because they assume that they act only as *transit* hosts and that most of its foreigners are moving ahead to another destination country. This might be the case in some eastern European countries with regard to movements to Germany (e.g. Poland) or in Latin America with regard to the movements to the USA (i.e. Mexico).

Furthermore, the official recording of illegal migrants is also part of a strategic game. Some countries might have incentives to record exaggerate figures to get international financial assistance or to legitimize political actions against illegal migrants. Other countries might be afraid of high figures because they could transmit the signal to foreigners that it is relatively easy to be an illegal alien in that particular country. A country with a high tolerance is more likely to be affected by illegal immigration than under similar conditions with strict enforcement of immigration laws.

Since nobody knows not even roughly how many illegal immigrants live in a country, one has to rely on other indexes and country-specific information. Procedures to quantitatively record illegal migrants which are used in one country may not be appropriate for estimations in another country, simply because the documentation or data used in the first case may not exist in the second country. One idea is to rely on border apprehensions. Espenshade (1995) concludes that for the period of 1977-1988 border apprehensions are a relatively exact tool for measuring illegal immigrant inflows. He estimates that the illegal immigration inflow is about 2.2 times the number of border apprehensions. However, this method can capture illegal Mexican inflow only and is not valid for examining visa-overstayers or abusers.[2] Furthermore, estimations concerning illegals in the USA cannot be transferred to western Europe for several reasons (for detailed arguments, see Röseler and Vogel, 1993):

1. The institutional arrangements on labour markets differ not only between the relatively free markets in the USA and the more regulated European cases, but also between the western European countries themselves.

2. Immigration policy in the European Union has become a topic of common concern only recently (see Baldwin-Edwards [1997] for a recent survey of the emerging European immigration regime). The Treaty of Amsterdam included the Schengen Agreement in the EU treaty and transferred some important competences from the national to the common EU level. In particular, the decision to abolish cross-border controls and to rely on external border controls is a far reaching step towards Schengenland. On the other hand, the internal enforcement, the weight of employer sanctions or the possibility to carry out amnesty programmes remains within national competencies.

3. In western Europe there are states which have a long tradition of immigration (like France) and countries like Greece and Spain which used to be typical emigration countries and are now facing large immigration. Therefore western Europe does not offer a homogeneous picture concerning illegal immigration. Each country faces its own national specific problems. For example, immigration pressure from eastern Europe is regarded as a bigger problem for Germany than for southern Europe, which is more concerned about illegal immigration from North Africa. However the transit migration flows of Kurds from Turkey, and of people from Albania to Italy and from there further on to Germany, shows how closely connected national migration policies have become.

4. The legal settings are different in all countries. The way in which controls are carried out is based on historically developed national traditions. For example, the wide use of an identification system in continental Europe makes controls within the country easier for the government compared to the USA. There, foreigners are supposed to be controlled only at the border which makes controls more difficult (see Steineck 1994).

Table 1 shows that estimates of the number of illegal aliens in Europe vary considerably. Furthermore, Table 2 gives some hints about the ratio of registered foreign-born population to unregistered foreign-born population. It shows that illegal immigration poses a big problem for southern European countries. These figures confirm a former estimation by Dell'Aringa and Neri (1989). They used a general equilibrium model in order to explain the expansion of the Italian underground economy and, connected with this, the growing demand for illegal workers. They estimate that more than half a million illegal foreigners were working in Italy in 1984.

TABLE 1

ESTIMATIONS OF ILLEGAL ALIEN STOCKS (THOUSANDS) IN VARIOUS EUROPEAN COUNTRIES

Country	1981	1986	1987	1988	1989	1990	1992	1994
Portugal			40-50	60	60-70		80	
Spain	51-76					170-260		
	367					88-132		
France							200	
Italy		580	572	300-450		600		1000
			350-1050	500-1000		700-1400		
Greece			40					
Germany							650	500
Switzerland							100	
							100-150	
Austria							40-100	70
Netherlands							50-100	
Belgium							40-90	

Source: Schoorl et *al.* (1996)

TABLE 2

ESTIMATIONS OF AFRICAN AND MEDITERRANEAN POPULATIONS IN EUROPEAN COUNTRIES (THOUSANDS)

Country	Year	Registered	Unregistered	Unregistered as % of registered population
Portugal	1985	35	22	63
	1990	43	28	65
	1994	57	36	63
Spain	1985	13	46	354
	1990	29	122	420
	1994	83	108	130
Italy	1985	62	262	423
	1990	117	590	347
	1994	310	697	225
France	1985	1603	29	2
	1990	1653	150	9
	1994	1633	175	11
Germany	1985	4488	176	4
	1990	5506	215	4
	1994	7180	277	4
Benelux	1985	1740	52	3
	1990	1870	69	4
	1994	2105	81	4

Source: Schoorl *et al.* (1996)

Nowadays, even countries of the former Soviet bloc like Hungary are becoming target countries for illegal immigration owing to the wage gap with neighbouring countries. Poland is used as a transit country to move from the easternmost part of Europe to the West. But some transit migrants stay longer than they originally intended in Poland and then start to work in the shadow economy (IOM 1995).

Furthermore, in East and Far East Asia illegal migration has started to become a topic of growing interest. Japan – a country closed to immigration – also faces illegal immigration by visa-overstayers or tourists entering and then seeking employment. Morita and Sassen (1994) estimate that bout 280,000 illegal aliens were working in Japan in 1991. The main sectors concerned are construction and manufacturing.

Australia seems to be the only country where a rigid entry policy and strict border controls have been successful tools in controlling illegal immigration. Birrel (1994) argues that, owing to the geographic isolation of the country, entries without inspection can be controlled more easily than in North America or in Europe. Visa overstayers and abusers have been expelled and deterred by strict application of legislation passed in the late 1980s.

4. WHY IS ILLEGAL IMMIGRATION A PROBLEM?

The economic analysis of illegal migration was originally closely related to the analysis of international smuggling and illegal trade to evade tariffs (Bhagwati 1981). Since the pioneering studies of Grossman (1984), Ethier (1986), Dell'Aringa and Neri (1989), Djajic (1987), Bond and Chen (1987) and Chiswick (1988), the welfare effects of illegal immigration have gained some specific analytical interest. Mostly, the analyses have concentrated either on the *employment* impacts of illegal immigration or on the effects of *illegality*. The first case does not differ much from the general migration discussion – whether legal or illegal. The second case comes close to the analysis of illegal work (such as in the underground economy) – independently of whether workers are citizens or foreigners.

In most cases, illegal immigration is judged to be a more or less severe problem. The logic of this evaluation goes back to the *general economic impacts* of the international movement of persons. To get a basic understanding of these impacts, it is not necessary to differentiate between legal and illegal migration. In a simplified world with economically identical people acting individually and independently of each other, and with perfectly and fully competitive markets with no common or public goods and no redistribution of income by taxes or social benefits, migration would be a positive mechanism to reach an efficient allocation of workers. In such a (neo-classical) framework, migration is an arbitrage phenomenon that overcomes local surpluses or scarcities in factor endowments. In a world with no national borders and no limits to the internationally free movement of labour, migration is welfare improving for the world as a whole. This is one of the clear results of the positive theory of international trade.

However, this is a very aggregated *cosmopolitan* view. It does not really consider the distribution of the gains from free migration. Moreover, the positive evaluation of migration effects is much more complex if we leave the (neo-classical) framework above. If we allow for unequal distribution of capital (i.e. wealthy and poor people), segmented labour markets (i.e. skilled and unskilled workers) and unemployment, or if we consider the existence of public goods, then free migration of labour could have negative effects – at least for some specific factors or groups. This is also true if we include externalities of migration.

The *pecuniary* externalities of migration should draw attention to the fact that macroeconomic allocational efficiency almost always has some negatively evaluated consequences on an individual microeconomic level. While the (re)allocational effects of migration are clearly positive on the whole, there will be winners and losers in the immigration and emigration country. To the degree that labour markets are segmented, competition between natives and immigrants for employment opportunities leads to distributional effects within the host country. Those who have invested capital in the immigration economy win, because labour becomes less scarce and therefore the average wage level will fall and the capital rent will increase. The native labour force that is complementary to the immigrant labour force might reach a higher productivity and will be better off with, rather than without, migration. However, the native labour force that is a substitute for the immigrant labour force will become more abundant and their average wage level will fall. Finally, it is also possible that an immigrant will push a native out of the labour market and thus make him unemployed.

Of course, we could show theoretically that the winners (i.e. the capitalists and the complementary domestic labour force) could more than fully compensate the losers (i.e. the unskilled). We could also argue that in most cases unemployment is the consequence of labour market inflexibilities, wage rigidities and structural inefficiencies. We could convincingly demonstrate that all these deficiencies have not much to do with immigration and that – on the contrary – immigrants can help to remedy these deficits. But all these valid arguments for immigration do not outweigh the individual evaluation of those directly concerned citizens (the unemployed or crowded-outs). Their perception is that a world with no immigrants would be a better world!

The same perception is the mother of many hardly correctible prejudices, myths and untruths about *non-economic externalities* of migration. Some natives dislike more or less arbitrarily and subjectively the presence of foreigners. They (emotionally) feel negatively affected by foreigners in their utility function. Consequently they lobby against foreigners even if immigrants would create positive economic benefits for the economy as a whole.

Of course, all these negative perceptions are even more strongly pronounced in the case of *illegal* migration. Illegal immigrants are an extreme provocation of the nation states and their laws and regulations. There are several more or less standard economic, legal and political arguments against illegal immigrants:

1. Illegal immigrants neither receive from nor pay into the national social security system. Illegal immigrants unlike legal immigrants are not integrated into this system. Therefore their direct impact on publicly financed activities is clearly negative. This argument has gained much attention in the recent US debate. Illegal immigrants are suspected of using public welfare programmes and education or medical treatment without paying taxes. Therefore they increase the tax burden of natives and legal immigrants (see Borjas 1995).

2. A rather legalistic string of arguments builds on the assumption that a state cannot tolerate illegality within its jurisdiction. If it does so, it suffers a decline in its legitimacy which spills over to other areas (e.g. tax honesty). This argument says that the state must enforce all given laws; however, it does not explain how the laws come into existence.

3. A similar argument says that legal immigrants had to wait for some time in order to get their rights to stay and to work (e.g. visas). The legal immigrants took the harder way to get into the receiving country whereas those coming illegally slipped in from the side without lining up properly. Therefore toleration of illegal immigrants rewards them and punishes those who took the legal way (see Hailbronner 1995).

4. Illegal immigrants are often pushed into the areas of the shadow economy. There is much concern that they tend to commit more criminal acts than other foreigners because they have less to lose and are more ready to accept risks. Hence, this line of arguments says that illegal immigrants commit more crimes and make life for natives and legal immigrants more dangerous (see Dell' Aringa and Neri 1989, for Italy).

5. Illegal immigrants have a weak legal position which gives them a weaker bargaining position, leading to concern that illegal immigrants are subject to exploitation. Arguments of this kind are often incorporated into systemic theories of migration. They say that in the case of producing tradable goods, exploitation of foreign labour takes place in the foreign country; in the case of non-tradable goods, cheap labour is imported into the industrialized country and exploited there (Morita and Sassen 1994).

6. Illegal immigrants are assumed to create competition for legal immigrants and minorities on the labour market. As far as illegals substitute for the work of legals, they decrease the possibilities for those who follow the rules.[3]

5. WHY DOES ILLEGAL IMMIGRATION EXIST?

Although illegal migration has some negative legal, economic and social aspects, and notwithstanding that it is a severe provocation for the legal system of nation states, it exists and has even grown in the past decade. The economic answer for this contradiction is twofold:

1. Illegal migration is a response to inefficient (i.e. too costly) market regulation. For some migrants and some employers it is economically beneficial to break laws and rules and to take the risks of being punished.
2. The optimal degree of illegal migration is greater than zero. This means that beyond a certain level the costs of avoiding illegal migration by control measurements becomes more expensive than the damage that is caused by illegal migration. Therefore it is cheaper for a society to accept some illegal migration but to 'save' the exorbitant costs of 'complete' border controls or the negative impacts of an extremely severe enforcement of internal controls.

The first point stresses the microeconomics of the market for illegal immigrants.[4] There is an oversupply of people willing to enter high-income countries. For whatever reason, the 'already theres' (natives, former immigrants) do not want to accept open borders and free immigration. They define an immigration law, declaring who is able to enter, stay and work, and what would be the consequences of breaking this law. Illegals can be detected by controls and they have to pay a fine when being caught. This fine can consist of several elements. They have to pay some money, they are arrested for some time, or they are taken to some far-off places in the sending country and therefore punished with the loss of time. But if the utility difference between host and receiving society is large enough, for some people the net present value of migration minus regular transaction and transportation costs of moving (as in the case of the legal migrant) minus the expected risk of being caught and punished remains positive. This means, they will offer their work in a host country even if this is only possible on an illegal basis. So we will have a *supply* of illegal foreign workers. But to become illegal workers in reality, there is also a need for a *demand* for illegal foreign workers.

The second point stresses the importance of a political economy understanding of illegal immigration. The politico-economic approach focuses on the endogenous formation of an immigration policy.

Individuals in the law-making process choose their action in order to maximize their own welfare. In the context of an immigration policy, individuals are in favour of immigration if they are more likely to gain economically. Those winners from legal and illegal immigration tend to be skilled workers and owners of capital. The losers are unskilled native workers. It has been shown analytically by Jahn and Straubhaar (1995) that if immigration law is a compromise between those two groups, they will bargain not so much over the law itself, but about the level of its enforcement.

Hillman and Weiss (1995) offer an explanation of why the obvious existence of illegal immigrants is tolerated. In their framework, illegal workers are locked into one specific sector producing a non-traded benefit. With more and more illegals entering the economy, the supply of labour in that sector will increase and therefore wages will decrease. These lower labour costs are of benefit to the rest of the society which therefore tolerates those illegal immigrants.

The fundamental element in the understanding of the determinants of illegal immigrants is the behaviour of employers. They represent the active part, the flow of illegal immigrants responds only to their behaviour and to the measures taken by the government. This view is justified, because the flow of illegal immigrants suggests that it responds flexibly and quickly to changing economic conditions and to enforced or comparatively relaxed controls.[5]

Employers of illegal immigrants can face severe penalties when they are detected by internal controls. Those fines are usually measured in money units. However, it should be noted that in practice other forms of punishment also exist, e.g. exclusion from public contracts. Consequently, employers hire illegal immigrants up to the point where the marginal benefit for them is equal to the marginal expected loss when such behaviour is discovered. For wage setting this means that illegals will get a salary below their marginal productivity and below the wage paid to legal workers.

It is now assumed that employers can and will make a rational choice between the expected penalty of employing illegal immigrants and the benefits arising from such employment. People not used to economic reasoning often reply that this is not the way *real world* decisions are undertaken because the employer is not able to compare the loss when he is sentenced to prison with (money) benefits he receives from employing illegal immigrants. But there must exist some transitive ordering between imprisonment and fines, because these two instruments are used simultaneously by judges. Therefore one should be able to compare (non-monetary) penalties and benefits.

Since they are cheaper for the employer, he can now employ more illegal immigrants for the same amount he used to pay to the former legally employed. Considering a neo-classical production function, output will rise if factor prices decrease. This rise in total production will benefit the qualified sector, if qualified and unqualified work are so-called 'q-complements'.[6] Saying that, the increase in total production and unqualified employed raises the productivity of the skilled sector. Taking the supply of qualified labour as fixed implies an increase in their wages.

The total revenue function then has an optimal point. Taking this revenue function as a welfare function means that there exists one socially optimal point of illegal immigration, which is not zero, meaning that *some* illegal immigration might prove beneficial to the society as a whole. Of course, this welfare improvement is based on a simple picture of the world. One might object that it does not include things other than money. By accepting some *illegal* immigrants one might feel negatively affected, because the government does not enforce its laws. This fact might decrease one's identification with this kind of society and thus lead to a loss in welfare.

The fact that the economically optimal level of illegal immigration is greater than zero stresses the need for a specific policy on illegal immigrants. Some illegal immigration is beneficial, too much is not. Illegal migrants have some qualifications not possessed by legal migrants and they will take job opportunities not taken by legal workers and will do other jobs more cheaply. So, at least for a certain level of illegal immigrants, they will increase the welfare of the receiving countries as a whole. As the benefits are not equally distributed in the society, a bargaining procedure will decide to what extent illegals are accepted and how severe should be controls and punishments. This leads to the questions of control and punishment.

6. WHAT COULD BE DONE?

A very intense and fruitful debate has emerged in political science as to whether democratic governments (or 'liberal states') can control immigration and cope with illegal (or 'unwanted') immigration (Freeman 1994, 1995, 1996, Brubaker 1995, Joppke 1996). In brief the answer has been that

1. liberal nation states and their democratic governments have the sovereignty to regulate immigration but are confronted with an increasing 'gap between a restrictionist control rhetoric and an expansionist immigration reality' (Joppke 1996:1) and that

2. the technical capacity to control immigration has increased but for politico-economic reasons (i.e. to serve clientelistic interests) governments self-limit themselves in the use of these capacities.[7] Migration policy appears to be cyclical, indicating that public pressure plays a major role in immigration law making.

Migration legislation can be located either at the external border or within the country. In the first case the legality of entrance is enforced. In the second case the legality of residence or work is examined. What are the economic consequences of such controls?

Border Enforcement

One way to detect illegal immigration could be to enforce external border controls. However, as stressed already in section 2, illegal employment and illegal residence do not necessarily imply illegal entry. At least in northern European countries, most illegal immigrants have entered legally and have then either abused their visa or extended their stay. Border enforcement, despite being an important control instrument, can catch only a limited number of illegal immigrants who actually enter illegally.

The issue of border enforcement is not confined to illegal entrance of foreign people. Border controls include the fight against *smuggling* and *organized crime*. They send out signals that 'borders are under control' and that not everybody or everything is allowed to enter. So border controls are not only effective through their apprehensions of illegal entrance. Their signalling effect is much more important. They give a sense of security to the people residing inside the country. At the same time, pictures of guards patrolling the border and catching people crossing a river in the middle of the night are more spectacular and draw attention to their work. This might deter further attempts.

Special attention is also given to traffickers of illegal immigrants. Facing tighter border controls, illegal immigrants might be willing to put their faith in a trafficker who helps them enter the desired country. Dramatic pictures of migrants locked into containers and left alone without food draw public attention and journalists' interest for a couple of days. In addition, professional traffickers are the direct enemy of border guards and pitilessly demonstrate the weak points of border enforcement and the slow response of officers to new holes in the border fence. Those points can explain why the fight against traffickers receives more and more attention by different governments and even leads to efforts in co-operation and harmonizing the fight against traffickers.

Labour traffickers appear as the scapegoat in illegal labour migration. However, their evolution as 'professionals' in the illegal migration business is a consequence of the demand which potential illegal migrants exercise and not their cause. The fight against labour traffickers has some justification because they violate national borders. One has to keep in mind, however, that their existence is a response to the demand for illegal entrance by people from other countries. These people are willing to pay money for their demand and as long as this is the case labour traffickers will always organize and find ways to take people to the place they want to go.

To summarize: Border protection is relatively costly and not very efficient for all the reasons we have mentioned in section 2. A complete control of the border is impossible to achieve. On the other hand border controls are extremely important for their signalling effects. People within the country feel safer, people outside feel not free to enter. So, the solution is to find an optimum. It needs some border controls but their costs should not exceed their potential benefits measured in terms of the apprehensions and deterrent effects.

Internal Controls

Internal control enforcements aim to detect illegal residents and illegal foreign workers. In this regard, the issue of illegal immigration becomes part of the more general issue of illegal work in the shadow economy and the fight against illegal immigration becomes part of the more general control of the underground economy. Illegal foreign workers and natives in the black economy cannot be distinguished *ex ante* anymore. Consequently, it needs something like an identification system to prove legal residence and the legality of work. Rules regarding the illegal employment of foreigners are in principle easier to enforce if a sensible work permit system exists. But on the other hand, this means that the illegal employment of foreigners is detected only at the cost of increasing work permit controls. Thus, all legal workers have to carry the burden of additional controls. Furthermore, this would also mean a general fight against the shadow economy: vested interest groups doing their business in or with the underground economy are not much in favour of such an intensified control of their activities.

There is a demand for seasonal workers and for people able and willing to do dangerous, dirty and unpopular jobs. In the highly regulated European labour markets with strong social networks, natives are neither forced nor willing to accept these relatively low-paid jobs with low social status. For this reason, many governments have created ways of legal entry for some foreigners to fulfil these activities. These provisions have two effects: on the one hand they ease immigration pressure by offering a legal alternative for illegal entry, but on the other hand they form a *channel of immigration* which is also used for illegal immigrant workers.

Employers and migrants still have strong incentives to abuse the provisions in order to save social security payments or to undercut minimum wage requirements. With the help of those agreements foreigners can enter legally. They have specific (seasonal or project related) work contracts but are not supposed to move or to over-stay. However, they have the chance to gather information necessary for subsequent illegal stay. They can build up economic and social networks with natives or relatives who have entered legally before.

In addition, these provisions make it harder for labour inspectors to check whether the employment of foreigners has a legal basis. With a variety of exceptions and special case regulations, controllers have a harder job to do and the detection of illegal practices is more difficult because the simple rule 'no work without a work permit' is not completely valid any more as the number of different work permits increases. Controls become especially difficult if foreign workers declare their status as 'self-employed' or show contracts with fictitious local *pro forma* firms.

Employer Sanctions

Besides the risk of being detected, the severity of punishment is the other policy instrument to react against illegal immigration. The higher the risks and the more severe the punishment, the lower the incentives to be an illegal or to employ illegal immigrants.

In the view of Todaro (1986) employer sanctions form the *key instrument* in decreasing illegal immigration. He shows that employer sanctions in the USA have led to a more dramatic decrease in illegal employment there than direct help given to Mexico in order to improve economic conditions in that country (see also Hill/Pearce, 1990 for a theoretical treatment of employer sanctions).

The question of employer sanctions relates to the more general question on the economics of crime.[8] Employing illegal immigrants is a criminal act. Economic incentives to offer and accept employment must be balanced by potential punishment for the employer and the employee. Fines which the employer has to pay when discovered employing illegal immigrants increases their costs making their employment less attractive, whereas fines to be borne by the illegal employee reduce his wages making his work less attractive.

A fundamental difference between Europe and the USA is that income from employment is taxed more heavily in Europe. Deductions for taxes and social security systems can reach up to 60 per cent of actual income offering another incentive for illegal work. The aspect of tax evasion and illegal employment is hardly discussed in the American literature whereas the relationship between the underground economy and illegal employment is more stressed in the European case (see for example Dell'Aringa and Neri, 1989).

Amnesties

Amnesties aim to abolish illegality by granting work and residence permits to a certain class of people. They provide the right to stay for a whole group of people and not to single persons on the basis of special case decisions. The residence and work status of illegals becomes legalized. By turning illegal immigrants into full members of society, they do not have to fear deportation anymore. Consequently, they are less likely to be exploited.

Amnesties mean that national authorities (government) acknowledge the existence of illegal aliens. Usually, not all illegal residents are included in amnesty programmes. Illegals have to qualify for amnesty. As a first step, they have to register themselves and thus have to reveal their illegality to officials. For various reasons not all illegals declare themselves:

1. Illegals might not trust government's announcements and prefer to stay hidden. If they declare themselves, they are subject to government controls and fear deportation.

2. Illegals might not be certain that their request will receive a positive answer. Usually, amnesties are tied to certain conditions. The illegal immigrant cannot be sure if he meets those conditions or if his documents are sufficient proof.

3. Immigrants engaged in illegal activities might prefer to stay in the underground making it harder for crime enforcement officers.

Thus, amnesties do not turn all illegal immigrants into legal residents. Normally illegal immigrants must have stayed in the country for some time. Sometimes, they are legalized only if they have found employment. But how should illegal immigrants prove the length of their not officially recorded duration of stay or their former working activities in the underground economy? For illegals it is hard to prove that they were employed for a period, or to prove their residence in the country, because they avoided all official contacts and private documents are easy to fake. So government officers have a high degree of discretion about whether they believe the foreigner or not.

People who were granted residence rights are usually young males.[9] Via the family reunification programmes they can then take their close family members into the country. This increases (legal) immigration. According to migration theory, other foreigners apart from immediate family members also establish ties to the receiving country. In the chain migration process, it is easier for those people to establish themselves in the receiving country, because they have more information and contacts. Even if they cannot expect to receive a residence or work permit in the near future, they could try to stay in the country illegally. They act the same way as their friends who emigrated earlier and succeeded. Why not do it the same way? Amnesties, therefore, can lead to further illegal immigration via the chain migration process.

The declaration of an amnesty programme also has a strong 'announcement effect'. It generates an important incentive for aliens to try to get legal residence and a work permit. Some foreigners might enter the country just to apply for amnesty.

Amnesties might also lead to the expectation that 'one amnesty leads to the other'. Thus, more illegal immigrants enter the country and this increase raises incentives for the government to conduct another amnesty programme if the first one was considered to be a success. Future amnesties become an important pull factor in the migration decision. Countries can enter a vicious circle of amnesties, more illegal immigrants, another amnesty, and so on.

Illegal immigrant workers once legalized leave the shadow economy and enter the formal economic sector. By doing so they and their employers have to pay social security and unemployment contributions. Thus, their work becomes more expensive and it is uncertain whether they will remain employed legally. After the amnesty the employer still has the incentive to recur to illegally employed labour in order to secure their lower costs. An amnesty does not remove the economic incentives that lead to the illegal employment of foreigners. As long as those incentives remain, illegal employment of foreigners will not vanish.

To make amnesties a useful tool in reducing illegal immigration, they have to be a credible one-time-only policy. If amnesties raise expectations for future legalization programmes they are of no use because they lead to an increased influx of illegal immigrants. Therefore amnesties are a good measure for countries where the situation of immigrants is not clearly defined. This is the case for southern European countries which changed from typical countries of emigration to immigration countries – attracting people from former communist countries, North Africa and the Near East. Their legal and bureaucratic framework was not prepared for this new immigration. The existence of illegal immigrants is tolerated by the state. Here, an amnesty together with a sensible reform of immigration legislation and enforcement is an option.

In countries with a well-regulated immigration system, such as France or Germany, such amnesty programmes are useless. In these countries, immigrants are or become illegal not by missing procedures but because they violate existing legislation. A general amnesty would not prove fruitful and can even increase illegal immigration via the chain migration process and due to raised expectations for future amnesties. This does not exclude that in special cases 'illegals' can be granted a residence permit or a toleration of their stay.[10]

7. WHAT SHOULD BE DONE?

Should we try to reduce or even stop illegal immigration at the borders or within the country by a stronger enforcement of residence and work laws? Or should we accept that illegal immigrants are an increasing phenomenon in the context of globalization and that we cannot cope with it? First of all, it has to be remembered that there are several good politico-economic reasons why democratic states accept unwanted immigration. This has something to do with the logic of client politics (Freeman 1994, 1995). Joppke (1996:7) sees for Europe that 'the legal rather than the political process explains why states accept unwanted immigration'.[11] But why are migration laws and regulations not enforced more strictly? This again might have something to do with 'client politics' and with the politico-economic powerplay of different vested interest groups.

Illegal employment of foreigners is a consequence and not the cause of specific (inefficient) law setting. It is the result of misleading economic incentives generated by labour market regulations and social security systems. Income taxes and financial contributions to the social security system drive a wedge between the productivity of the worker and his net wage. In net payment the employee receives less then he earns and the employer has to pay more than he gets. As long as this wedge exists, employers and employees always have the incentive to negotiate their proper work contract without giving the public coffer its piece of the cake. On the other hand, the social security system allows natives to refuse lower paid jobs. If domestic labour is not available on the official labour market, employers have to turn to illegal sub-markets. Thus, the only long-term strategy available to lower illegal immigration is to remove the economic incentives to employ illegal migrants! But this is a more general advice to the too rigid and regulated European labour markets: it will need enormous politico-economic efforts and take some time to reform and cure these deficits. Thus, for a rather short-term strategy we suggest the following steps:

1. If citizens (voters!) really dislike illegal immigrants, why not just sanction much more severely against the employers of illegal (foreign?) workers? The answer is that the economy as a whole, and especially some specific sectors, urgently need illegal (foreign) workers to fulfil some low-paid, unskilled, dirty and risky jobs. So, illegal work is also a consequence of misleading labour market regulations. If there is a gap between economic reality and (moral) legislation, people have strong incentives to defraud and to work in the informal underground economy. Consequently, the first suggestion to fight illegal migration is to deregulate the European labour markets. Bridging the gap between productivity and net payments is one way to reduce illegal practices on the labour market. That means reducing direct taxation of income and social security contributions from the employee and the employer implying a shift to increased taxes on consumption.

2. Illegal migrants could be detected either at the border or in the labour market. The main difference is the cost sharing. External controls give the whole task to the federal state and their officials (i.e. border patrols, border check points) and nowadays in Europe, it transfers the problem to the border countries of Schengenland. Internal controls make employers also responsible. They have to check whether their workforce is legal. If they do not take seriously their responsibility, they will also be punished. This means that internal control shares the costs between the public and private sector. Hence, the second

suggestion could be to shift as much as possible the controls from the external border to the internal enforcement of labour market regulations.[12]

3. Internal controls can be enforced by the intensity of controls and the severity of expected punishment. Relatively random-walk checks combined with strong employer sanctions would again shift the control costs from the public to the private sector. Employers would have an incentive to check carefully themselves the legal status of their workforce. Consequently, such a strategy fights illegal labour market practices in general. So, our third suggestion is to increase dramatically the sanctions against employers of illegal foreign workers.

SOME CONCLUDING REMARKS

The control of entry, stay and work of foreign people is a principal issue of national sovereignty. Illegal immigrants challenge national control mechanisms and are an extreme provocation to national authorities. They test border guards and once inside the country penetrate the underground economy. A simple and easy way for politicians to bare action against illegals is an increase in external border controls or spectacular raids to catch illegal foreign workers within the country. Once they realize the inefficiency of such control-oriented policies, amnesties are the next helpless attempt to cure the problem of illegal migration. However, amnesties decrease the stock of illegal immigrants by legalizing them. But after a while, the number of illegals increases again, as historical experience has evidenced. Amnesties just do not work out the way they are supposed to do.

An economically much more efficient way to handle illegal immigration and illegal work starts at the economic roots of illegal employment of illegal foreigners. This means first, that national labour markets should be made more flexible. Illegal immigrants work very often without written *de facto* contracts. Why not allow them or others to work *de jure* under the same conditions? If labour is not available on the official labour market, employers have to recur to illegal sub-markets. Opening up the labour market and giving easier access to newcomers is an appropriate strategy.

Illegal employment of natives and of foreigners is the consequence and not the cause of inefficiencies in the labour market. Finding and eliminating the cause and nature of those inefficiencies presents the only possible long-term strategy to lower the economic incentives for illegal immigration. A good labour market policy is the only valid strategy fighting illegal employment and will more or less automatically cure the most obvious problems of illegal migration. Or to put it briefly: make European labour markets work efficiently and most of the negative impacts of the illegal work of foreigners will vanish!

NOTES

1. Some seminal papers can be found in Pozo (1986) and the discussion has been enlarged competently by Chiswick (1988); for more recent results see Schmidt, Stilz and Zimmermann along with several other papers in the Special Issue on illegal migration of the *Journal of Population Economics*, 1998.
2. Warren (1994) suggests that visa overstayers and abusers represent roughly one half of the stock of illegal immigrants in the USA, the other half consists of people who have entered the country illegally. In this second group Mexicans are the great majority.
3. Djajic (1997) gives a deep insight into the economic effects of illegal immigration. He considers short and long-run effects. In the short run, more illegal workers employed in the underground economy lead to an increase in wages of the skilled workforce. The wage effect for legal unskilled workers depends on whether illegals are complements or substitutes for them. In the long run, there is no change in wages if both natives and illegal immigrants are employed in the shadow economy. Illegal immigrants are simply absorbed. If only foreigners are employed, wages for skilled and unskilled natives increase. Thus, this model specification illustrates the possibility that 'all native workers may benefit from illegal immigration as the inflow of foreign workers enables them to enjoy larger scarcity rents' (Djajic 1997:112).
4. Jahn (1997) offers an analysis of the economic interests of different actors present in the market for illegal immigrants.
5. Using a cross-country approach, Bratsberg (1995) shows that illegal immigration flows are more sensitive to changes of GNP per capita than legal immigration. Therefore illegal immigration depends even more than legal migration flows on the economic conditions in the sending and receiving countries. Consequently it can be seen as a very flexible reserve of labour.
6. 'q-complementarity' in a rough everyday sense means that one would expect that as one has more unskilled labour one would be willing to pay more for a marginal unit of skilled labour; i.e. wages for skilled workers would increase.
7. Marie (1994) tends to support Freeman's (1994) view that government's ability to detect and punish illegal work has increased and now is more credible than 20 years ago. For France, it should be noted that natives form the greater part of the underground economy. Illegal employment seems to be demand determined and jobs can be offered to natives to work illegally and to illegal immigrant workers. There is no line to draw between the two cases. In economic terms, natives and illegals are perfect substitutes in the underground economy. Therefore the fight against the underground economy as a whole provides the better way to fight illegal alien employment
8. For a classical approach see Becker (1968). A survey on the economics of enforcement applied to environmental issues is Gawel (1993) whereas Entorf (1996) surveys recent developments in the economics of crime and punishment.
9. From some regularization programs that have been conducted in France, Italy, Spain and Portugal (for an intensive presentation of the French case see the Raport au Premier

Ministre (1992)) and from the OECD (1989) reports we know that illegal immigrant workers tend to be young males employed in specific sectors already characterized by a high proportion of legal immigrants employed – suggesting that employers have a preference for foreign workers.

10. Regularization programs have been conducted in France, Italy, Spain and Portugal. In France, official labour immigration ended in 1974. Only family reunification and entrance of seasonal workers was permitted. After several minor programmes, about 140,000 aliens were granted residence permits in 1981. The regularization programmes were decided in the framework of a law in Italy, Spain and in the USA whereas for France they were formulated as ministerial orders. It is noteworthy that the initial conditions and duration were eased during the operation in most countries giving the enacting authority more discretion over how to deal with unforeseen cases. However, this discretion was limited by the aliens' possibility to appeal – giving them some more confidence and security.
11. 'Europe has closed its doors to new immigration over twenty years ago. Postwar immigration to Europe has been a non-recurrent, historically unique process. The immigrants acquired in this process were not acquired by will, but by default' (Joppke 1996:23).
12. Ethier (1986) shows that with decreasing marginal effectiveness of controls relative to the resources invested, a mixture of both types of controls is optimal. If employers can distinguish legal from illegal immigrants, legal workers are advantaged by internal controls. However, if employers are not able to tell the difference between the two groups such a policy will harm all unskilled workers and benefit skilled workers because costs for unskilled workers in general increase. An increase of external controls benefits those workers who are likely to be confused with illegal aliens, e.g. legal immigrants from the same country, because they are less likely to be discriminated by the employer who might fear to hire illegal immigrants. Those ideas have been extended by Bond and Chen (1987), Djajic (1987) and Yoshida (1996).

REFERENCES

Baldwin-Edwards, M. (1997): 'The Emerging European Immigration Regime: Some Reflections on Implications for Southern Europe', *Journal of Common Market Studies*, 35, pp.497–519.

Becker, G.S. (1968): 'Crime and Punishment: An Economic Approach', *Journal of Political Economy*, 76, p.169–217.

Bhagwati, J.N. (1981): 'Alternative Theories of Illegal Trade: Ecocomic Consequences and Statistical Detection', *Weltwirtschaftliches Archiv*, Vol.117, pp.409–27.

Birrel, R. (1994): 'Immigration Control in Australia', *The Annals of the American Acadamy of Political and Social Sciences*, pp.106–17.

Bond, E.W. and T. Chen (1987): 'The Welfare Effects of Illegal Immigration', *Journal of International Economics*, 23, pp.315–27.

Borjas, G.J (1987): 'Immigrants, Minorities and Labor Market Competition', *Industrial and Labor Relations Review*, 40/3, pp.382–92.

Borjas, G.J. (1994): 'The Economics of Immigration', *Journal of Economic Literature*, 32, pp.1667–717.

Borjas, G.J. (1995): 'The Economic Benefits from Immigration', *Journal of Economics Perspectives*, 9, pp.3–22.

Bratsberg, B. (1995): 'Legal versus Illegal US Immigration and Source Country Characteristics', *Journal of International Economics*, pp.715–26.

Brubaker, R. (1995): 'Comments on 'Modes of Immigration Politics in Liberal Democratic States', *International Migration Review*, 29, pp.903–08.

Chiswick, B. (1988): *Illegal Aliens (Their Employment and Employers)*. Kalamazoo, Michigan (W.E. Upjohn Institute).

Collinson, Sarah (1993): *Europe and International Migration*, London: Pinter

Cornelius, Wayne A., Philip L. Martin and James F. Hollifield (1994a): 'Introduction: The Ambivalent Quest for Immigration Control', in Cornelius, Wayne A., Philip L. Martin and James F. Hollifield (eds.): *Controlling Immigration: A Global Perspective*, Stanford: Stanford University Press, pp.3–41.

Crane, K., B.J. Asch, J.Z. Heilbrunn and D.C. Cullinane (1990): *The Effect of Employer Sanction on the Flow of Undocumented Immigrants to the United States,* The Rand Corporation and The Urban Institute Press.

Dell'Aringa, C. and F. Neri (1989): 'Illegal Immigrants and the Informal Economy in Italy', in Ian Gordon and A.P. Thirlwall (eds.): *European Factor Mobility (Trends and Consequences)*, Basingstoke: Macmillan, pp.133–47.

Djajic, S. (1987): 'Illegal Aliens, Unemployment and Immigration Policy', *Journal of Development Economics,* 25, pp.235–49.

Djajic, S. (1997): 'Illegal Immigration and Resource Allocation', *International Economic Review*, 38, pp.97–117.

Entorf, H. (1996): 'Kriminalität und Ökonomie: Übersicht und neue Evidenz', *Zeitschrift für Wirtschafts- und Sozialwissenschaften,* 116, pp.417–50.

Epstein, G.S., A.L. Hillman and A. Weiss (1998): 'Creating Illegal Immigrants'. CEPR Discussion Paper, 1796 (January 1998), London.

Espenshade, T.J. (1995): 'Using INS Border Apprehension Data to Measure the Flow of Undocumented Migrants Crossing the US-Mexico Frontier', *International Migration Review,* 29, pp.545–65.

Ethier, W.J. (1986): 'Illegal Immigration. The Host-Country Problem', *American Economic Review* 76, pp.57–71.

Freeman, G.P. (1994): 'Can Liberal States Control Unwanted Migration?', *The Annals of the American Acadamy of Political and Social Sciences,* 534, pp.16–29.

Freeman, G.P. (1995): 'Modes of Immigration Politics in Liberal Democratic States', *International Migration Review*, 29, pp.881-902.

Freeman, G.P. (1995a): 'Rejoinder', *International Migration Review*, 29, pp.903–08.

Freeman, G.P. (1996): 'A Reply to Perlmutter', *International Migration Review*, 30, pp.389–93.

Gawel, E. (1993): 'Vollzug als Problem ökonomischer Theoriebildung', *Zeitschrift für Wirtschafts-und Sozialwissenschaften*, pp.597–627.

Grossman, J.B. (1984): 'Illegal Immigrants and Domestic Employment', *Industrial and Labor Relations Review*, 37, pp.240–51.

Hailbronner, K. (1995): *Möglichkeiten und Grenzen einer europäischen Harmonisierung des Einreise- und Asylrechts*, Baden-Baden: Nomos Verlag.

Hill, J. and J. Pearce (1990): 'The Incidence of Sanctions Against Employers of Illegal Aliens', *Journal of Political Economy,* 98, pp.28–44.

Hillman, A.L. and A. Weiss (1995): 'Why Illegal Immigration is Illegal and Why it Exists.' Paper presented at the CEPR Workshop on illegal migration, Halkidiki, Greece, September 15-17, 1995.

IOM (1995): *Transit Migration to Poland*, Geneva: International Organization for Migration.

Jahn, A.E. (1997): 'Wer hat Interesse an illegaler Beschäftigung? Niemand will sie ... missen', in Deutscher Gewerkschaftsbund (ed.): *Illegale Beschäftigung in der Europäischen Union*, Düsseldorf: Gewerkschaftliche und staatliche Handlungsmöglichkeiten.

Jahn, A.E. and T. Straubhaar (1995): 'On the Political Economy of Illegal Immigration'. Discussion Papers in Economic Policy, 52. Hamburg: University of the Armed Forces.

Joppke, C. (1996): 'Why Liberal States Accept Unwanted Immigration', paper presented at the Conference 'Effects of Policy on Migration Patterns and the Integration of Immigrants, Department of Demography, Humboldt University Berlin, November 1–2, 1996.

Kubat, D. (ed.) (1993): *The Politics of Migration Policies*, 2nd edition, New York: Center for Migration Studies.

Marie, C.V. (1994): 'From the Campaign against Illegal Migration to the Campaign against Illegal Work', *The Annals of the American Academy of Political and Social Sciences*, 534, pp.119–32.

Morita, K. and S. Sassen (1994): 'The New Illegal Immigration in Japan', *International Migration Review*, 28/1, pp.153–64.

OECD (1989): 'Comparative Analysis of Regularisation Experiences in France, Italy, Spain and the United States', in SOPEMI Report 1989, Paris: OECD.

Perlmutter, T. (1996): 'Bringing Parties Back In: Comments on 'Modes of Immigration Politics in Liberal Democratic Societies', *International Migration Review*, 30, pp.375–88.

Pozo, S. (ed.) (1986): *Essays on Legal and Illegal Immigration*, Kalamazoo, Michigan (W.E. Upjohn Institute).

Rapport au Premiere Ministre. Haut Conseil à l'Intégration (1992): *Les Étrangers et l'Émploi*, Paris.

Röseler, S. and D. Vogel (1993): 'Illegale Zuwanderer – ein Problem für die Sozialpolitik?' ZeS Arbeitspapier. Zentrum für Sozialpolitik, Universität Bremen.

Schmidt, C., A. Stilz and K.F. Zimmermann (1994): 'Mass Migration, Unions and Government Intervention', *Journal of Public Economics*, 55, pp.185–201.

Schoorl, J.J. *et al.* (1996): 'Migration from African and Eastern Mediterranean Countries to Western Europe', paper presented at the Mediterranean Conference on Population, Migration and Development. Council of Europe, Strasbourg.

Steineck, A. (1994): *Ökonomische Anforderungen an eine europäische Zuwanderungspolitik*, Baden-Baden: Nomos-Verlag.

Todaro, M.P. (1986): 'A Theory of Illegal International Migration from Developing Countries', Working Paper of The Population Council, New York.

Warren, R. (1994): 'Estimates of the Unauthorized Immigrant Population Residing in the United States by Country of Origin and State of Residence', Immigration and Naturalization Service, Washington D.C.

Yoshida, C. (1996): 'The Global Welfare of Illegal Immigration', *Indian Journal of Economics*, 74/303, pp.538–50.

Illegality, Enlightenment and Ambiguity: A Hot Italian Recipe

GIOVANNA ZINCONE

Italian immigration and immigrant policies are studied in this article to single out some features of democratic decision-making that we tend to underestimate. As we will try to demonstrate, democratic policies are not driven only by politicians' desires, or the need to comply with public opinion as postulated by economic and pluralistic theories of democracy; they are not simply inspired by the defence of vested interests, as neo-elitist and neo-Marxist theories would suggest, nor are they mainly shaped by persistencies, as neo-institutionalists maintain. All of these theories unveil some aspects of the decision making logic, but neglect one – the 'enlightened side' of the democratic process. Even contentious matters are partially sheltered from mass moods and potential populism by the 'enlightened' counterbalancing of civil servants and expert committees, or by the one-sided 'benevolent' pressure of agencies – such as leftist unions and voluntary associations – specialized in defending weaker strata. The role of pressure groups and civil servants[1] is well known in policy studies: what I wish to underline here is their capacity to simultaneously defend weak interests and adjust national legislation to conform with international agreements. The liberal principle that suggests the protection of basic rights from majority rule competence is normally played by judges. The magistracy has proved able to partially contrast legislation aimed at limiting the rights of asylum and family reunification, and also able to extend citizens' rights to resident foreigners even in the absence of valid residence permits (Hollifield 1994; Baldwin-Edwards and Schain 1994; Haut Conseil de l'Immigration 1990). In Italy this role was played by traditional lower strata pressure groups such as voluntary associations and unions, by civil servants and experts who formed together a relatively stable policy network.

As everywhere, the regulation of flows and the provisions aimed at incorporating foreign people have been reflecting the political perception of the issue: a perception that rapidly moved from under-evaluation to over-evaluation. This notwithstanding, these policies did not merely adapt to public alarm; they did not simply become more severe as by and large happened in other immigration countries. Whereas the policy of migration flows and repression of criminal behaviour connected to immigration became actually more strict, in accordance with Italian integration into the Schengen area, social policies for immigrants became increasingly liberal.

From the observation of the Italian case we can deduce five interesting features or characteristics of democratic decision making that are sometimes underestimated.

1. *The crucial role played by experts and civil servants.* In the case examined here, they were in some ways able to moderate public opinion that was showing a growing sense of discomfort towards immigration, on the one side; on the other, weak interest group pressure – reluctant to give up the cover of clandestinity and a strict compliance with the rule of law with regard to foreign criminals. The 'enlightened' dimension of democracy is probably far more widespread than traditional theoretical frameworks would suggest. The 'policy community' theory (Kingdon 1984) comes close to the syndrome that I intend to focus on, when it underlines the role of already existing expert networks. Expert and social worker networks – according to this theory – wait until they find a political opportunity to have their proposals listened to and implemented, they look for a sort of 'window' that could connect their virtual ideas to actual policy making. Still, the policy community theory does not take into due account the role of high level public administrators and innovative political leaders in integrating already existing policy community networks, thus playing a crucial policy steering activity. In the so-called transition between the First and the Second Republic, the Italian political system faced a major change of the political elite in parliament and in government; the relative lack of experience of the new elite increased the role of experts and high level civil servants. The present consolidation of the new elite and a relative restoration of party government is decreasing both the role of experts and civil servants in government.

2. *The innovating role of the periphery.* This is more neglected than the first characteristic. It refers to the fact that the origin of many rights, here of many immigrants' rights, can be traced back to practices introduced at local level through the combined action of local civil servants, voluntary

charitable associations, social workers, union representatives and researchers. This may suggest a flow of innovation from the periphery to the centre, which is usually considered irrelevant or less relevant relative to the centre to periphery direction.

3. *Working 'around' the law*. This third characteristic is virtually ignored. Local practices are often aimed at 'going around' the law, at 'honestly cheating' national legislators. Practices do not just implement and adapt legislation – as any good student of law would tell us – they also act *contra legem*, against the law: they can erode unwanted provisions and initiate new ones. It might be that this kind of benevolent public illegality is more widespread in southern Europe, especially in the Italian political system; however, it is not exclusive to this country or this region of the Western world, nor is it confined to immigration matters. Again, as agents of these benevolent *contra legem* practices we find charitable associations, social service workers and unions. *Contra legem* practices are not confined to the third sector, nor are they always inspired by benevolent action towards immigrants. Local *questure* [metropolitan police headquarters] and central government departments may obstruct progressive legislation and effectively dismantle it.

4. *Structural ambiguity*. Italian immigration policies can also play the function of a privileged observatory to notice a common characteristic of democratic decision making – the strategic propensity for 'self-contradiction', a sort of convenient ambiguity in law making. Contradictory patchwork policies, inconsistency between proclaimed principles embodied in legislation and actual implementation, are likely to flourish especially in the case of party systems like the Italian, which produce shrunk and heterogeneous governmental majorities. Even though no majority may be said to be completely homogeneous, the Italian case is quite peculiar in this respect. Furthermore, ambiguity is particularly convenient when hot matters like immigration are concerned – matters that cannot ignore opposition views.

5. *Policy continuity*. A final puzzling feature emerges from the analysis of immigration policies in Italy. Policy-making swings between persistency and emergency, the reproduction through the inertia of old attitudes and provisions not in tune with new social situations on the one side, and a flash reaction to impressive events on the other (Bolaffi 1996). Both these types of behaviour contrast with the 'enlightened attitude' of planning

innovative large, inclusive, long-lasting laws. The Italian capacity to deal with immigration whilst adhering to some liberal principles can be explained not only by the 'enlightened element' represented by the understated but crucial role played by experts and civil servants, and by the 'charitable element' due to the voluntary sector, but also by a recent Italian exceptionalism – the continuity of a series of centre-left governments, with the short interruption of Berlusconi's cabinet. Furthermore, even during this one centre-right government, the head of the department responsible for immigration policies was confirmed in office, and this minister was a relatively progressive social worker, according with the convention of assigning social policy responsibilities to individuals endowed with some sense of social solidarity. The uncommon eclipse of the Right from the government, and of right-wing personalities from the Social Affairs Department, may have contributed to preventing Italian immigration policies from experiencing the brisk U-turns observable in many other countries.

Italian immigration policies were able to move on the double track: on the one hand, increasing repression of illegal and criminal behaviour in tune with international relations of the country; on the other, the increasing extension of rights to immigrants – even undocumented immigrants. This balanced policy was made possible because of institutional changes and electoral reforms that moved the main focus of policy-making from parliament to the cabinet. At this level, policy-making is more open to civil servants' suggestions and experts' opinions.[2]

The electoral reform was more clearly majoritarian and candidate oriented at city level[3] thus widening the political role of mayors, and the so called 'mayors' party' was, and is, active in pressing for a more severe and repressive policy against immigrants' criminality and for more liberal social policies. We could also have assessed that the relatively liberal attitude of Italian policy-makers as far as immigrants' rights are concerned was due to the limited extent of the phenomenon and a consequent low concern in public opinion. This is unfortunately not the case, as even this relatively small number of immigrants has proved able to produce remarkable reactions in public opinion.

According to the latest official data of the Interior Ministry, on 31 December 1997 there were 1,240,721 foreigners legally resident in Italy. On the same date, the legal immigrants from non-EU countries in Italy numbered 1,072,596. If we count only those coming from Eastern Europe and developing countries, we have a figure of 972,462 – to which we should add some other 200–300,000 undocumented people from the same areas.[4] Summing up, we can roughly estimate a 'problematic immigration basin' of some 1,200,000–1,300,000 foreign people. We can define it as problematic since it is more likely to generate needs of cultural integration and social protection. It is a relatively small basin, but this is not the opinion of Italian people.

According to the European Commission 1997, 62 per cent of Italian as against 29 per cent of Spanish people believe that 'our country has reached its limits; if there were to be more people belonging to these minorities we would have problems' (EU15, 65 per cent). In a Eurobarometer poll of 1993, Italians had already achieved the highest score among European people in answering that immigrants in their own country were 'too many' (Italy being one of the European countries where the percentage of immigrants was lower at the time). In a more recent survey (European Commission, 1997), only 35 per cent define themselves as not at all racist (EU15, 34 per cent); by contrast Portugal scores 58 per cent, Spain 49 per cent and Greece 43 per cent. Italians reach also a medium score, in comparison with other European countries, as far as racist attitudes are concerned. That is why recent Italian immigration policies have been aimed at controlling the stock of immigrants from developing countries, as well as providing means of integration and social protection. This does not mean that policy-makers have succeeded in reaching their goals.

In the next paragraph we briefly analyze the evolution of migratory flows toward Italy, and the main political initiatives of the 1980s. Then, in the second part of this article, we focus on recent legislation, both immigration policies (entries, stay, expulsions) and integration policies (nationality law, civil, social and political rights). We will use this analysis to give evidence of our hypothesis about the main features of democratic decision making processes.

MIGRATION FLOWS AND THE PERCEPTION OF THE PROBLEM IN THE 1980S

Immigration flows to Italy started after the 1974 oil crisis, when other European countries – notably Germany, Britain and France – announced the closure of their borders. Flows were then partially diverted from the economically and socially more attractive northern and central Europe to southern Europe. Inflows to Italy consisted mainly of those who previously would have gone to France, a deflection which has been favoured by vicinity to the main French immigration source, the Maghreb, and by the continuing 'open door' practices. The level of immigration was initially quite insignificant, until the more affluent European countries kept open the two possibilities of political asylum and family reunification.

In the late 1970s immigrants to Italy were still mostly people of Italian origin coming back from Europe and South America[5] even though domestic labourers from Asia and Africa were employed in big cities and seasonal workers from Maghreb were recruited as fishermen in southern regions (ISTAT 1992). Furthermore, especially in central and northern cities, a consistent growth in the numbers of university students and political refugees was detected: they were mainly Iranian, Kurd, Palestinian, Jordanian from the Middle East; Somalis and Eritreans from Africa; and Brazilians, Chileans, Uruguayans and Argentines from South America. For non-European political dissenters, it was difficult to enjoy the legal status of refugee in Italy, since it was automatically given only to people coming from Communist Countries, according to the so-called 'geographic clause' (or 'proviso') with which Italy had signed the Geneva Convention and that was repealed only in 1990.

Italy discovered itself to be a country of immigration at the beginning of the 1980s. The 1981 Census revealed an unexpectedly 'high' number of foreign residents (210,937) and presences (109,841) on Italian territory, but the issue of immigration did not immediately reach the political agenda. Immigrants recorded in the 1981 Census were mainly of Italian origin (Melotti 1993) and in a reasonable economic condition. They were not in need of either cultural or economic integration.

The biggest influx of immigrants of non-Italian origin dates from between 1984 and 1989, when some 700–800,000 people entered the territory (Mauri and Micheli 1992), among them 300–350,000 without a regular permit. Thus, during the 1980s Italy shared with Germany the primacy of the largest inflows within the EC.

Even when the big influx from North Africa was already underway, the Italian Government continued an open door policy. As a traditional country of emigration, Italy had difficulty in perceiving immigration as a social problem. Only a small minority of the Italian people – as shown by surveys – used to perceive immigration as risky (Bonifazi 1991). Nevertheless, some problems had to be solved. A large percentage of immigrants were undocumented, the legal entitlements of immigrants in Italy were still to be defined, and a process of integration had yet to begin.

In 1986, the Government tried to face these problems with Law no. 943 of 30 December (renewed through Act no. 81, 1988). The aim of the act was to legalize and regulate the situation of immigrants in Italy and to prevent illegal immigration rather than to restrict access and cut down inflows. Two committees were created on that occasion. The first was attached to the Ministry of Foreign Affairs[6] and had the purpose of regulating flows, controlling illegal immigration and repressing organizations working in that field. The hypothesis that inspired the committee's activity was based on the experience of Italian emigration abroad: legal immigration was caused by the pull effect of labour demand, illegal immigration was due to the hidden economy.[7]

The second committee, with a consultative role, was attached to the Ministry of Labour and Social Security and it should have been composed, among others, of six representatives nominated by the main non-EU immigrant organizations.[8] Since it was difficult to select the most representative immigrant associations, the number of seats assigned to them was conspicuously enlarged. Some sixty people were admitted and the logic of their appointment was in some way inspired by clientelistic criteria. One can imagine the consequences of this move for the political relevance of the committee. In fact, it was abolished three years later, as was the first one.

The fact that the main consultative committee was attached to the Ministry of Labour and that the Migration Flows Committee was aimed at regularizing the import of manpower indicates that Italian politicians and civil servants were still looking at immigrants as 'workers plus their families'. The inertia forces were then prevailing in immigration policy-making: it tended to interpret current Italian immigration in the light of past Italian emigration. The bulk of the first provisions in fact treated immigrants as workers; they were intended to protect nationals' employment from the 'unfair' competition from foreigners. Nationals were given priority in employment opportunity and non-EU workers were prevented from moving freely from one kind of job to another. Entry and work permits were given after having checked the lack of national manpower for those jobs. Non-EU foreign citizens wanting to work in Italy were supposed to register in special placement lists at Italian consulates in their own countries. These lists, in reality, were never drawn up. The cost of migrant labour was equalized and even made higher in comparison with domestic labour by making employers pay more expensive social security contributions for non-EU alien workers. No serious effort, however, was made to eliminate the illegal employment of migrant workers in the hidden economy. Thus, the focus of Italian migration policies at that time was still restricted to the employment issue, although many immigrants were not in fact entering the workforce, at least the registered workforce.

Yet, the 1986 Act was intended also to foster integration; it stated for instance that immigrants should have free opportunities for learning Italian. At the same time, it favoured the protection of ethnic identities and decided that courses of native languages should be available (Art. 9). However, no public money from the central state budget was reserved for these initiatives, and the law, while emphasizing good purposes, did not provide for the concrete means to implement them. The meagre local finances were charged of these and other new duties connected to immigration. The discrepancy between noble principles underlying the legislation and actual implementation was emerging.

Immigration policies at central level had a first turn in 1989; by the end of the decade, the perception and political conceptualization of the issue had changed. The impact of relevant immigrant flows started to be dramatically visible in large cities and in southern agricultural areas. The lack of accommodation, the consequent squatting by immigrants, the aggressive reactions of the nationals living near the occupied buildings, homeless immigrants subject to aggression by extreme right-wing youngsters, the illegal labour market and people living in brutal conditions were all features of an uneasy situation which reached a peak when a black labourer, Jerry Essan Masslo, was assassinated in Villa Literno (Calabria), in October 1989. Immigration appeared abruptly on the political agenda as an emergency issue and it was deeply reconceptualized. The new guiding principles behind Italian migration policy were to give to immigrants already present in Italy the opportunity to lead a decent life and to strongly reduce inflows. Drastically limiting new arrivals was considered a precondition for the social rescue of those already in Italy.

Thus, Italian Governments' political attitudes toward immigration started to converge with other European countries, *at least in principle*. In fact, the decree of 30 December 1989, which later become law (Law 28 February 1990, n. 39) embodied this new political attitude, but more as a rhetorical stance than through concrete measures. Italy decided to be a 'cautious country of immigration'. In conformity with the Schengen Treaty[9] the Martelli Law abolished the special clause attached to the Geneva Convention[10] thus accepting asylum seekers; on the other hand, Italy made visas compulsory for people coming from 'high emigration risk areas'.[11] It also introduced proper accommodation and a minimum income level as criteria for residing on Italian territory.

As regards the problem of regulating inflows, Law no. 39 of 28 February 1990 indicated not only economic reasons (the lack of national workers in some trades) or cultural preferences (people of national origin) as criteria for establishing priority in entering and legally residing in Italy , but it asked a Flows Committee[12] to decide how many workers from non-EU countries could enter Italy every year. Priority in the right to a work permit was first given to national and EU citizens, then non-EU unemployed residents, then non-EU immigrants already resident but with a different residence permit, and lastly non-EU citizens still resident in their own countries. All these constraints resulted in a decision to cut the inflow of workers to a small number.[13] This conclusion suggested that the Committee should extend its competence so as to adjust the quota of non EU citizens to be admitted every year according to the arrivals for family reunions and for humanitarian reasons – both to be included within the yearly quota.

The Committee may or may not have given sensible advice during the following three years; its decisions were either overwhelmed by emergencies like the influx of refugees from Albania or eroded by ineffective implementation. After the first crisis in Albania (October 1990 and March 1991), those in ex-Yugoslavia (since Autumn 1991) and Somalia (September 1992), the Italian Government felt obliged to host people in danger. A new status, the 'asylum for humanitarian reasons'[14] was introduced (Bonetti 1993), following the example of northern European countries. The award of this status to categories and groups depends on decisions taken by the Italian government and can be given, and withdrawn, at will. It is therefore a more discretionary political instrument than the status of political refugee. At the end of 1994, foreigners present in Italy for humanitarian reasons were 46,290; people with this legal status grew to 55,684 in 1995 and decreased to 45,930 in 1996 (Caritas 1997:95). The figures of permits for humanitarian reasons tend obviously to reflect emergency trends (see Tables 1 and 2).

In February 1997, political crisis and turmoil in Albania, together with active support from the local mafia, brought a new massive landing on the Apulian shores.[15] To these boat-people some 17,000 temporary permits were given, valid just until August 30 of that year, but they were extended for 90 more days to allow a gradual repatriation; a large proportion in the meantime had just disappeared, i.e. they became illegal residents.[16]

As the recent annual report of the Central Commission for the Recognition of the Status of Refugee (CCRR, *Commissione Centrale per*

TABLE 1

IMMIGRANTS BY AREA OF ORIGIN (1992–97)

	1992	1993	1994	1995	1996	1997
EU	146,918	152,954	141,577	164,003	152,092	168,125
Non-EU	778,254	834,451	781,129	827,416	943,530	1,072,596
of which:						
ADCs	120,395	122,567	107,696	101,594	90,972	100,134
LDCs	657,859	711,844	673,433	725,822	852,558	972,462
TOTAL	**925,172**	**987,405**	**922,706**	**991,419**	**1,095,622**	**1,240,721**

Source: Caritas 1997:69 (data of the Ministry of the Interior)

Advanced Developed Countries (ADC): Andorra, Australia, Canada, Japan, Gibraltar, Iceland, Israel, Leichtenstein, Malta, Monaco, Norway, Switzerland, USA, Vatican City, and, until 31/12/1994, Austria, Finland, Sweden

Less Developed Countries (LDC): all the others

TABLE 2

THE 31 COUNTRIES WITH THE HIGHEST LEVEL OF EMIGRATION TO ITALY (1995–97)

	1997	1996	1995	% CHANGE 1996/95	1997/96
Morocco	131,406	119,481	94,237	26.79	9.98
Albania	83,807	63,976	34,706	84.34	31.00
Philippines	61,285	57,071	43,421	31.44	7.38
USA	59,572	54,659	60,607	-9.81	8.99
Tunisia	48,909	44,821	40,454	10.79	9.12
Fmr Yugoslavia	44,370	44,259	51,973	-14.84	0.25
Germany	40,079	36,515	39,372	-7.26	9.76
Romania	38,138	31,673	24,513	29.21	20.41
China	37,838	29,073	21,507	35.18	30.15
Senegal	34,831	31,870	23,953	33.05	9.29
Poland	31,329	27,375	22,022	24.31	14.44
France	28,333	25,585	27,273	-6.19	10.74
Sri Lanka	28,162	24,920	20,275	22.91	13.01
Great Britain	26,771	24,779	27,694	-10.53	8.04
Egypt	26,171	23,785	21,874	8.74	10.30
Peru	24,362	21,738	10,025	116.84	12.07
Brazil	23,008	19,887	22,053	-9.82	15.69
India	22,620	19,417	14,629	32.73	16.50
Croatia	20,464	18,865	18,944	-0.42	8.48
Switzerland	18,611	17,923	18,327	-2.20	3.84
Spain	18,549	16,842	17,847	-5.63	9.52
Ghana	18,032	16,379	12,550	30.51	10.09
F.Y.R.O.M.	16,504	16,419	15,426	6.44	0.52
Greece	15,728	13,688	14,821	-7.64	14.90
Nigeria	14,243	11,229	6,343	77.03	26.84
CSI	13,604	10,184	10,197	-0.13	33.58
Algeria	13,086	9,812	4,020	144.08	33.37
Somalia	12,172	11,235	17,839	-37.02	8.34
Bangladesh	12,101	11,145	5,541	101.14	8.58
Bosnia-Herz.	11,866	11,068	10,224	8.26	7.21
Dominican Rep.	11,403	10,384	8,652	20.02	9.81
First 31 countries	*987,354*	*894,985*	*777,480*	*15.11*	*10.32*
TOTAL	**1,240,721**	**1,095,622**	**991,419**	**10.51**	**13.24**

Sources: Caritas 1997:69; Caritas 1998:79 (Data of the Ministry of the Interior)

il Riconoscimento dello Status di Rifugiato) has stated, the allowance of temporary permits and of those for humanitarian reasons accounts for the decreasing number of asylum seekers: 1,766 in 1994, 1,738 in 1995, only 675 in 1996, and 4,960 in 1997 (Caritas 1997:116.; Caritas 1998: 106). Italian authorities have moderated their severe attitude on this matter. The rate of acceptance was only 4.88 per cent of asylum seekers in 1992 (336 people); but in 1995 it increased to 16.7 per cent and to 22.1 per cent in 1996 (Caritas 1997: 92). Since the number of requests had considerably decreased, by the end of 1995 the residence permits given under this title (to refugees and people waiting for asylum to be granted) were only 10,352, 1 per cent of the total of permits, and they had decreased to 0.4 per cent (3,902) by the following year (Caritas 1997:92). Owing to recent changes, the requests rose again to 1,518 in 1997 (up 132 per cent) and to 1,963 at 15 June 1998 (+182 per cent). Asylum seekers figures are doomed to increase further for three reasons (*Documento programmatico*, 1998): because the new Law (no. 40, 1998) foresees the possibility of receiving a work permit for people whose asylum requests were refused, have appealed and have being waiting for a decision for more than two months; because the Dublin Convention will increase the number of people seeking asylum in other European countries whose first country of arrival is Italy; and finally because the Napolitano-Turco Law will hopefully make clandestine entries more difficult.

The small number of asylum seekers in the past can be explained by the fact that relatively restrictive criteria on this matter have always been coupled with more permissive attitudes towards undocumented immigrants. Many people were able to enter as clandestine or with a tourist visa and overstay, then regularize their position under the three amnesties enacted in the last ten years. The 1986 Law allowed the legalization of 118,349 people, the 1990 Martelli Law of 234,841, the Dini Decree (D. l. 18 November 1995 no. 489)2[17] of 248,501 (see Figure 1).

The Martelli Law was just an apparent turn in the Italian policy of easy entry; it can in fact be considered as the strongest message that illegal entry to Italy and subsequent legalization were the easiest way to immigrate into Europe. Amnesty was announced with considerable advance while border controls were not reinforced: it became easy to obtain proof of having arrived in Italy before 31 December and regularize on the spot. The Martelli Law, against its proclamed intentions, gave incentives to new clandestine entries to Italy: it can be considered as one of the best examples of discrepancy between rhetorical

FIGURE 1

IMMIGRANTS IN ITALY SINCE 1989. THE AMNESTY EFFECT.

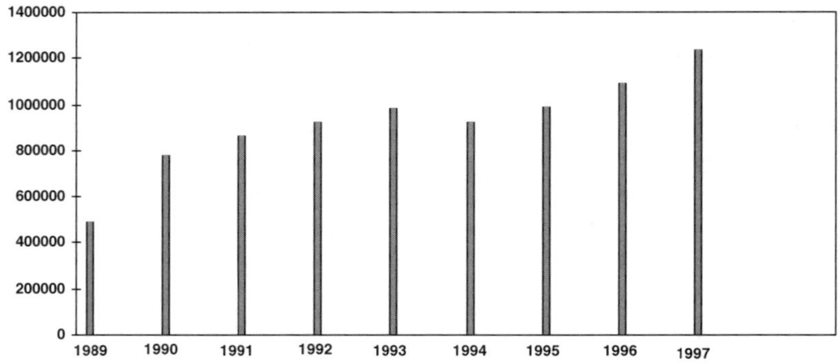

Source: elaboration on data of the Ministry of the Interior

principles, proclaimed aims of legislation and actual outcomes. Preparation and implementation of the Martelli Law shows the important role played by Italian unions and Catholic voluntary associations in defending immigrant interests – illegal immigrants' interests in particular. These 'one-sided pressure groups' were active in reshaping the Martelli Law and in providing immigrants with the necessary proofs to be legalized. This is also a case of benevolent law cheating. Preparation and implementation of the Martelli law also singles out the possible contrast between high level public administrators more interested in complying with international treaties and western European moods, on the one hand, and lower strata pressure groups more interested in advocating immigrants' needs, on the other hand.

Beside attracting actual new immigrants, amnesties produce a false 'new migration' statistic effect. In the period 1981–97, we observe a quasi-regular yearly increase (between 5 and 12 per cent) with some positive and negative peaks. The three main positive peaks follow the legalizations: up 27.1 per cent in 1987, after the first amnesty (Law 30 December 1986 no. 943); up 59.3 per cent in 1990, after the second amnesty (Law 28 February 1990 no. 39) (Pastore 1998:72); 10.51 per cent in 1996 (Caritas 1997). The analysis of more recent data shows that the last amnesty has produced more than 250,000 false 'new immigrants'. The periodical cleaning-out of expired permits and multiple applications brought a negative peak of down 24 per cent in 1989.

The policy of closing the front door to legal entry while keeping the back door for illegal entry half open was finally pushed into change. Recurrent illegal arrivals especially from Albania, petty criminality (prostitution, burglary, drugs smuggling) characterized the new waves:[18] they were upsetting public opinion and the risk of spreading anti-immigration attitudes became real and consistent.

RECENT DEVELOPMENTS: FROM CONTRI'S BILL TO LAW NO. 40, 6 MARCH 1998

The turning point can be dated back to 1993, when a first attempt was made to prepare a general reform not only of the Martelli Law but also of the entire legal treatment of non-EU foreigners. It was initiated by the then Minister of Social Affairs Fernanda Contri, under the Ciampi Government (April 1993–January 1994). The minister charged a special committee, composed of experts and heads of civil service departments, with writing the new Bill. In this decision and in the choice of core members of the committee, a special role was played by the chief of the department, Guido Bolaffi; despite the change of governments, ministers and political majorities, he has remained in this post. This fact – as we have already stated – helps to explain the high degree of continuity of Italian immigration policy.

The expert committees and the political action of the heads of departments have also played a special and stronger role in Italian decision making in the recent period of political transition, characterized by a consistent change in the political elite. The fall of the Berlin Wall (9 November 1989) and the definitive democratic option made first by the Italian Communist party (Council of Direction, October 1989 and the Rimini Congress, January 1991) and then by the formerly neo-fascist MSI (Fiuggi Congress, February 1994), together with the 'clean hands' judges' action (started by Di Pietro on February 1992), deeply reshaped the Italian party system. Old parties were disbanded, traditional cleavages (pro/anti-communism) became obsolete, new cleavages were then able to rise and find political representation.

New autonomous local parties had already started in the 1980s, but they gave birth to a larger federated Northern League (*Lega Nord)* only in the early 1990s. The crisis of the Socialist Party and of the Christian Democrats, because of the magistrates' action, and the disquieting presence of the Northern League left space for a new moderate party, *Forza Italia* (Go Italy). The new party was initiated at the end of 1993 and officially set up in 1994 by the owner of the three main private television networks – Silvio Berlusconi. The centre-right coalition included either new parties like *Forza Italia* and *Lega Nord* (which eventually split from the coalition) or parties for the first time in government, such as *Alleanza Nazionale* (the 'post-fascist' group). The centre-left coalition also included parties for the first time in government, such as the post-communist PDS (now DS), plus small parties re-born from Christian Democratic ashes; these governments were obliged to promote new leaders not yet compromised with scandals and corruption. If we sum up the turnover of 1992 (43 per cent) and the turnover of 1994 (71 per cent) we can get an idea of the dramatic recent renewal of the Italian political elite (Cotta and Verzichelli 1996: 380).

Ministers in office for the first time are more ready to accept the professional support of prominent civil servants and experts. The committee appointed by Fernanda Contri was able to prepare a complete reform project in less than six months. In March 1994, a perhaps too extensive bill (172 articles) on immigration was presented. The Bill introduced some relevant changes, such as basic public health provisions and public education – even for undocumented immigrants.

The same Bill, for the first time in Italy, proposed the right to local voting for immigrants who had been legally residents in Italy for more then five years. The fall of Ciampi's government and the rise of Berlusconi's (April–December 1994) prevented the Contri Bill from becoming law. The core of its proposals were included in the Turco-Napolitano bill (after the name of the Ministers of Social Affairs and Interiors) presented on 19 February 1997[19] and was approved, after a long and distressing parliamentary debate on the 6 March 1998.

The New Immigration Policies: Expulsions, Entry and Residence Permits

Some of the measures of the Contri Bill were already included in the Dini decree (18 November 1995), named after the then prime minister (January 1995–April 1996), head of the cabinet that came after Berlusconi's. Its mandate was to deal with only the most pressing problems (avoidance of a political crisis during the Italian presidency of the European Union, preventing further rise in public debt) and to prepare new elections.

The distinctive character of the Dini Decree, when compared with both the Contri Bill and the present Napolitano-Turco Law, consisted of restricting the opportunity for appeal in cases of expulsion on the grounds of *ordre public*; this has occasioned some critiques in terms of constitutional compatibility and has since been amended.

We start by summarizing here the main novelties introduced by Law no.40, 6 March 1998, on expulsions, entry and residence permits. The other parts of the law will be analyzed later when we deal with immigrants' citizenship rights in Italy.

In order to control clandestine entries, the Law foresees the possibility of detaining illegal immigrants in special 'centres of residence and assistance'; this is a typical example of compromise and ambiguity, since the Law (art. 12) does not specify their method of operation. Until now their uncertain nature can be underlined by the fact that they are run by voluntary associations (such as the Red Cross) and patrolled by the police. Detention in special centres can be applied not only to people caught illegally crossing the Italian borders and to people already requested to leave the country, but also to undocumented residents. A partial exception is made for those illegal residents who had come to Italy before the Law was enacted (as shown by their passport validation): this category of undocumented aliens can only be ordered to leave the country within 15 days – a fairly useless measure. However, on the basis of a local *Questore* (Sheriff) discretionary decision, and with the consent of the local judge, they too can be interned (art.11, par 15).

In practice, a large proportion of illegal immigrants already present in Italy may be put in the new special detention places or left free, according to the local police authority discretion. This is a typical case of a 'self-contradictory', ambiguous and discretionary piece of legislation. It is highly questionable because of the uncertain nature of the centres, and the discretionary power left to the *Questore*. It was the result of a compromise between the right-wing parties on the one hand, who wanted to make possible the expulsion of all undocumented foreigners and the left-wing of the majority coalition (backed by lower strata pressure groups) on the other, that wanted to concentrate the expulsion efforts on criminals and leave the undocumented undisturbed. The Right wanted clandestine immigrants caught at the borders to be put in prison when it is possible to identify and expel them, and the Left was not prepared to consider clandestine entry as a crime. The same quarrel divided left-wing parties in government and centre and right parties in the opposition in August 1998, when the 30 days term of detention was elapsing for many unidentified clandestine immigrants. The ministers of the interior (Napolitano) and of social affairs (Turco), both belonging to DS, backed the decision to set them free – though making it clear that further police measures would be taken against them.

The Turco-Napolitano Law foresees three kinds of expulsion. The *administrative expulsion* (art.11) is decided by the minister of the interior for reasons of *ordre public* and state security or by the prefect of police both for *undocumented* aliens and for foreigners *suspected* of belonging to criminal organizations. In the first case the indicted can appeal to the administrative court, in the other cases to normal judges. The deadline for the appeal is in any case only five days for those people still in Italy and 30 days for those already expelled. The *expulsion for security reasons* (art.13) is decided by a judge and concerns people *already convicted for relevant crimes* and it does not erase the penalty; whereas the *expulsion as alternative to the penalty* (art. 14) is applied to people *involved in minor crimes*.

The introduction of more severe measures towards undocumented people was due to the growing belief that illegal residence and criminal behaviour 'go hand in hand'. Though illegality is of course not a sufficient condition for becoming a criminal, in 1997, 75.8 per cent of foreign people arrested proved to be illegally resident (Blangiardo 1998:48).

The Turco-Napolitano Law reproduces Contri's project and the Dini Decree's severe provisions aimed at combating the smuggling of immigrants.[20] It also confirms another provision already present in Contri's bill and Dini's decree: an important incentive is given to the victims, often young prostitutes, to rebel against criminal organization and denounce their exploiters. This consists of the chance of receiving a permanent permit and of benefiting from special assistance programmes (art. 16). The measure has produced good results.

Law no. 40, 6 March 1998 also makes clearer the conditions required in order to reside in Italy legally. Every three years the president of the council (art.3) has to present to the council of ministers and then to parliament an immigration flows plan, whose quantity will be decided taking into account labour market needs.

Sponsorship is the most important innovation introduced by legislation in the field of entries (art.21). Italian citizens and foreigners (legally resident in Italy), regions, local administrations, unions and a list of recognized voluntary associations can guarantee and support immigrants 'looking for a job'. To those 'sponsored' immigrants a temporary permit can be issued within the planned quota. Legal entry is thus made simpler by the new Law. Furthermore the residence permit can become permanent (art. 7). After five years of legal stay in Italy, those foreign people who have not been indicted for crimes, can apply for a permanent permit card. The card should represent – at least in intention – a tool for integration, because only people who can stay as long as they want can plan a future in the country. Many of the provisions that we will illustrate in the next paragraph are inspired by the same logic.

So is the easing of family reunion requirements. Measures that should facilitate family reunion were already present in Contri's project and Dini's decree. We can date the change in this matter to 1993, when a series of circulars obliged the departments involved to answer the request of reunion within 90 days, to use the most rapid means of communication among the various offices, and to deliver the decision to the families (Zincone 1994: 96; Caritas, 1995: 134). In 1992 family reunions were only 6,518, but in the first half of 1993 they numbered already 8,564. At present, there is a positive trend: they were 13,943 in 1995, and 13,665 in 1996 (Caritas, 1997: 156), 27,785 in 1997 (Caritas 1998: 185): about 25 per cent of residence permits for non EU foreigners are in the category of family reasons.

TABLE 3

RESIDENCE PERMITS (AS OF 31 DECEMBER 1997)

Reason for stay	
Employment	720,243
Family reasons	230,450
Religious matters	58,372
Study	56,759
Tourism	47,360
Elective residency	45,852
Self-employment	36,586
Adoption	9,706
Asylum seekers	5,128
Others	30,265
TOTAL	**1,240,721**

Source: Caritas 1998:103-106 (Data of the Ministry of the Interior)

Moreover, the Turco Law widens the categories of relatives to which this permit can be given: parents and also those relatives within the third degree of relationship such as uncles, aunts, great-grandparents and great-grandchildren, who, because of their handicaps, cannot work and support themselves (art.27). Thus, we start giving some substance to the idea that Italian immigration policies are quietly converging with other

TABLE 4

RESIDENCE PERMITS, PROPORTIONS BY CATEGORY OF REASON FOR STAY

Reason for stay	**1990** (%)	**1995** (%)	**1997** (%)
Employment	46,2	52,3	58,1
Family reunion	12,5	17,7	18,6
Religious matters	5,0	5,0	4,7
Tourism	8,8	4,9	3,8
Elective residency	5,6	4,4	3,7
Self-employment	3,1	3,9	2,9
Others	18,8	11,8	8,2
TOTAL	**781,138**	**991,419**	**1,240,721**

Source: Caritas, 1998:109 (Data of the Ministry of the Interior)

countries' policies as far as the repression of illegality and criminality is concerned, but they are also diverging with regards to integration measures.

One important piece of the integration puzzle consists of avoiding putting immigrants in need of breaking the law. The use of sponsorship will hopefully avoid, for instance, an improper use of tourist visas, so easier long-term residence permits for relatives will avoid their illegal overstaying; similarly, allowing the reunited parents and asylum seekers to work will no longer force them to enter the illegal economy. The difficult process of establishing obedience to the law in Italy is taking three forms in this, as in other fields: a more active magistracy, the incorporation into new legislation of previously *contra legem* practice and statuses, the abrogation of pieces of legislation too difficult to comply with.

Naturalization and Intermediate Rights

As in many other European countries, Italy has always followed by and large a *jus sanguinis* model. This model fitted the case of an emigration country, it allowed the retention of bonds with Italians who had emigrated. More surprisingly, the *jus sanguinis* character has been reinforced after Italy perceived its new condition of being an immigration country.[21] The Nationality Law (5 February 1992, no. 91) is more generous towards foreigners of Italian origin and EU-citizens, but less generous than the previous legislation towards other categories of foreigners. The period of residence required by the previous law (15 June

1912 no. 555) was five years for everybody; now it has been raised to ten for non-EU citizens, and reduced to four for EU-citizens and to three for people of Italian origin. The present Minister of Social Affairs, Livia Turco, is planning to make naturalization for non-EU citizens easier. The same law – following the self-contradiction principle – also introduced a *jus soli* element when it foresaw the possibility for foreign children born in Italy, and legally resident in the country for some time, to become citizens at the age of 18. The liberal principle of double citizenship was introduced as well. The two progressive elements of the law were made void by the obstruction of public administration. An immediate inscription to the register of births instead of the hospital certificate was required. The Ministry of the Interior using an administrative decree signed by Under Secretary Gasparri (of National Alliance) (22 November 1994) ruled in a matter such as nationality that is protected by the rule of law (*riserva di legge*). It decided that for people from countries that do allow double citizenship the applicant has to renounce diplomatic protection of the country of origin and virtually that citizenship. The obstructionist attitude of part of the public administration prove the possibility that law changing in Italy is not always due to a benevolent attitude towards immigrants, but also by the opposite attitude. This could also explain the low rate of naturalization. In fact, naturalizations in Italy are very few at the moment, as is normal in the first phase of the migration cycle (Böhning 1972; Bonifazi 1991).

Italy in the mid-1990s is still characterized (though not uniformly) by a situation in which immigrants have come recently, and still plan to – and sometimes do – go back to their native countries. In 1992, the year of the new nationality law, there were just 4,408 naturalizations, 3,869 of which were through marriage. In the following years there has been a progressive though modest increase: they were 6,544 in 1993, 6,613 in 1994, 7,442 in 1995 (6,396 of them by marriage), 6,961 in 1996 (6,059 of them by marriage) (Caritas, 1997:177), 9,221 in 1997 (Caritas, 1998:98).

Since the chances of getting a regular permit and renewing it vary from region to region, the chances of being naturalized, and consequently of acquiring political rights, differ from place to place. This potential differentiation of naturalization and political rights goes together with a potential differentiation of political rights at the local level.

The Italian legal system, for the moment, does not foresee local voting for non-EU nationals. At the beginning of the 1990s, public opinion on this subject seemed to be divided, 45.5 per cent for, and 45.8 per cent against (Bonifazi 1991); a more recent survey conducted by CIRM (February 1997) reported 52 per cent in favour, 33 per cent against, and 10 per cent uncertain. Both the Contri and the Turco Bills embodied local voting for documented immigrants after five years of legal stay. This was one of the rights that should be connected with the 'permanent card'. Art. 38 of the Turco Bill, that should have introduced local voting also for non-EU citzens, was removed and its approval posponed because the Constitutional Committee of Parliament decided against its constitutionality.[22] A project of constitutional revision has already been presented (AC 4167), but it is unlikely to be passed in a short time. Anyway, once again Italian immigration policies are in many respects moving against the mainstream: none of the European countries have planned to introduce the right to vote for immigrants after the 1980s, with the exception of Belgium after the killing of a Moroccan girl by a paedophile. The same country still has to implement the Maastrict Treaty and give local voting rights to EU citizens.

In some Italian cities, immigrants enjoy the right to vote in consultative referenda. Act no. 142, 8 June 1990, allows individual cities to adopt autonomous statutes. Cities such as Turin (title II, art.9) and Bologna (title II, art.3) have allowed foreigners who have legal residence to take part in local referenda. In Rome this is possible only after five years of regular residence (title II, art.3), whereas in other towns (such as Milan) the proposal was rejected. In general, city councils governed by progressive majorities voted for all sorts of forms of representation for immigrants: Bologna, Napoli, Catania, Modena and Nonantola (a small town in the Province of Modena) introduced one added (co-opted) city councillor. In Turin, the councillor has been added at neighbourhood council level. Turin, La Spezia and Modena adopted elective consultative bodies. The popular investiture did not provide these bodies with higher influence however. This is the case of the elective consultative committee in Turin, elected on 19 June 1995; in the following November it protested because it had not been consulted in many relevant circumstances, and a month later members of right-wing parties asked for its abolition, because it was considered both useless and quarrelsome.

Thus, as we have seen, access to intermediate political rights varies from town to town. A similar observation, as we will see, applies to public provision and social services. Many of those creative, often *contra legem* practices so crucial in Italian immigration policy-making, come from the same few towns (Bologna and Turin, in particular). What are the factors responsible for local innovative policies?

Varying *political attitudes* towards immigration is one; i.e. local political majority. Milan, which is relatively more reluctant to extend provisions to immigrants, was the first major city conquered by the *Lega Nord*; i.e. with a majority belonging to the party that has the strongest anti-immigrant stance. Milan's current majority, which does not include the Northern League, is a centre-right coalition including *Alleanza Nazionale*. The 'converted' post-fascist party has not taken a clear anti-immigration stance at central level, although it tends to oppose immigrants' rights, political rights for instance; besides, it has often raised anti-immigrant issues at local level.

It is not only the political colour of the majority of the city council and of the mayor that matter, however, but also the different *efficiency of local administrations and services*. For example, in 1990 Rome housed 20 per cent of non-EU foreign residents and granted 22.1 per cent of all residence permits. The region of Latium – whose capital is Rome – consequently received the largest share of the funds that the Martelli Law made available for temporary accommodation for immigrants, but the local authorities were not able to spend this money.

Strength and attitudes of voluntary associations (mainly Catholic) and *their relations with the local administrations* are also crucial variables in determining immigrants' treatment. The very right of residence depends on the efficiency of the local *Questore*, on the informational support and on the compliance of local union and voluntary associations, which can provide declarations and certificates. Similarly, the chance for innovative practices to be introduced depends on a synergic relation between local majorities, local civil servants, local unions and voluntary associations. The relevance of this 'synergy factor' applies in particular to the delivery of social services and to integration policies.

Social Problems and Social Policies

Ambiguity and contradiction within the national legislation – the space left for discretionary implementation, needed to keep quiet radical wings of both majority and opposition – make possible the differentiation at local level. This remarkable differentiation contrasts with the Italian institutional framework which is still highly (though increasingly less) centralized. The Italian case suggests that the location of immigrant policy implementation at the local level is inevitable: it is there that problems arise, are perceived, and must be faced.

Ambiguity and contradiction also produce inconsistency in law enforcement and, secondly, opportunities for arbitrary behaviour and corruption. Some employees of the Italian consulate in Nigeria are being investigated for allegedly selling visas, others are suspected. Undocumented immigrants' relative immunity in several of their trades is supposedly linked to some policemen's rewarded blind eye. Discretion and corruption are not typical of immigrants' treatment, as they represent a quite widespread syndrome.

Immigration can help the understanding of political systems, as it puts the system under stress and highlights its deficiencies. For the same reason it also brings significant changes to the system. Political and social structures have to adapt to the functional and cultural needs of the immigrants. Immigration can therefore be taken as an agent of political change.

Social policies can provide evidence for the peculiar phenomenon of high local variation in the institutional framework of a formally centralized state, thus acting as *reagent*, but they are even more appropriate for focusing on immigration as an *agent* of change.

The specific legal situation of immigrants (non-citizens and sometimes illegal residents) tends to 'informalize' social and political rights; i.e. to let them be used by people who are not fully entitled to them. Specific cultural needs (religious, linguistic and historical) tend to 'culturalize' social and political rights, and bring them more in tune with different ethnic traditions. Immigration, finally, produces nationalistic reaction and can reinforce either national or regional identities (Barbé 1995, 1997; Diamanti 1996a, 1996b). As immigration in Italy is still fairly recent and large ethnic minorities have yet to settle down permanently, the process of informalization in this country is more advanced than the process of culturalization, even though the reactionary process has already started – especially as far as local electoral campaigning, and more generally political struggles, are concerned.

The process of informalization is particularly evident in the provision of social services, as in the case of accommodation. City administrations provide temporary lodgings. This service, which was developed to address the problem of initial temporary accommodation, was in fact used for stable residency by poor immigrants who took advantage of the free facility. The very poor and needy immigrants, often undocumented, cannot officially use public lodgings. They can however apply to the voluntary sector, which in turn benefits from public funding. Officially the local authorities do not finance illegal immigrants' care, but can turn a blind eye to the allocation and use of public money by voluntary associations. On the one hand, the new law asks municipalities, voluntary associations, charities and other private or public organizations to promote private and public collective social temporary lodgings – i.e. hostels open to both Italian and non-Italian citizens. On the other hand, the present government is sending clear signals to voluntary associations that there will no longer be tolerance of their open attitude towards clandestine immigrants. Voluntary associations are consequently becoming more cautious (Roatis 1998).

Fortunately the problem of initial temporary accommodation for legal and illegal immigrants is becoming less acute: as the first waves of immigrants get established, they give hospitality or help in finding accommodation for newcomers. In the free market, at least, immigrants are weak economic actors. A large number of immigrants rent without contract or subcontract; many live in houses below minimum standards (Tosi 1996). Research on cities like Rome and Palermo confirms that immigrants live in the most run-down part of the town and share the same housing problems as weaker strata of the Italian population (UNESCO-MOST Programme, 1998c and d). More detailed research on Milan shows that difficulties in finding proper accomodation concerns only minorities coming from Maghreb and to some extent from Eastern Europe, whereas immigrants from the Philippines, Sri Lanka, Peru, El Salvador (mostly employed as domestic workers) live with their employers in good neighbourhoods. Also the Chinese are quite well-accommodated: 6.2 per cent of them already own their apartments (UNESCO-MOST Programme 1998e).

As far as stable accomodation is concerned, Law no. 40, 6 March 1998, assigns to documented immigrants the same right to public housing, with the same conditions, as to Italian citizens. This is despite the fact that public housing is an extremely scarce resource in Italy, receiving a very small percentage of social expenditure. In the field of lodgings, as well as in other social matters, central legislation incorporates local provisions and practices.

Regions like Piedmont and Emilia-Romagna had already allowed immigrants to apply for public lodgings. In Emilia-Romagna's capital, Bologna, 1 per cent of flats were assigned to immigrants in 1992 (A. Lostia, G. Tomaino, 1993). By the end of 1994, 2,015 foreigners out of 13,289 residents in the town (15.2 per cent) were housed in publicly financed lodgings;1,479 of them (11.1 per cent) were still in temporary lodging centres (UNESO-MOST Programme, 1998a). In Turin the most recent available figures concerning public housing applications (23 October 1995) showed that 1,870 out of the 10,930 applicants were non-EU nationals, corresponding to 17.11 per cent of the total (UNESCO-MOST Programme, 1998b).

In 1993, local voluntary associations working in this sector in northern Italy set up a 'Network for Social Housing' (RIAS, *'Rete di Iniziative per l'Alloggio Sociale')*. Its headquarters is located in Genova and it is aimed at easing immigrants' access to the private housing market. This is the case of the *Diogene Project*, undertaken in 1995 in Turin by the Cicsene (*Centro Italiano di Collaborazione per lo Sviluppo Edilizio delle Nazioni Emergenti* – Italian Centre for collaboration on the Housing Development of Emergent Nations), with the financial support of the EU, the Piedmont Region and the Municipality of Turin. It consists of a guarantee fund at the disposal of those associations who sub-let flats to immigrants' families, acting as guarantors toward Italian owners. For the moment, only 40 contracts have been signed under these special conditions. The relative failure of the project is probably due to the financial limits of the guarantee, which covers a maximum of three months rent defaulting, along with any legal expenses and damages caused by the tenants.

Law no. 40, 6 March 1998, while embodying these legal local experiences, has also limited the chances of undocumented immigrants finding accomodation in publicly funded lodgings. In the case of lodgings, previous *contra legem* local practices were not incorporated in the new Law: hostels are open only to documented people, and the undocumented can be housed only in the special centres while waiting to be expelled. The Law cannot of course prevent voluntary associations from going on with *contra legem* practices, but – as we have already noticed – Government dissatisfaction is already having some consequences for voluntary associations' behaviour.

Early experiences of the newly introduced special centres aimed at holding and restraining illegal immigrants who are awaiting expulsion are revealing many difficulties in peacefully preventing people from escaping; since clandestine entry is not a crime and since the centres are not real jails, escaping from them is also not a crime. The police have had to use guns to stop upheavals and escape in many centres. This notwithstanding, the Prodi government was reluctant to reform the ambiguous nature of the centres because of the opposition of the radical wing of its majority and lower strata pressure groups. After the fall of the Prodi government and the formation of that of d'Alema, the strengh of the permissive wing of the majority grew: the minister of the interior (a left-wing catholic) declared that illegal inflows must not be dramatized.

Generally speaking, the treatment of illegal immigrants in Italy is extremely generous: tough local practices concerning housing have been embodied in the Law only in so far as they were legal. By contrast, *contra legem* local practices have been embodied in national legislation where public health and education are concerned.

It has always been possible, with the mediation of unions and voluntary associations, for undocumented immigrants to be treated in public hospitals by finding the 'right' doctors or departments prepared to offer common therapies. The treatments could be concealed under the heading of emergency and pregnancy care, as these are free of charge for any person present on Italian territory. In Turin, as in other 'progressive' municipalities, a specific voluntary association providing care to undocumented immigrants ('*Camminare Insieme*', 'Walking together') was, and is, financed both by its members' pockets and by the local administration.

The reform of the Italian health service (Law no. 421, 23 October 1992 and Law no. 502, 30 December 1992) made these *contra legem* practices more difficult to be continued, since it assigned specific financial resources to the Local Health Units (ASL, *Azienda Sanitaria Locale*), thereby making financial controls stricter. Laws 421 and 502 also discontinued the practice of the central government administration covering local debts: moreover, a general manager was made legally responsible for making good use of limited resources. Local units were consequently obliged both to limit *contra legem* practices and to make a more parsimonious use of their resources. Many hospitals, therefore, had to reduce the informal care given to illegal immigrants. To avoid leaving those immigrants without health care, Decree n. 489, 18 November 1995, art. 13 allowed undocumented immigrants not only access to emergency and pregnancy care – which was already given – but also to treatment for serious illness and accidents, as well as free preventative prescriptions. The Turco-Napolitano Law extends (art. 33) free public health care to undocumented children.

The voluntary sector still provides health services for not only undocumented but also documented immigrants, who find it easier to address this provider instead of 'consumer unfriendly' Italian public services. A recent survey has singled out the bad functioning of public services and public administration as the main cause of complaints made by immigrants in Italy (Ires-Piemonte, 1998).

Employed immigrants enjoy the same public health treatment as national workers, i.e. they are automatically registered in the local health units of the national health service. A long succession of decrees, a 'sausage-like' series of provisions – as they were defined by the then head of the Health Ministry Development Bureau – was issued to cover the expenses of unemployed immigrants on placement lists (Zincone 1994), but this sausage is at risk of being 'sliced off' by the general reduction in public spending in Italy. In fact, according to the Contri Bill art. 131, immigrants enrolled on placement lists were required to subscribe to the National Health Service: that means that they were supposed to pay, as the Italian unemployed do. The Turco-Napolitano art. 32 reproduces this same provision.

Widened access to the public health service for undocumented immigrants is an example of the role played by local *contra legem* practice in transforming Italian legislation; it also confirms a sort of 'enlightened' dimension characterizing present Italian immigration policy, owing to the peculiar influence of voluntary associations, unions and experts in decision-making processes.

Some attempts at 'culturalization' of health services for legal immigrants have also been made. For instance, female staff belonging to the same ethnic group as the patients, have been hired by some clinics in Turin to take care of Islamic women. The experiment did not prove successful, because the sense of privacy was felt to be more at risk when people of the same ethnic community were involved (Lostia and Tomaino, 1993a). Greater success occurred with the introduction of 'cultural mediators' in 'forerunner' cities like Turin and Bologna: they are not mere translators or interpreters, they are supposed to act as intermediaries, as bridges linking the cultural worlds of the immigrant and the Italians (Lostia and Tomaino 1993a, 1993b). Cultural mediators are often immigrants themselves, provided with a high level of education, often a university degree.

By 1992, regions like Emilia Romagna (capital Bologna) and Piedmont (capital Turin) had already started special training course for cultural mediators, with the direct involvement of immigrants associations (UNESCO-MOST Programme 1998a and b). Cultural mediators have been employed by health services, jails, courts, local authorities, and special bodies like the Foreigners and Nomads Bureau or the Non-EU Minors Bureau. The *Documento Programmatico* (immigration policy plan) of 1998 allocates part of the budget devoted to integration measures to cultural mediation programmes.

When we move our analysis from cultural rights to religious rights for new immigrants, these are comparatively weak. They are hopefully improving together with a general improvement in the situation of religious minorities in Italy. Traditional religious minorities in Italy, like the Waldensian Church or the Lutherans or the Jewish Communities,[23] were only recently allowed to join the Catholic Church with the possibility of receiving part of the 0.8 per cent allocation of income tax.[24] The opening of a Mosque in the holy city of Rome in 1991 provoked strong reactions from conservatives.[25] The Prodi Government had already started (June 1998) a procedure for an agreement with the Italian Islamic Community. The difficulty in this case – as happens generally where relations with the muslim community are concerned – is due to the lack of a single organization to negotiate with and donate public funds; thus the Government has to wait until the many local and different communities are able to find agreement and build an umbrella association.

Multiculturalism is moving forward more quickly in the field of education. Ministery of Education Circular n. 205, 27 July 1990 foresaw not only that foreign students should be taught the history and culture of their country, where possible, but even that schools or classes without foreign students should promote multicultural information and attitudes. For these reasons, the District Education Office was requested to organize training programmes for teachers in co-operation with local authorities and universities. These administrative guidelines were embodied in recent legislation.

Ministry of Education Circular no. 301, 8 September 1989, and Circular no. 205, 27 July 1990, suggested putting up to five students of the same origin in the same class, in order to avoid isolation and segregation. This kind of desegregating measure was abandoned in recent legislation, whereas another integration measure included in the same circular was kept and reinforced both by Law no.40 and *Documento programmatico* 1998, that is, the introduction of extra hours to teach Italian and fill foreign students' 'knowledge gaps'.

In education as well as in public health the process of *informalization* has been, until its embodiment in recent legislation, far more advanced than the process of *culturalization*. This is the most clear case of the role played by local practice in starting the public decision-making process. The syndrome of embodiment into national legislation of *contra legem* practices applies in particular to education. Since 1993, individual Education District Offices like Milan or Turin[26] started to allow students without permits to attend classes while 'waiting for the permit' to be given. Unions and voluntary associations had previously persuaded some liberal school heads to accept undocumented children informally (Zincone 1994).

Although Italy had signed the 1989 UN Convention on the Rights of the Child (and had introduced it into Italian legislation by Act no.176, 27 May 1991), Ministry of Education circular no.400, 31 December 1991, still required students to possess residence permits in order to attend school. A circular of the Ministry of Education (no. 5, 12 January 1994), made at the request of the Ministry of Social Affairs after pressure from open-minded local authorities, asked all Education District Offices to admit immigrant children to school – even if they were undocumented. A second circular (no. 386, 4 April 1995) entitled undocumented pupils to receive diplomas. As the same circular made clear, school attendence does not give entitlement to legalization. The Dini Decree and the subsequent Turco-Napolitano Law (art. 36) confirmed the right to education for all foreign children present on Italian territory.

The results of this set of measures have been positive. The number of foreign students enrolled in Italian schools has risen considerably. Between the 1983–1984 and 1990–1991 school years the increase amounted to 17.8 per cent in nursery, 29.8 per cent in elementary, and 202 per cent in intermediate schools.[27] Growth is decidedly higher according to more recent data: between 1992–93 and 1994–95 there was a 38.5 per cent increase of foreign students; 34.5 per cent in elementary schools, 43.8 per cent in intermediate and 42.1 per cent in high schools (Caritas, 1997:159). Between 1993–94 and 1994–95 the number of Italian students showed a decrease of 320,000 whereas foreign student have increased by 13,000. 0.5 per cent of the students enrolled into Italian schools are now foreigners, 0.7 per cent when we consider elementary schools only, with peaks of 1.7 per cent in big cities like Milan.

We can notice again the same decision making pattern, which goes from *contra legem* local practices to their embodiment into national ministerial circulars, and then into decrees and legislation fostered by low strata pressure groups, backed by liberal, high-level civil servants. Experiments are made at local level due to the co-operation between innovative social workers (here, school heads) and civil servants (for instance, local directors of education), approved and imitated by progressive central state civil servants, who convince ministers to act through circulars and eventually to present a bill of law. The bill is prepared, as in the case of Contri and Turco, by a committee made up of experts chosen by the minister and the head of the department. The same bill is likely to be criticized by radical wings of low-level pressure groups, by radical parties sometime belonging to the governmental majority; to be attacked the opposition, and eventually to pass with some compromise and amendment.

These low-level pressure groups (unions and voluntary associations – mainly Catholic) play a crucial role also in immigrants' everyday life, in providing easier access to public services. To pressure the local health units or the District Education Office, to get in touch with the more compliant doctors or teachers in order to obtain *contra legem* provisions for undocumented immigrants, and to ease the approach with the Italian bureaucracy, have been important functions of unions, as well as of pro-immigrant and voluntary associations. The same people are often members of more than one organization. For example, a leading member of a pro-immigrant barristers' association is a representative of Caritas at the same time. Plural membership helps in keeping pro-immigrant associations, unions and charities in tune.

Political Actors: A Slow Process of Integration and a Rapid Process of Polarization

Unions and pro-immigrant associations are also a means of political participation and channels of representation. The rate of unionization of immigrants, which was quite low in the early 1990s (Zincone 1994), appears now to be increasing. This is just an estimate, since there is no indication of nationality on the application form. In 1993, in fact, immigrants who were members of Italian unions were about 100,000. In 1993, CISL (the second largest union, centre left) declared that 30,000 out of its 3,600,000 members were immigrants (Zincone 1994). In 1997, CISL declared 70,000 immigrants as members of trade organizations, with another 32,000 belonging to the Anolf, *Associazione Nazionale Oltre le Frontiere* (National Association Beyond Borders), an organization specifically for both employed and unemployed immigrant workers. CGIL (Italian Confederation of Labour, the largest union and left-wing) declared 60,000 foreign members in 1996. For 1998 until today, we have only regional data: 9,000 members in Emilia-Romagna, 8,000 in Lombardy, 6,000 in Piedmont.

During the 1980s and 1990s, Italian unions did not force immigrants to subscribe and, at the same time, much union activity was devoted to helping immigrants with illegal working status to sue their employers and legalize their situation. In this respect, foreign workers used to behave as 'free-riders': they made use of the unions' advocacy and, although they paid a minimum for the services received, did not pay full membership fees (Zincone 1994).

The last two amnesties confirms the 'free-rider' hypothesis. In Turin, many immigrants addressed the CGIL and CISL Immigrant Bureaux in order to be helped in the legalization procedures, but they did not subscribe according to the assessment of the officials of the Bureaux (Mohammed Kivar and Lamine Sow). Unions are investing in the future: they are promoting a sort of free affiliation, giving membership cards at a very low price or even free, with the aim of gaining real members once immigrants have found stable work (Mottura and Pinto 1996:166). We do not know whether such a strategy will prove successful.

Both the CISL and the CGIL have immigrant bureaux at district and regional level, and an Immigrants Committee at national level. In 1996 the *Coordinamento immigrati*, which was the main assembly for the participation of immigrants at the central level in the CGIL, was substituted by a National Committee (*Commissione Nazionale*) and a Standing Committee (*Commissione Permanente*). The first one is composed of local and national members of Immigrant Bureaux, plus a number of experts, and acts as a consultative body. The second, made up of local and central representatives, is a political body: it decides the Union's immigration policies. UIL, *Unione italiana del lavoro* (close to the Socialist Party and non Catholic centre parties) used to be the third largest Italian confederation. The crisis of the Italian Socialist party, due to the 'clean hands' judges' action, has been reflected in the UIL: this accounts for the difficulty the Confederation faces in providing recent data on immigrant members. Like the CISL and unlike the CGIL, the UIL has always favoured organization by trade rather than by place. In this union, immigrants have joined trade organizations instead of local organizations, and they have been represented on the main executive bodies: in 1993 they constituted 10 out of 400 in the National Assembly, 1 out of 100 of the Central Committee and 1 out of 60 of the Executive Board. Foreign workers were also adequately represented in regional and local directive and executive boards (both in territorial and in trade unions). As mentioned above, at the moment, this union is facing a phase of internal restructuring, and immigrant recruitment is neglected.

Unions could influence immigration policy-making as members of key committees or because by law their opinion has to be heard. The Committee that should have decided about the inflow rate according to the Martelli Law (art. 2:3) was made up of representatives from the Departments of the Interior, Labour, Budget and Foreign Affairs who had to consult unions. Law no.40, 1998 (art.3) details the main unions to be consulted to elaborate the *Documento Programmatico* and to establish the quantity of inflows.

Unions used to be members of the '*Consulta nazionale per i problemi dei lavoratori extra-comunitari e delle loro famiglie*' (Consultative Committee for migrant workers and their families) attached to the Ministry of Labour (Law of 30 December 1986, art. 2). This body was abolished in 1993 and then reinstated on 26 February 1996, together with a new Consultative Council set up on 11 July 1995, attached to the CNEL (National Council for Economics and Labour) where voluntary associations and unions are represented .

The Single Act (*Testo Unico*) approved recently (23 July 1998) by the Council of Ministers combines new and old legislation concerning foreign non-EU citizens in Italy, but did not abolish the new Council,[28] attached to the CNEL. Law no. 40 introduces *Consigli territoriali per l'immigrazione* (Territorial councils for immigration) that according to the Single Act, will take the place of the old inefficient *Consulte*. The new bodies must include representatives of the regional institutions, of local administrations at town and district levels, of those voluntary associations that take care of immigrant welfare, as well as of the unions and employers' associations (art. 3, par. 6).

Unions do not appear among the members of the new committee that is in charge of promoting integration, although they are likely to be invited (art. 44).[29]

Unions participate in the management of the Italian welfare system and thus it is through them that immigrants' interests might be better represented and defended. All things considered, we can draw the conclusion that, even before having been granted local suffrage, immigrants receive a sort of political representation through unions, voluntary associations, progressive parties. This is more an 'acting for' than a 'standing for' kind of representation in Hannah Pitkin's terminology; i.e. these organizations take care of immigrants' interests although immigrants are not properly represented. The many immigrants present in Italy exercise no mandate over the few people who are members of consultative bodies or executive boards, often appointed through a process of co-option.

Unions and progressive parties are still quite closely linked in Italy. Not only unions but also left-wing parties encourage immigrants to become members – leftist unions and groups even accept illegal immigrants. Parties also have ancillary associations devoted to immigrants' political recruitment. Immigrants seem less reluctant to join them than to join parties (Zincone 1994). Still, it is not a consistent phenomenon. Immigrants have also their own associations, but their role is still weak, because of their structural inconsistency: they cannot rely upon any stable source of money, often they have no premises, and their turnover is consequently very high (Caponio 1996).

The Turco-Napolitano Law introduces a Register of Immigrants Associations that will enjoy special rights, such as representation on consultative bodies and acting as 'sponsor' for the issuing of temporary residence permits (art. 40: 2).

Immigrant interests also found a peculiar means of representation in the early 1990s, when a federation of pro-immigrant associations (many of them branches or groups close to unions, progressive parties and churches) was able to set up a specific pressure group. The organization '*Patto per un Parlamento antirazzista*' (Alliance for an anti-racist parliament), created in 1992, was able to present and back 208 candidates at the parliamentary elections of 5 April 1992. 69 of these were elected. We do know how much their election was due to the *Patto*'s help. They were joined by some other members of Parliament and up to the elections of March 1994 the group could count on 90 MPs out of 950 (70 in the Chamber of Deputies and 20 in the Senate). They belonged mainly to leftist parties (Zincone 1994; Perlmutter 1998). The reform of the electoral system and the consequent formation of a 'tripolar' party system (Northern League; the centre-right cartel called *Polo della Libertá*, and centre-left cartel which has chosen the Olive Tree as its symbol) made difficult or redundant such transparty alliances, and the *Patto* consequently dissolved.

With the background of this process of political integration that seems to involve rather some brilliant immigrant personalities than the bulk of common people, a process of political polarization of the party system is taking place. In a brilliant article, Ted Perlmutter (1996:245) concluded:

> The Italian case poses two challenges to the general framework for immigration politics. It has found mainstream (pro-system) parties willing to politicize the issue and extremist (anti-system) parties willing to de-politicize the issue.

In contrast to this thesis, not only did *Alleanza Nazionale* (post-fascist party) and *Lega Nord* (a quasi-secessionist party) strongly oppose the Turco-Napolitano Law, but they also made use of immigration as a profitable electoral issue. Why did Perlmutter not notice this fact? First, because the politicization of the issue by right-wing parties has started and still largely remains at the local level. The Northern League was an aggressive anti-immigration political entrepreneur already in the 1993 local elections, then moved its action from the periphery to the centre.

Secondly, we must distinguish between the building of policy agendas and the ignition of electoral issues. On the one hand, pro-system parties in government may decide, pressed by the periphery-centre mechanism we have widely described, to face immigration problems (agenda) early on, in order to de-emphasize the electoral issue. On the other hand, internal (extreme wings of the majority) and external oppositions will try to oppose a legislation they do not appreciate and eventually make use of popular discontent; thus they can ignite a fierce parliamentary debate and shift the main locus of the political debate from parliament to the media, from policy making to electoral campaigning. They can make the issue shift from policy agenda to electoral campaigning.

The immigration issue can also be used to cut or build political alliances. Claudio Martelli, a Socialist minister, used his 1990 Law as a friendly gesture towards the Communist Party, thereby dissociating himself from the then Secretary of the Socialist Party Bettino Craxi, who was steadily allied with the Christian Democrats. Similarly, in mid-August 1998, former 'clean hands' prosecutor Di Pietro, a conservative member of the Olive Tree centre-left coalition, proposed defining clandestine entry as a crime punished by repatriation within 24 hours of clandestine immigrants to their presumed countries of origin (namely Tunisia), even using force to deal with possible opposition from the presumed countries of origin. The move can be interpreted as a conciliatory gesture towards conservative milieu.

Alleanza Nazionale (the post-fascist party, which has steadily underlined its distance from the xenophobic European Right) reacted to Di Pietro's declaration with a far more sensible proposal of three points:

- to extend the term of detention in the special centres (from 30 to 60 days),
- to make the declaration of false identity and the destruction of identity cards a crime, which would imply according to Italian criminal code the possibility of imprisonment, and
- to define clandestine entry a crime, in order not to discourage asylum seekers.

The internal right-wing of *Alleanza Nazionale* sharply rejected the proposal. By contrast it was backed by the Secretary of the party, Gianfranco Fini. Fini has always been very careful not to be confused with the anti-system Right, and has succeeded in being accepted by the Gaullist regroupment at European Parliament level – and he has used racism and immigration moderation as an indicator of his democratic reliability.[30] Immigration can be used to draw new political borders between and within parties; to build and destroy alliances. Radical parties can be tempted to alternate on this matter: moderate stances when they need to acquire a democratic legitimation or raise their coalition potential; extreme and vocal stances when they want to strengthen their electoral appeal. Moderate parties in government can alternate liberal policies (when they want to attract or keep progressive parties in their coalition); conservative policies, when they want to please conservative groups. Immigration stances are a most visible indicator of what political track a party, a faction, or a single leader intends to take.

SUMMING UP

We could say that immigrants in Italy have started the usual process of social integration through public education, social services, and – as Reyneri shows in this issue – through legal and more often illegal work. This process is reliant upon the consistent help of voluntary associations (mainly Catholic), open-minded civil servants and unions which are smoothing access to social services and legalization. Immigrants have also started the usual process of political integration through unions and ancillary associations of parties (mainly leftist).

This integration process is fostered by a legislation comparatively liberal not only towards documented, but also towards undocumented immigrants. This peculiar feature of recent immigrant legislation in Italy is due to the recent huge turnover of the political elite and the reinforcement of the executive. These have left space for low-level pressure groups' advocacy, for civil servants and expert policy networks. This space is doomed to shrink as the new party government becomes more self-assured and stable. Unions, voluntary associations and progressive civil servants have proved able to start innovative practices at local level, often with the purpose of going round the constraints imposed by law. These local *contra legem* practices have moved from periphery to centre and, step by step, have been institutionalized (by means of ministerial circulars, decrees and laws).

Italian law is often 'trespassed' and not always for benevolent purposes. The innovative character of the 1992 Nationality Law was neutralized by circulars, decrees and obstructionist practices. Italian laws can easily be trespassed since they tend to be vague and contradictory; their ambiguity is caused by the necessity of combining opposite pressures by internal extreme wings of the majority and by a vocal and strong opposition.

A centre-right opposition that was a majority after the 1994 elections, and still would be such if it were not for the split of the Northern League, is making a strong political challenge to the present centre-left government and making electoral use of the anti-immigration issue especially at local level. The immigration issue, being high 'values intensive' is also used within parties' cartels and even within the same party as an instrument to change political positioning along the left-right spectrum, to build or destroy alliances. Parties with dubious democratic credentials such as Northern League and *Alleanza Nazionale* tend to commute between extreme anti-immigrant stances at the local level and more moderate attitudes at the central level, to commute between more radical stances when elections are coming closer and more moderate positions when they want to raise their coalitional potential.

The political use of anti-immigration attitudes was made possible also by the inadequacy of legal instruments to repress immigrant criminal behaviour and clandestine entries. That is why the new Law provided some instruments to repress illegality, such as 'Centres for residence and assistence', but these centres (half hostels and half prisons) are proving less effective than the Government had hoped.[31] And both internal and external oppositions are making good media use of their relative failure.

Furthermore while Prodi's government had already enacted a first 20,000 people flow decree in June 1998 and a second 38,000 decree at the beginning of September and had already decided (pressed by low-level lobbying) to devote the second 'instalment' to legalizing people already in Italy before the new law, the present D'Alema government – less influenced by experts and civil servants and even more influenced by low strata lobbying – have decided to adjust the 1999 flows decree so that all irregular immigrants present in Italy before March 1998, and who can get a registered job, can be legalized. At the same time the criteria to prove presence in Italian territory before the fixed date were relaxed, and a stream of illegal immigrants started to cross Italian borders in order to be legalized. Unfortunately the future of immigrant policies in Italy depends on the capacity of the present government to provide a mix of efficient repression and valid integration. If it does not succeed in achieving this difficult task – and it can well happen – the anti-immigrant attitude will further increase in public opinion, it will represent a rewarding electoral profit for already active 'racist entrepreneurs' and this will put an end to the quasi-virtuous circle of recent Italian immigration policies.

NOTES

1. The specific role of high level civil servants in Italian immigration law making has been already underlined by Veugelers (1994).
2. As a reaction to the fascist regime that had ruled Italy from 1922 to 1943, the post-fascist electoral system used to be highly proportional. In a scale of proportionality conceived by Mac Rae, on a scale that goes from one to 11, Italy scores nine. The Chamber of Deputies used to be elected through competing party lists and preference votes, whereas the Senate was apparently just a single member majority system, since the votes of those constituencies in which no candidate had reached 60 per cent of the suffrage, i.e. the large majority of Italian Senate districts, were redistributed according to proportional criteria. The deflatory process started with the reduction of preference votes from five to one; it was the outcome of a referendum held in 1991 and promoted by 'Comitato per il sì' (Committee vote yes) led by former Christian Democrat Mario Segni. Another referendum (18 April 1993) changed the Senate electoral system into a 'first past the post' one, since it abolished the threshold of 60 per cent of suffrage to get the seat. The Chamber of Deputies electoral system had to be changed accordingly (Law n. 277, 4 August 1993). For this Chamber, 25 per cent of seats are assigned through a proportional system to the parties that have reached a 4 per cent threshold at national level. In the 1994 elections, for the first time, Italian voters were asked to choose between two electoral cartels, a centre-left and a centre-right one. The secession of one of the centre-right winning coalition parties (the Northern League) from the cabinet caused the fall of the Berlusconi government and the formation of a government based on a majority different from the one voted by the electorate. The victory of the centre-left in 1996 gave birth to a relatively more stable coalition, although this also was always under the threat of secession of its extreme left-wing (Rifondazione Comunista). Political rights in the renovated Italian political system are less deflated and less effective than they pretend to be. The peculiar position of the Northern League strongly rooted in areas of the North East and highly mobile in its political alliances produces a sort of 'three polar system', a system composed of three partners. The 'tripolar' format of the Italian party system in the 1990s not only makes the electorate mandate loose, but also unclear. The heterogeneous character of electoral cartels and governamental coalitions contribute in expaining the contradictory character of legislation. This not withstanding, the executive acquired more autonomy from the legislature both at central and local level.
3. According to Law no.81, 25 March 1993, and Law no 415, 15 October 1993, mayors are elected through ballotage between the two candidates that have received more votes at the the first turn; the winner can count on a majority prize that enables her to count on 60 per cent of council seats. The reform widened big city mayors' power and influence at national level.
4. See *Relazione sula presenza straniera in Italia*, Ministero dell'Interno (Home Office), 1998. This kind of data is by definition controversial and an object of disputes. According to ConfCommercio (National Association of Traders) undocumented people could be between 600,000 and 800,000. Osservatorio statistico di Milano, (Milan Statistical Observatory) suggests some 150.000. Caritas believes they are about 250-300,000 people (Caritas di Roma, 1997; pp. 113-114).
5. Between 1971 and 1980, for the first time since 1861 (when Italy had became a nation-state) the migration balance was negative (108,234 espatriated people versus 112,150

repatriated, most of them coming from European countries (the positive sign of the balance was due to European movements – 83,540 expatriated people versus 89,908 repatriated, outside Europe the balance was still slightly negative – 24,694 espatriated people versus 22,242 repatriated; Caritas, 1995: p. 77).

6. It was made out of representatives of the Ministries of Foreign Affairs, Labour and Social Scurity, Home Office, three people from workers' and three from employers' unions.
7. As Reyneri notes in his article in this issue, employment opportunity in the informal economy affects also legal flows and immigrants who have already enjoyed amnesty thus becoming legal.
8. Plus four representatives of the unions, three of the employers' associations, four experts nominated by the Ministries of Education, Foreign Affairs, Finance and Home Office.
9. Italy signed the Schengen Treaty on 27 November 1990 and ratified it on 30 September 1993. The Treaty came into force on 26 March 1995, while Maastricht came into force on 1 November. But in fact Italy was not allowed to enter until 27 October 1997, due to the lack of proper legislation and technology to treat personal data and then enter SIS (Schengen Information System). Compliance with Schengen requirements was achieved by Law, 31 December 1996, n. 675.
10. Articles 17 and 18 of the Geneva Convention, 28 July 1951 were ratified by Act no. 722, July 1954.
11. As a consequence of Italian Acceptance of International treaties, the Minister of Foreign Affairs (Circular no. 0002, 18 February 1991) defined five categories of countries subjected to different visa regulations, countries included in each category change continuously.
12. The new balance of power within the new committee favoured the main Ministries (Labour, Foreign Affairs, Public Budget and Finances, Home Office) which should consult other political actors, such as unions and the National Council of Economy and Labour, but in fact could steer the decision. The proposal of the committee should have been communicated to the involved parliamentary commissions and after 45 days, having heard their opinions, could become law. .The decision should have been issued each year by October 30. In fact the Committee was never able to decide in due time.
13. For instance, 31,629 work permits were delivered to non resident people in 1992, 69 per cent of them to domestic workers (source: Ministry of Labour)
14. According to Law no. 390/1992,these permits allow work, unlike the ones given to political refugees that up to Law no.40, 6 March 1998 were prevented from working.
15. The most tragic case was that of a ship rammed by an Italian patrolling vedette boat, on 28 March close to Otranto's shores; sixty clandestine people lost their lives.
16. Decree no. 60, 20 March 1997, converted in Law no. 128, 19 May 1997, allowed the Questure to issue temporary entrance permits (*nulla osta provvisorio di ingresso nel territorio nazionale*) to Albanian people escaping the dramatic situation of civil war in their home country. 10,425 people have benefited from such a temporary permit. According to the Ministry of Domestic Affairs, up to August 1997, 6,517 people were repatriated, among them 449 were 'given an incentive' with 150 thousand liras cheque each. Albanian citizens who left the camps giving notice to the authorities were 5,806, those who left secretly 3,066. Only 1,685 Albanian citizens have sought political asylum.
17. This decree that included many important measures that we will describe afterwards, was renewed with the Decree, 18 January 1996, n. 22, again with the Decree of 19 March 1996, no. 132 and that of 18 May 1996, n. 269).
18. Leftist scholars (see Palidda 1994, 1996; Pastore 1994) have tried to de-emphasize the phenomenon, but they recently had to admit the real presence of criminals especially in the more recent waves (Ires- CGIL, 1997).
19. Opposition parties especially the Northern League and the former neo-fascist Alleanz Nazionale (National Alliance) presented 700 amendments.

20. (Art.10 par.2; three years of jails and $17,000 especially when it is made by a racket (art.10 par.3; from 4 to 12 years of jail and $17,000 for each alien smuggled) and it involves minors to be recruited in the criminal labour market and women destined for prostitution (art.10 par.3 from 5 to 15 years of jail and from 26,000 to 142,000 dollars for each illegally imported alien).
21. We must add that Italy is still more a country of emigration than of immigration (not as far as flows are concerned but as resident stocks)
22. Art. 48 of the Italian Constitution, first paragraph says. 'The electorate includes all citizens, men and women, who have reached full age. The article intended to exclude the possibility of preventing women and minorities from voting.
23. Beside the State, the Waldensian and Lutherans, Seventh Day Adventists, Assembly of God in Italy, and the Jewish Community participate in the '8 per thousandth' part of income tax.
24. The Waldensian Church was able to raise a considerable amount of money due to support from a large number of non-believers and liberal Catholic tax payers. The agreement with the Jewish community was signed only in 1997 and it is still not known how successful they will prove in fundraising.
25. Irene Pivetti (of the Lega Nord), then Speaker of the Chamber of Deputies, was rumoured to have attended a special mass devoted to expiating the sacriligious event.
26. Milan District Education Office circular no.21790, 21 May 1993; Turin District Education Office circular no. 517, 27 May 1993.
27. One out of three immigrants under age regularly present in Italy are born in Italy (Bontempi et al., 1993).
28. It has the same name and almost the same composition (art. 42, cc. 3-4).
29. The Committee includes representatives of the Departments of Social Affairs, Ministery of the Interior, Foreign Affairs, Education, Justice and Employment, plus ten experts.
30. Fini's moves proved successful in raising external consent. The Minister of Interior member of Democratici di Sinistra (Democratic Left) post-communist party, Giorgio Napolitano, promised to take the AN proposal into serious consideration. The government opening to AN proposals provoked in turn the upheaval of Fausto Bertinotti, secretary of Rifondazione Comunista, the radical leftist party, whose vote of confidence is crucial for Prodi's Government survival. Secretary Bertinotti made use of immigration together with unemployment issues to give evidence of the conservative nature of Prodi's Government and of the consequent eventual necessity to open a crisis in the lack of relevant political changes.
31. Ministry of Interiors denies the failure, it declared (20 August 1998) having expelled 465 clandestines detained in the new centres; since 8 August, promised to reach the amount of 600 by the end of the month, but did not tell how many were able to escape from the centres, nor how many came to Italy without being detected.

REFERENCES

Baldwin-Edwards, M. and M. Schain (1994): 'Introduction', in Baldwin-Edwards, M. and M. Schain (eds): *The Politics of Immigration in Western Europe*, London: Frank Cass.

Barbé, C. (1995): *Interazioni etnocentriche. Quali, in che modo, con quali conseguenze?*, Mimeo, Conference on: Immigrazione, stereotipi, pregiudizi, Università La Sapienza, Rome, April 5–7.

Barbé, C. (1997): 'Il drastico irrobustimento dell'identità nazionale in Italia', *Quaderni di Sociologia*, 31/1.

Bohning, W.R. (1972): *The Migration of Workers in the United Kingdom and the European Community*, Oxford: Oxford University Press.

Bolaffi, G. (1996): *Una politica per gli immigrati*, Bologna: Il Mulino.
Bonetti, P. (1993): *La condizione giuridica del cittadino comunitario,* Rimini: Maggioli Editore.
Bonifazi, C. (1991): 'Gli italiani e l'immigrazione straniera', in R. Palomba (ed.), *Crescita zero*, Firenze: La Nuova Italia.
Caponio, T. (1996): *Associazionismo e integrazione politica degli immigrati. Un'analisi comparata*, dissertation, University of Turin: Faculty of Political Science.
Caritas di Roma (1995): *Dossier statistico '95*, Roma: Anterem.
Caritas di Roma (1997): *Dossier statistico '97*, Roma: Anterem.
Caritas di Roma (1998): *Dossier statistico '98*, Roma: Anterem.
Cotta, M. and L. Verzichelli (1996): 'La classe politica: cronaca di una morte annunciata?', in M. Cotta and P. Isernia (ed), *Il gigante dai piedi di argilla*, Bologna: Il Mulino, pp.373–408.
Diamanti, I. (1996a): *Il male del nord: Lega, localismo, secessione*, Roma: Donzelli.
Diamanti, I. (1996b): *Territorio e politica: una mappa elettorale (molte Italie e molti Nord)*, paper presented to the conference: «Politics and Society in Italy», Italian Association of Sociology, Political Sociology Section, Turin, May 8–10.
Documento programmatico, (1998), Roma, Presidenza del Consiglio, Dipartimento Affari Sociali.
European Commission (1997): *Racism and Xenophobia in Europe,* Eurobarometer Opinion Poll, n.47.1, presented at the closing conference of the European Year Against Racism, 18–19 December.
Haut Conseil de l'Immigration, (1990), *Premier Rapport*, mimeo, Paris
Hollifield J.F.(1994): *Entre droit et Marché,* in Badie and Wenden, *La défie migratoire*, Paris, Presse de la Fondation Nationale de Science Politique.
Ires-CGIL (1997): 'Lavoro, genere, etnia', Quaderni Ires-CGIL, Torino.
Ires-Piemonte (1998): *Il filo di Arianna,la città, i servizi, gli immigrati a Torino*, Città di Torino.
ISTAT (1992): *La situazione* del paese, Rapporto annuale, Roma.
Kingdon, J.W. (1984): *Agendas, Alternatives, and Public Policies*, London: Harper Collins publishers.
Lostia, A. and G. Tomaino (1993a): 'I diritti sociali', in G. Zincone (ed.), *Orientamento alle politiche dell'immigrazione in Italia*, rapporto CNR.
Lostia, A. and G. Tomaino (1993b), *I diritti sociali degli immigrati extracomunitari*, Mimeo, conference on: Il governo dell'immigrazione nelle città: bilanci, prospettive e proposte, ISMU, Milan, November 17–18.
Mauri, L. and G.A. Micheli (1992): *Le regole del gioco. Diritti di cittadinanza e immigrazione straniera*, Milano: Franco Angeli.
Melotti, U. (1993): 'Migrazioni internazionali e integrazione sociale: il caso italiano e le esperienze europeee', in M. Delle Donne, U. Melotti and S. Petilli (eds.), *Immigrazione in Europa: solidarietà e conflitto*, Roma: Cediss.
Ministero dell'Interno (1998): *Relazione sulla presenza straniera in Italia e sulle situazioni di irregolarità*, Roma.
Mottura, G., and P. Pinto (1996): *Immigrazione e cambiamento sociale. Strategie sindacali*, Roma: Ediesse.
Palidda, S. (1994): *Devianza e criminalità tra gli immigrati*, Milano: Fondazione Cariplo-Ismu.
Palidda, S. (ed.) (1996): *Délit d'immigration. La construction sociale de la déviance et de la criminalité parmi les immigrés*, national chapters by P. Tournier, H.J. Albrecht, F. Brion, B. Agozino and S. Palidda, Bruxelles: C.E., Collection COST A2 Migrations.
Pastore, F. (1994) *Produzione normativa e costruzione sociale della devianza e della criminalità tra gli immigrati*, in Palidda, S. (ed.) (1994), op. cit.
Pastore, F. (1998): 'Normativa e politiche migratorie nazionali, tra ritardi e carenze

storiche', in L. Davico, F. Pastore and G. Ronca (eds.), *Torino, città di immigrazione. Le politiche possibili*, Torino: Comitato Giorgio Rota.

Perlmutter, T. (1996): 'Immigration Politics Italian-style', *South European Society & Politics* 1/2, pp.229–52.

Perlmutter, T. (1998): *The Lessons from Italian Politics in the early 1990s: Parties or Interest Groups as the Agent of Immigration Policy,* Center for European Studies, New York University.

Pitkin, Hannah F. (1972): *The concept of representation*, Berkeley: University of California Press.

Roatis, M. (1998): *Il trattamento degli immigrati irregolari*, dissertation, University of Turin: Faculty of Political Science.

Tosi,A. (1996): *La casa: tra integrazione ed esclusione sociale*, mimeo, conference on: Immigrati. Stranieri o nuovi cittadini, Torino, 8-9 Novembrer (Comune di Torino, Ministero per la solidarietà sociale).

UNESCO MOST PROGRAM (1998a)*: Multicultural Policies and Modes of Citizenship in European Cities, Bologna, Italy.*

UNESCO MOST PROGRAM (1998b)*: Multicultural Policies and Modes of Citizenship in European Cities, Turin, Italy.*

Veugelers (1994): 'Recent Immigration Politics in Italy: A Short Story', in Baldwin-Edwards, M. and M. Schain (eds): *The Politics of Immigration in Western Europe*, London: Frank Cass.

Zincone, G. (1994): *Uno schermo contro il razzismo*, Roma: Donzelli.

The Mass Legalization of Migrants in Italy: Permanent or Temporary Emergence from the Underground Economy?

EMILIO REYNERI

UNDOCUMENTED MIGRANTS ENTERING A LARGE UNDERGROUND ECONOMY

At present, immigrants from Africa, Latin America, Asia and eastern Europe are estimated to number slightly more than 1,100,000 people, or little more than 2 per cent of the Italian domestic population. The residence permits granted as of December 1997 to citizens from undeveloped countries number about 950,000, but they do not include children or undocumented migrants, who are still numerous notwithstanding three acts of legalization (in 1986, 1990 and 1996). The number of migrants who applied for legalization rose to almost 600,000, nearly two-thirds of migrants now legally living in Italy. The comparison does not take into account that many may have availed themselves of more than one legalization, or that there are no figures for returns; however, it gives a rough idea of how few migrants entered Italy holding a residence permit.

The first legalization, in 1986, required migrants to be irregularly employed by an employer willing to 'regularize' them, but applications from job seekers were also accepted. Fewer than 120,000 migrants were legalized, but not even 45 per cent were able to hold a labour contract. To apply for the second legalization, in 1990, migrants were required only to have lived in Italy before the end of 1989. About 220,000 migrants were legalized: 21,000 as wage earners, 13,000 as self-employed and more than 180,000 as job seekers.

This article is based on the findings of a wider comparative research project 'Migrants insertion in the informal economy, deviant behaviour and the impact on receiving societies' (Migrinf), financed by the European Commission-TSER programme.

Roughly speaking, if we consider that legalizations mostly granted permits for work reasons and that 40 per cent of all permits were granted for reasons other than work, we can infer that almost all migrants holding a work permit in 1991 had received it through a legalization. On the other hand, prior to 1986 no procedure existed for entering Italy for employment, except for housekeepers. This remained the case even afterward, as the quota system was not fully implemented and, since 1990, with the exception of housekeepers (10-12,000 per year), very few people were entitled to enter Italy with a work permit (3-4,000 per year, mostly holding a fixed term labour contract). Few migrants failed to apply for the 1990 legalization. Yet many more entered Italy afterwards, both illegally (clandestinely crossing French or other borders or landing on Mediterranean beaches) and legally (holding a short-term visa and then overstaying). The number of undocumented migrants began to increase again also because many migrants who were legalized in 1990 failed to renew their two-year permits of stay, as they lacked regular jobs (Reyneri 1998c).

The Characteristics of Migrants

The great majority of migrants, both men and women, are of working-age and actually work in Italy, although mostly in the underground economy – even many of those with work permits and entitled to take a regular job. The role of the underground economy in illegal migration to Italy is very important, but as cause rather than effect (Reyneri 1998b). The location of migrant workers in the underground economy is usually seen as an indicator of an oversupply of migrant labour, caused by migratory flows merely due to a push-effect from the sending countries. This is not the case for Italy.[1]

Italy has carried out a strict policy towards refugees, to such an extent that only 20–30,000 people from Bosnia were received. As regards Albanians, even the two temporary 'invasions' are to be seen in social and economic terms as much as political. Besides, people from Albania and former Yugoslavia have not reached even one-quarter of overall immigration. Migrants have come from countries that have not suffered dramatic events, such as Morocco, the Philippines, Tunisia, Senegal, Egypt, Brazil, India, Poland, Romania, Peru, China, Ghana and Nigeria.

According to all surveys (see Reyneri 1997a for a review), many, perhaps the majority, are highly educated youths and/or have a middle class origin, and the working situations they left were often fair or even good by the standards of their country of origin. In a field-study (Reyneri

1998a) migrants who applied for the last legalization in Milan were classified, rather evenly, into four groups: the 'under-privileged' with low social status and little education; the 'underachievers' with little education but middle-high class origin; the 'upwardly mobile' with high educational level but low social status; and the 'privileged' with high educational level and middle-high class origin.

Most migrants entering Italy are, therefore, the elite youth of their own countries, who were most exposed to the lure of the material well-being and freedom that the countries of destination represent. They are those who most intensely felt the disparity between expectations and reality, and had the personal and material resources necessary to support the costs of emigrating. The large variety of the so-called migratory projects confirms this picture (Reyneri 1998c). Besides the usual 'temporary and targeted migration', many urban and educated young people are attracted by the 'downtown mirage', with its confusion, shop-window lights, distractions, welfare and sexual freedom. Other migrants, exposed to 'anticipating socialization' carried out by Italian television, aim at immediately adopting high consumption standards. Finally, many people from North Africa and eastern European countries are seasonal or 'commuter' migrants. All these were not escaping for survival, but looking for upward mobility. So, the situation of the receiving country does matter.

Scarce Competition with Domestic Job-Seekers

A high rate of total unemployment does not mean that there is no demand for immigrant labour. The Italian unemployment pattern penalizes women, young people living with their parents and the well-educated, while protecting 30–50-year old men, heads of households and the uneducated (Reyneri 1998d). The unemployment rate of Italian middle-aged men is the lowest in Europe. The large majority of Italian job-seekers are women and young people, who are frequently living under their family's roof, with their fathers holding gainful employment or receiving a pension. Furthermore, the relative advantage of educated youth is far lower than in most European countries; thus uneducated young people out of work are relatively less abundant and few Italians are really in competition with migrant workers for low-level jobs, as is confirmed by the scarcity of conflicts concerning employment. Finally, in some northern regions the total unemployment rate is the lowest in Europe and there is near to full employment for middle-aged men as well as for uneducated youths suited to unskilled jobs. As internal migration from the high unemployment in the southern regions has been negligible since the mid-1970s, a demand for immigrant labour does exist. In fact, after the 1990 legalization, migrants are increasingly concentrated in regions where the unemployment rate is lower.

A Large Domestic Underground Economy

The underground economy has long been well-rooted in Italy as well as in all southern European countries (Mingione and Magatti 1994). According to National Accounts estimates, Italian wage earners not registered on the firms' pay rolls, along with those self-employed lacking the required permits, numbered about 2,900,000 as of 1995, or equal to 13.6 per cent of people in employment. The trend is downward, since in 1980 there were almost 3,500,000 irregular jobs, representing more than 16 per cent of total employment. In contrast, the number of workers holding a part-time second job is steady at around 4 million people, although there is a sharp increase in moonlighters who are working in industry and services: in 1995 they numbered 3,200,000, equal to 15 per cent of people in employment (Reyneri 1998c). The proportion of irregular labour in northern Italy remained below 8 per cent, in central Italy it slightly exceeded 11 per cent, but in the South it was over 25 per cent (Eurispes 1995). The most affected sectors are agriculture and construction, followed at some distance by the garment industry, repair firms, transport and entertainment.

The National Accounts estimates support the hypothesis that migrants have been replacing domestic workers in the underground economy. The growth of non-resident foreign workers compensates for the decrease in domestic irregular workers, so that from 1980 to 1995 the proportion of domestic regular employment remains almost steady at around 83 per cent. Furthermore, if we exclude housekeeping (which accounts for more than 40 per cent of non-resident foreign workers and less than 1 per cent of domestic irregular ones), the distribution by economic sector of non-resident foreign workers is almost parallel to the distribution of domestic irregular ones.[2]

Migrants' Insertion in the Underground Economy

The evidence on migrants' insertion in the Italian underground economy is clear. The incorporation of migrants into the regular labour market increased substantially in recent years; nevertheless the change in the ratio between wage-earners registered for social security and migrants entitled to work as employees remains important: from 37 per cent to 60 per cent over the period 1994 to 1996 (Reyneri 1998c). Although this ratio is likely to be underestimated, this undoubtedly means that many documented migrants are working irregularly, because unemployment is not high among people who can rely neither on the help of relatives nor on public subsidies.

All local surveys of immigrants show a huge proportion of irregular employment, even among those who could have a regular labour contract since they hold residence and work permits. A wider picture of migrants' employment conditions is given by the controls carried out by inspectors from the Ministry of Labour (Reyneri 1998a; 1998c). From 1991 to 1996 the proportion of irregular non-EU wage-earners at the national level was never lower than 31 per cent, i. e. more than twice as much as domestic workers. The percentage is always lower in the north-eastern and central regions, which are characterized by a growing integration of migrant workers in regular manufacturing jobs. In contrast, it is above the national average in the South, Latium and Lombardy (where the large metropolitan areas of Rome and Milan prevail) and it is increasing in the de-industrialized regions of the North West. The proportion of irregular migrant wage-earners is generally higher in hotels and catering, cleaning, housekeeping and the retail trade, whereas it is lower in transport and industry.

Not all the irregular migrant wage earners are, nevertheless, without documents. According to the Ministry of Labour inspections, they are generally divisible into two almost equal groups: those who hold a permit of stay for work reasons and those who do not. Combining these data with other sources (residence permits granted for work reasons, wage-earners registered by Social Security, National Accounts estimates), we have been able to estimate both how many migrant workers are irregular and also how many irregular workers either do, or do not, hold a permit of stay.[3] Tables 1 and 2 show the estimates for 1994 and 1996 (Reyneri 1998c).

TABLE 1

IMMIGRANTS IN EMPLOYMENT. 1994

Stay	registered	non-registered	Total
Legal	211,000	138,000	349,000
Illegal	—	341,000	341,000
Total	211,000	479,000	690,000

Source: Our estimate on data from Istat, Caritas, Ministry of Interior, Ministry of Labour.

TABLE 2

IMMIGRANTS IN EMPLOYMENT. 1996

Stay	registered	non-registered	Total
Legal	391,000	166,000	557,000
Illegal	—	182,000	182,000
Total	391,000	348,000	739,000

Source: as for Table 1.

In 1994, only one out of every three immigrants who were working had a registered job, with the others working either without a labour contract or without a proper self-employment permit. The percentage of those registered reaches 60 per cent if we consider only those with a valid permit of stay for employment reasons. Finally, a little less than half of those working did not have a valid residence permit. The percentage of undocumented migrants among those working irregularly was 70 per cent, although many probably had a permit granted for other reasons (family, tourism, etc.). In 1996, just after the legalization, the scenario was quite different, though still critical. 'Only' one of two migrants was working either without a contract or a valid permit to do so. The percentage of registered workers among migrants with a permit for work reasons is more than 70 per cent. Thus, almost one-third of non-registered migrant workers had no legal impediments to getting regular jobs. Finally, just one-quarter of those actually working do not have a residence permit. The percentage of undocumented migrants among irregular workers drops to a little more than half.

The 1996 estimation undoubtedly under-estimates the incorporation of migrant workers in the regular labour market, as many migrants who applied for the legalization were not registered before 1997 with the Ministry of Interior or for social security. Yet, the emergence from the underground economy attributable to the 1996 legalization is likely to be temporary, as we will see below.

How Undocumented Migrants are Attracted by the Underground Economy

Some inquiries have already shown that many migrants entered Italy illegally because they envisaged it as a country where living and making money were easy even without a residence permit. Recent field work in Milan (Reyneri 1998a)[4] lets us go deeper into this topic, as migrants were asked why they entered Italy. The great majority answered that they had friends or relatives who had come here before them. However, many knew other receiving countries; so they were able to make a comparison with Italy. In any case, the expectations the immigrants had regarding Italy before they left their countries of origin fit exactly with its stereotype: a country where it is easy to live and to make money even without a permit, so that it is worth the hardships, expenses and risks to get around border checks.

Few migrants said that they chose Italy because it was the easiest and/or cheapest country to enter, contrary to widespread belief (Foot 1995). Instead, the opinion was widely held that remaining in Italy is relatively easy, because inspections are few and even if caught, immigrants are rarely deported. Many also mention the possibility of availing themselves of legalization. The picture that emerges is of a country where, sooner or later, immigrants become legal, so it is against their interests to respect the orders of expulsion. Official records confirm that very few of those who are issued expulsion orders are actually deported: one or two in every ten. Moreover, those who had ignored expulsion orders were not excluded by the legalization. The situation, however, should change from now on, as the new immigration act approved in February 1998 specifies immediate deportation for people who entered Italy illegally.

Although only a few of the migrants knew the difference between 'regular' and 'irregular' jobs, the prevailing view was that work was easy to come by in Italy, so money could be made even without a permit. Some immigrants explicitly mentioned this state of affairs as an explanation for choosing Italy. Many of the Albanians knew of Greece, where it was easy to find work without a permit, as well. However they preferred the Italian underground economy because of the higher earnings to be had. The opportunity for irregular jobs was cited as a reason for coming to Italy by many Moroccans, who should be familiar with Spain and who often travelled through that country illegally to reach Italy. In any case, the general consensus among immigrants from the Mediterranean basin is that Italy's underground economy offers the most job opportunities and the highest earnings.

If immigrants who illegally entered Italy are able to stay easily earning in its large underground economy, this does not necessarily mean that all of them are living according to their expectations. Irregular and odd jobs let migrant workers survive, but do not fulfil their hopes. Nevertheless, the impact on migratory flows is almost nil. Among migrants declaring themselves to be in difficult situations, not one even vaguely hints at the possibility of returning to his country, and they all say that their negative opinion would not prevent their friends and relatives who remain at home from emigrating also. Emigration is a sort of bet between those who leave and those who stay. Whether it is a family investment or an escape, those who emigrate feel obliged to show those who stayed behind that the hardships they have suffered were worth it. The migrant will try to avoid coming home without money at all costs, because he would be a 'walking dead man' among his friends and relatives. He is thus forced to prolong his stay, even if life becomes increasingly difficult.

For the same reasons, the migrant tends to paint a rosy picture of his situation to those who have remained at home. The emigrant can justify his choice only by concealing the negative aspects of living and working conditions in the country of destination. Thus, if many of the interviewed migrants say that they would not advise anyone to come to Italy, it would mean that they are really in dire straits. However, everyone adds that their advice wouldn't be heeded and would not at all serve as a deterrent. Apart from the frequent contradiction between verbal and non-verbal communication in the messages given by the migrants when they return home, their negative comments would be ignored anyway, because it would be interpreted as a sign of hostility or rivalry. The immigration network thus stimulates additional immigration, regardless of the information it transmits.

The new immigration in Italy is seldom a success story, as was true for the previous one in the traditional European receiving countries. The well-known self-sustaining effect of the migratory chain is, nevertheless, prevailing (Portes 1995).

THE OUTCOMES OF THE 1996 LEGALIZATION: PUSHING MIGRANT WORKERS OUT OF THE UNDERGROUND ECONOMY?

For the 1996 legalization, quite rigid requisites were established to force migrants to emerge both from illegal stay and the underground economy. In addition to demonstrating their past presence in Italy, migrants had to have been irregularly employed in the last six months, to have an ongoing irregular labour position or a written job offer by an Italian employer. In order to prove the existence of either the previous jobs or the job offers they declared, a large amount of money had to be paid to social security (up to two or three months' wages for a migrant worker), supposedly by employers, but in fact often by migrants themselves. A large number of migrants, nevertheless, succeeded in availing themselves of legalization and the number of regular hirings of migrant workers more than doubled on a yearly base. Does this mean that migrants really emerged from the underground economy as well as from illegal stay? Unfortunately, both of the aims of the legalization were only partially and transitorily achieved, as an analysis of administrative data shows.

Reducing as Well as Reproducing Illegal Stay

The third legalization surpassed the far less restrictive second one, claiming the record as the largest legalization ever carried out in Europe. In 1995, migrants from undeveloped countries were estimated at nearly 1,000,000 and those not holding a permit at about 40 per cent (Censis 1995; Ismu 1996). As more than 256,000 applications were filed, of which 93 per cent were approved, those 'excluded' should have numbered a little over 150,000 or about 40 per cent of those who could have applied. The proportion of migrants who did not avail themselves of the legalization was lower in northern Italy, where migrants have more opportunities of finding regular jobs and at the same time are subject to stricter control by the police. On the contrary, in the South the number of illegal stays was far larger before the legalization and became even larger afterward. Moreover, field-work in Milan (Reyneri 1998a) shows that there were differences between one migrant group and another. For two of the most closely-knit groups, the Chinese and the Senegalese, practically everyone applied. The groups with the highest number of exclusions seemed to be those with the lowest solidarity – Albanians, Moroccans, Tunisians and Egyptians. Co-operation within groups was essential in finding an employer who was willing to offer a labour contract and the funds needed to pay social contributions.

Furthermore, each legalization exerts an important attraction on people still living in sending countries. In the city of Milan, migrants without residence permits decreased by only 20 per cent during 1996 (Ismu 1997). This contrasts not only with data on the impact of the legalization in the North West (which includes Milan) but also with the opinions of observers and the migrants themselves, who maintain that few were excluded. The fact is that the 1996 estimates of illegal migrants included those who entered after the deadline and were not entitled to apply for the legalization. This means that the legalization's impact was greater than it appears, but it was partially offset by new inflows. Moreover, according to the Ministry of Labour's inspections, the percentage of migrants without a permit of stay, paradoxically, did increase from 1995 to 1996, and the overall proportion of unregistered migrant workers dropped only because of a drop in the number of people who are classified as irregular for other reasons. These figures can be explained only by new arrivals of migrants, attracted by the hope of getting legal status. Consequently, in implementing the new immigration act approved in February 1998, the Government was engaged in adopting a 'soft' procedure to once more legalize a large part of the old as well as of the new undocumented migrants, estimated at 200,000.

Which Jobs Were Legalized

Eleven per cent of the migrants legalized in 1996 were officially unemployed, whereas only slightly more than 3 per cent were definitely hired. As to the great majority of job offers (almost 86 per cent), we do not know how many reflect actual hirings, although a sizeable sum in social security payments had to be made. The not inconsequential differences in the regional distribution of these three categories confirm the different work situations of immigrants. In north-eastern and central Italy (those regions characterized by industrial development based on small firms), there is a greater percentage of hirings and a lower percentage of migrants registered on the unemployment rolls. These are the areas that present the best opportunities for regular jobs. The opposite is true in north-western regions, suffering from the manufacturing crisis, and in the South, where the chances of finding regular employment are very few.

The share both of fixed term jobs and of part time jobs could emphasize how steady, as well as real, was the employment declared in the applications. However, the first is not a good indicator. Only one in four jobs was for a fixed term contract, just the same level as those of normal hirings of both immigrant and Italian workers in the mid-1990s. The reason for a relatively high share of permanent jobs is evident. In the context of the legalization, there were two contrasting forces at work: although a fixed term job reduced the amount of social security contributions to be paid, usually by the migrant, it resulted in a permit of stay for a shorter period of time, while a permanent labour contract qualified migrants for two-year permits of stay. Therefore, the migrants' interest in paying less was balanced by the interest to get permits for a longer stay.

Part-time work offered a way to reduce social security payments without reducing the period of the residence permit and, predictably, it was more largely implemented, although we have data for the Milan metropolitan area only. In Milan province more than 85 per cent of labour contracts declared in the applications were for part-time work. The percentage of part-time work was more than 94 per cent in housekeeping and 92 per cent in cleaning and porterage. In these sectors, there are structural reasons that justify shorter working hours, but levels between 60 per cent and 80 per cent were registered in the industrial and service sectors also, where men (most migrants in these sectors are male) usually work full-time. A comparison with the normal hiring trends for immigrants confirms the very unusual nature of this preponderance of part-time positions.

If these data hold true for the rest of Italy, as is very likely, they would reveal an impressive phenomenon. As, except for the case of cleaning/porterage and housekeeping, real job offers are almost never part-time, there are two possible interpretations of this very high part-time percentage. And neither sheds favourable light on the success of the legalization in integrating migrants into the Italian labour market. One is that these are false labour contracts, or at least contracts designed specifically to fulfil the requirements of the legalization. In this case, the part-time contract would have represented the savings of the immigrant, who had to pay all of the social security contributions. The other possibility is that these are actually full-time jobs, which were only partially legalized, so that the employer did not have to give up entirely the great advantage of not paying the social security contributions.

In the latter case, the emergence from the underground economy would have been only partial, whereas in the former, the emergence is illusory. Even if this was not the case, however, we must ask ourselves if this emergence will be permanent or if it will only be a temporary change. In any case, the combination of contract length and working hours, in the Milan area, confirms a more stable integration of migrant workers in manufacturing, construction and hotels/catering, as well as housekeeping. On the contrary, some urban service sectors (from transport to cleaning firms) are the ones in which immigrants work with the least job security.

A further indicator seriously questions the actuality of many jobs declared in the applications: the high proportion of housekeepers. Housekeeping accounts for fully 40 per cent of the occupations, whereas industrial jobs (including construction) total slightly more than 21 per cent and agricultural jobs less than 14 per cent. There is, also, a sizeable number (more than 7 per cent) of immigrants hired as cooks, waiters and barmen in hotels, bars and restaurants, and still more (almost 18 per cent) were hired in the service sector, as porters, janitors, watchmen, sales clerks and quite a few as office workers.

The territorial differences are fairly consistent with what we know of the various occupational niches filled by immigrants and is also reflected in the distribution of regular employment. Manufacturing and construction reach 46 per cent in north-east Italy and 40 per cent in the central regions, where the strong demand for blue collar labour and the lack of local manpower favour the immigrants' insertion in the regular labour market. In these areas the percentage of housekeepers is relatively small, from 17 per cent to 25 per cent, because there are no big cities, but also perhaps because few migrants were forced to resort to the housekeeping stratagem in order to be legalized. In contrast, in the South one-third of the jobs are in agriculture. In Latium, where the metropolitan area of Rome dominates and neither manufacturing nor agricultural jobs are plentiful, housekeeping reaches 60 per cent. The percentage of housekeepers is greater than 40 per cent in Lombardy (over 52 per cent in Milan), the north-west regions (Turin and Genoa) and the South (Naples, Bari, Catania and Palermo). This may be due to the twofold effect of large cities: an important demand for maids by households and a serious pressure to look for 'arranged' jobs, as we will see below. The percentage of bar and restaurant workers changes little: this service sector is almost uniformly distributed in Italy today, and it seems to provide employment for immigrants in almost the same proportion everywhere. Finally, other services are more frequent in northwest Italy and particularly in Lombardy. In the Milan metropolitan area, they reach 26 per cent and include business and office workers as well as the usual menial unskilled jobs.

... And How Many Might be Supposed to be False?

Compared with the regular jobs held by migrants, as registered by social security, the occupations declared for the legalization show an over-abundance of housekeepers and a relative scarcity of manufacturing/construction and agricultural jobs. The low number of agricultural jobs declared by legalized migrants can be explained by the lower impact of the legalization in the South, as well as by the difficulty of obtaining a job offer in agriculture during the winter. That leaves the relative excess of housekeeping and the low number of manufacturing and construction jobs to be explained. The hypothesis that illegal migrants were working more in housekeeping than in manufacturing and construction is supported by a 1993–94 survey (Natale and Strozza 1997), but it is not at all enough to explain the huge mismatch between regular employment and the jobs declared in the applications for the legalization.

The suspicion that the applications did not correspond to the real state of affairs, because housekeeping was the 'cheapest' category to apply for without having a real job and manufacturing the most 'expensive', is confirmed by the unusually high proportion of housekeepers in some immigrant groups. In the metropolitan area of Milan housekeeping reaches extremely high proportions (from 75 per cent to 94 per cent) in groups who have traditionally occupied the sector (Filipinos, Peruvians, Mauritanians, Sri Lankans, etc.), but also accounts for considerable proportions (around 50 per cent) of jobs held by Czechs and Slovaks, Ex-Yugoslavs and Brazilians, who were not previously inclined to these occupations. Furthermore, it seems really very odd that 20 per cent of Albanians and Moroccans and 15 per cent of Senegalese and Tunisians should be registered as housekeepers, because these groups consist mostly of men and were usually completely excluded from the sector.

According to a 1993–94 survey in selected areas (Natale and Strozza 1997), over a third of illegal migrants were self-employed, higher than legal migrants, because most of them were sidewalk vendors. All of these people, as well as the almost 20 per cent of migrants who were unemployed, were forced to look for a job as employees in order to avail themselves of the legalization. This leads us to believe that, because of the legalization requirements, more than half of the migrants lacking residence permits were obliged to search for a job offer, rather than having a job as an employee that could be legalized. Because it is estimated that only 40 per cent of immigrants were excluded from the legalization, it is reasonable to think that at least 15 per cent of the applications approved were actually based on false labour contracts or jobs specifically created for the purpose of legalization.

The rough estimate of at least 15 per cent of applications being false and not reflecting true labour contracts, is basically confirmed by the results of the controls conducted by Labour Inspectors. In fact, of the 23,000 applications checked (almost 10 per cent of all applications), slightly more than 20 per cent were false. However, these inspections finished after a few months and they almost never led to actual interventions: an amendment to the legalization was approved which allowed the granting of a permit for registration in the unemployment rolls, even if the job offer reported was not implemented by the employer. So, as regards the few rejected applications, the principal reason was the lack of documentation demonstrating the applicant's presence in Italy before the deadline, although some evidently false jobs were rejected, too (such as ones where the same employer was cited by too many applicants).

The First Impact on the Labour Market

During the four months of the legalization process, the number of jobs declared by immigrants in their applications was distinctly larger than the labour contracts stipulated by legal migrant workers during an entire year. Therefore, the legalization did cause a huge and sudden increase in the regular hirings of migrant workers: we can estimate that the amount more than doubled, based on the yearly base. However, several Labour Offices have found that a few months and sometimes even a few weeks following the legalization's deadline, many of the labour contracts declared had been terminated; this certainly represents an underestimation, because employers were not obliged to notify anyone of the termination. This information is consistent with the increase in immigrants registered on the unemployment rolls, indicating that for many a legal labour contract and the insertion in the regular economy were only a temporary change.

From December 1995 to March 1997, the registered unemployed increased by almost 70 per cent – from 98,000 to 166,000. Given that labour contracts for immigrants also increased substantially, driven by the economic recovery, the increase of 67,000 registered unemployed can be attributed entirely to the legalization. Of these, 18,000 were already registered as unemployed at the time of the legalization and the remaining 50,000 account for about one third of the almost 150,000 who were either hired or declared a job offer by an employer. Therefore we can estimate that a third of the immigrants who had obtained a regular job for the legalization lost it within a few months, re-joining the ranks of the unemployed or, more likely, returning to the 'underground' economy, despite their new status which would qualify them for a regular labour contract. It would, thus, appear to be a repetition, on a much larger scale, of what had already occurred after the 1990 legalization.

The increase in the number of unemployed immigrants is particularly large in the regions where manufacturing is declining in north-west Italy, as well as in the South (about 250 per cent), but is minimal in the north-eastern regions (only 30 per cent), where more immigrants have been able to find regular work in the small and middle-sized factories. Once more we find confirmation that these are the regions where there is a demand for regularly-hired immigrants, whereas in all other regions, once there is no longer a pressing need to find or 'buy' a regular labour position in order to obtain a permit, many return to their usual irregular jobs.

An important demand for regularly-hired migrants comes from households, too. Among migrant groups less prone to return to the underground economy after the legalization, we find the groups most involved in housekeeping and in helping elderly people (Filipinos and Peruvians), those most 'sustained' by their communities (Chinese) and those who have achieved the highest degree of integration (Egyptians, Somalis, Poles and Romanians). Instead, a greater propensity to return to irregular jobs exists for Moroccans and Senegalese, but also for Tunisians, Nigerians, ex-Yugoslavs. Albanians cannot be classified because of their high turnover.

THE OCCUPATIONAL PATHS CAUSED BY THE 1996 LEGALIZATION: A CASE STUDY IN THE METROPOLITAN AREA OF MILAN

The analysis of the administrative data concerning the 1996 legalization raises serious doubts about the job offers declared in the applications. Interviews with migrants and key persons in Milan (Reyneri 1998a) let us understand better how so many migrants succeeded in availing themselves of legalization – even those who were not qualified for it – and what occurred to them after legalization.

How Migrants Succeeded in Applying for Legalization

The ways in which migrants obtained legalization can be classified as follows:

1. In most cases, the immigrant declared either a previous real job or a real job offer; i.e. not obtained with the sole purpose of getting a permit of stay. Nevertheless, these cases, though they do correspond to actual work performed, do not always fit the model that the legalization was intended to rectify. First, the actual working conditions and wages may be different from those declared (to the benefit of the employer): for instance a part-time job was declared whereas the real job is full time. Secondly, the employer may make the immigrant pay the whole of his social security. Thirdly, when a former employment relationship is cited, the immigrant could have returned

to the world of odd jobs and illegal work – such as street peddling in the case of the Senegalese.

2. Some respondents had a very difficult time finding a job that would qualify them for legalization. These immigrants were excluded from the world of irregular work as well, because they usually worked as street vendors, black market cigarette sellers or were engaged in other marginal – even illegal – activities. To cope with these problems, some immigrants looked for a labour contract drawn up solely for the purpose of obtaining the residence permit. Even when this actually led to a real job, it was viewed as a temporary situation in one's normal occupational path. In order to 'create' these relationships, they had to rely on friends or find an Italian prepared to help them get hired, mostly as maids (which required the lowest social security payments), or for part time jobs. All this supports the serious misgivings caused by the disproportionately large number of male migrants who succeeded in legalizing themselves as housekeepers. It is not possible to know how many were fake, or were filed by employers trying to help out the immigrants (women who were struck by their difficulties, but also priests, who occasionally increased the number of their assistants).
3. In other cases, the immigrants 'arranged' to 'buy' labour contracts for the legalization. When someone openly talks about 'buying a contract' to satisfy the requirements of the legalization, they are referring to a completely fraudulent situation, without any real job behind it and sometimes without even a real employer. The migrants who resorted to 'arranging' a false labour contract were mostly those who were able to earn money in self-employed jobs, or who were engaging in illegal activities (from selling black market cigarettes to selling drugs) and intended to continue. In fact, they did not have the time to try to actually find a real job offer, nor to do the job involved. On the other hand, they did have the necessary funds to pay more, because in addition to the social security payments, they also had to pay the prospective employer for making a false declaration, and usually a middleman, too, either immigrants themselves or Italians.

In a qualitative study with a limited and not random sample, it was impossible to measure the relative frequency of these alternatives. However, although the first was clearly the most frequent, the interviews both of immigrants and key persons indicate that the second and third alternatives were also utilized by many migrants. The doubts raised by administrative data are, thus, confirmed.

What Occurred after the Legalization

Migrants' behaviour after they had obtained their residence permit, which gave them access to regular jobs, were as different then as in the ways they succeeded in being legalized. The stories related by migrants interviewed in the Milan metropolitan area, allow us to outline the occupational paths after legalization and, in particular, emphasize that there was a close correlation between the way in which migrants became legal and their subsequent work situation.

Those who filed a false labour contract were usually involved in either odd jobs or borderline street vending (from counterfeit brandname goods to black market cigarettes) and often continued doing this after obtaining their permits. The very fact that they did not look for a real job to obtain a permit indicates that either they did not want to enter the regular labour market or were unable to. For these people, it made little difference if they 'bought' their labour contract or if they were helped by a friend or fiancée, who agreed to hire them as maids. The image of the cigarette vendor, street peddler or odd job/handyman, who gets his permit by 'buying' a labour contract but continues to do what he has always done, is common among Moroccans, but is not unknown among the Senegalese, too.

Some were forced to return to their jobs as street vendors after working in a regular job with a fixed term contract. These immigrants attempted to enter the regular job market, but were unable to do it. There are not enough cases to draw reliable conclusions, but it is interesting to note that these do not include immigrants who worked as street vendors or cigarette sellers for an extended period. Instead, they are usually immigrants who worked at odd or casual jobs, who are trying to find better jobs after having got their residence permits. Finally, there were the few who, after having declared a false job, looked for and found a regular job. None of these had ever been a street vendor.

Among migrants who had declared a real job, a peculiar situation is held by those who 'arranged' a work contract specifically for the legalization, because this was a sign of their desire to leave the world of street vending and odd jobs. In fact, none of these, for a few months at least, 'backslid' into street vending or odd jobs, although some have gone back to working 'irregularly' and others are looking for a better and/or higher-paying job.

The way in which social security contributions were paid is a key to understanding what happened after the legalization to immigrants who declared a real, not expressly sought, job in their own applications. In fact, many applicants paid all of the social security due even in these cases. When an immigrant reports that his employer paid for his social security, according to the law, he underscores its exceptional nature – usually attributed to a good relationship between the migrant and the employer. For many, it was a sort of blackmail: either they agreed to make their social security payments or the employer would refuse to sign the job offer for the application.

When the employer paid the social security contributions, the migrant almost always stayed at the same job. In these cases, the employer and the migrant have established a mutually rewarding relationship. The employer was willing to pay the social security due, because he needed the immigrant worker. In other words, he was employing him irregularly because he had no permit of stay – not to save on labour costs. When the legalization made it possible, he legalized the worker's status, although it involved a sharp rise in the labour cost. On the other hand, by remaining with the same firm, the immigrant shows that he views his situation as acceptable in terms of both wage and working conditions, even if they often involve heavy work and/or long hours, and even if he is qualified for much better positions.

If, instead, he was forced by his employer to make his own social security payments, the migrant is very likely to abandon the job that helped him get his permit and look for a better paying one and/or one with better working conditions. In these cases, the employer had hired the illegal migrant in order to cut down on labour costs and is not interested in keeping him on if the employer must pay the full cost. The willingness to sign the job offer without charge is presented to the migrant as a favour. At the same time, the 'irregular' employer, who exploits non-registered workers, makes it clear to the migrant that he will not want to keep him on if he is going to have to sustain the full labour cost. The immigrant worker, of course, knows the restrictions placed on his bargaining position by his former situation: now that he has a permit of stay, he will look for a better job.

There are, thus, three typical sequences which illustrate the real effects of the 1996 legalization (see Table 3).

On the other hand, few of the migrants interviewed in Milan refer to the chance of getting a regular job as an advantage of the legalization, although this should have been its primary motivation. This does not mean at all that most migrants want to work irregularly, even though there is a sizeable minority who choose to continue working in marginal or irregular jobs to get higher earnings. Migrants are all well aware of the

TABLE 3

	Job before	Legalization	Job after
A	street vending *selling cigarettes* odd jobs	fake work contract	street vending *selling cigarettes* odd jobs
B	steady but non- *registered job*	employer paid social *security*	kept the same job *declared for permit*
C	steady but non- *registered job*	immigrant paid social *security*	looking for new job

distinction between regular and irregular jobs, and their job searches have given them a good idea of their respective opportunities on the labour market. The great majority believe that there are few job opportunities for migrants outside the underground economy. The few who say that there are some regular jobs available talk about jobs that Italians are reluctant to take – from assisting the elderly to heavy factory work, construction jobs and cleaning or restaurant jobs. Some migrants stress the growing difficulty of finding work, even in the underground economy. Others state that the opportunities for street vending have diminished substantially. Increasing difficulties in finding jobs in various services (from cleaning companies to waitering jobs) probably show that they are somewhat saturated. In contrast, the main advantage, quoted by all migrants interviewed, is that the permit allowed them to return to their country of origin for a visit. This is not necessarily a signal of a desire to settle in Italy, as the possibility of periodic returns also gives migrants with seasonal or odd jobs considerable savings on living expenses during the slack periods.

LEGALIZING MIGRANTS AND THE UNDERGROUND ECONOMY TRAP

The 1996 legalization succeeded in getting nearly 250,000 migrant workers to emerge from illegal residence as well as from the underground economy. As a matter of fact, this success, however, was less significant even in the short run. Many undocumented migrants were not able to apply, mainly because they were taking occasional low paid jobs and they had not enough money to pay the social contributions, as was required to get a fictitious job offer. In not a few cases the accepted job offers were fictitious, as they were either 'bought' or 'arranged' by migrants who were going on working in the underground or even illegal economy. In other cases the emergence from the underground economy was partial, as irregular full time jobs were legalized as part time ones. Furthermore, some migrant workers lost their jobs just after the legalization, as they were fired or resigned, and they had to find a regular job, a difficult task even for those holding a permit.

Problems will be much more evident in the long run. Apart from the new illegal entries attracted by the legalization itself, the number of undocumented migrants is expected to increase again considerably when those migrants legalized in 1996 have to renew their two-year permit, showing that they are regularly employed. It is estimated that almost one-third of the residence permits granted to migrants legalized in 1991 were not renewed two years later (Istat 1998). A similar phenomenon is likely to repeat oneself, although at a lower level because the labour demand for regular migrant wage-earners undoubtedly increased in recent years, mainly in manufacturing. However the main source of new illegal immigrants will be the underground economy, which goes on exerting a strong pull effect.

While migrants cannot be said to have created the submerged economy, which in Italy is a deep-rooted domestic phenomenon, migrants' propensity to accept unregistered jobs has contributed to its continuation. Most migrants are employed in labour-intensive jobs which, because of low levels of technological innovation and growth in productivity, run the risk of being priced out of the market if workers were paid at union rates. In Italy, perhaps more so than in other European countries, the regular labour cost ladder is narrow and minimum union wages are relatively high. So the only way to adjust the labour cost of these jobs to their productivity is to make them irregular, thus saving on indirect costs (taxes and social contributions) and sometimes even on direct wages. As the demand for a labour force amenable to giving up the guarantees of regular jobs is likely to increase, once such a labour supply runs out within the national borders, the scene is set for immigration from undeveloped countries.

Because of their huge involvement in the 'black labour market', immigrants are, nonetheless, caught in a vicious trap between the crisis of the welfare state and the re-emergence of the underground economy. The welfare state was based on universalistic, anonymous and acquired solidarity to provide the safety net and care functions which families and communities could no longer offer. Once the welfare state enters a crisis, part of its function is transferred back to family and community networks and particularistic forms of solidarity re-emerge, which exclude outsiders and, primarily, immigrants. The mechanism that starts this crisis may be the same that brings about the re-emergence of the submerged economy. Since social services are increasingly expensive, the costs of such solidarity grow endlessly and the view that it should be reserved for persons seen to be 'alike', not to outsiders – although they, too, pay taxes and contributions – becomes increasingly widespread. The situation worsens if most migrants work within the submerged economy, since this strengthens a vicious circle between welfare and fiscal crisis, a growth of irregular jobs, an increasing incorporation of migrant workers into the underground economy, a growing attitude of rejection towards immigrants and a more and more strict immigration policy.

Italy was entered by migrants in a warped way: they were attracted by large opportunities for working in the underground economy, the internal police checks were poor and so were the social provisions for their integration. Their insertion into the labour black market makes people forget that their working contribution is important and it causes their stigmatization, while the lack of any migratory policy causes a very negative self-selection, attracting more migrants who are prone to deviant behaviour, etc. So, the reactions of the receiving society become less and less tolerant. In few years, public opinion in Italy has changed from a well-disposed attitude to a rough rejection and the repression of migrants by the police and justice system has increased greatly (Palidda 1998).

After the 1996 legalization the control of borders became far more strict and the new immigration act made deportations easier. However, penalties for firms employing undocumented migrants were not harshened, nor the inspections increased. The opportunities of new entries for work were extended, but a more open quota system provided for by the new immigration act is not yet implemented. So, the pull effect caused by the domestic underground economy is expected to remain steady, as the case of the United States shows (Passel 1996).

In conclusion, from a policy point of view, the informalization of employment in Italy, as well as in other European countries, plays a crucial role in understanding what occurs with migratory inflows and their impact on receiving societies. Public opinion, politicians and state agencies devote a lot of care and resources to the control of the external borders of the European 'fortress'. If only they would devote as much care and as many resources in addressing the downgrading of their own labour markets, whose 'black employment' is the extreme feature.

NOTES

1. The findings of a comparative research project, on which this article is based, allows us to confirm this hypothesis also for other new receiving southern European countries.
2. Reyneri 1997b and 1998b show a detailed picture of jobs for migrant workers in Italy, both regular and irregular.
3. The assumptions and the procedures of calculation are shown in Reyneri 1997b; 1998c.
4. In the Milan metropolitan area about 15 per cent of all applications for legalization in Italy were submitted and more than 11 per cent of non-EU people in Italy live there. Besides interviews with key persons, 85 open interviews were conducted with migrants from Morocco, Egypt, Tunisia, Senegal, Albania and China, who had either been legalized or even had remained illegal. Interviewed migrants were chosen both to present the widest possible range of immigrant responses to the legalization and to give a more detailed 'close-up' of marginal subjects, who are most prone to remaining 'trapped' in the underground labour market.

REFERENCES

Censis (1995): Sopemi Italian report, Rome, Mimeographed.

Eurispes (1995): *Rapporto Italia 1995*, Rome: Koiné edizioni.

Foot, J. (1995): 'The Logic of Contradiction: Migration Control in Italy and France, 1980–'93', in Miles, R. and D. Thranhardt (eds.), *Migration and European Integration*, London: Pinter.

Ismu (1996): *Secondo rapporto sulle migrazioni*. Milan: Franco Angeli.

— (1997): *Terzo rapporto sulle migrazioni*. Milan: Franco Angeli.

Istat (1998): *La presenza straniera in Italia*, Rome.

Mingione, E. and M. Magatti (1994): Report on informal employment in the countries of the European Union. Unpublished paper.

Natale, M. and S. Strozza (1997): *Gli immigrati stranieri in Italia*. Bari: Cacucci.

Palidda, S. (1998): Research report on immigrant deviant behaviour in Italy and in particular in Milan. Migrinf: Second Italian Report. Mimeographed.

Passel, J.S. (1996): 'Recent Effort to Control Illegal Immigration to the United States', Working Party on Migration, Oecd, Paris, 13–14 June.

Portes, A. (1995): 'Economic Sociology and the Sociology of Immigration: a conceptual overview'. In A. Portes (ed.) *The Economic Sociology of Immigration*, New York: Russell Sage Foundation, pp.1–41.

Reyneri, E. (1997a): 'The Characteristics of the Immigration'. Migrinf: First Italian Report. Mimeographed.

— (1997b): 'Migrant Workers in the Italian Labour Market'. Migrinf: First Italian Report. Mimeographed.

— (1998a): 'Permanent or temporary emergence from the underground economy?' The impact of the 1996 legalisation on the insertion of immigrants in the Italian labour market. Migrinf: Second Italian Report. Mimeographed.

— (1998b): 'The Role of the Underground Economy in Irregular Migration to Italy: Cause or Effect?', *Journal of Ethnic and Migration Studies*, Vol.24, No 2, pp.303–21.

— (1998c): 'Addressing the Employment of Migrants in an Irregular Situation: The Case of Italy', Technical Symposium on International Migration and Development, U.N., The Hague, 29 June–3 July 1998.

— (1999): 'Unemployment Patterns in the European Countries: a Comparative View'. DML on-line, No.1 (www.lex.unict.it/dml-online).

Immigrants in the Spanish Labour Market

UBALDO MARTÍNEZ VEIGA

In Spain, the tradition has long existed of meeting in a particular square or street to offer services or to transmit job hunting information. The 'Novisima Recopilacion' states that 'All carpenters, masons, workers and day-hands, other men and women and others seeking shelter and hire, should come out of the places they are in to where it is customary to hire them, each at daybreak with their tools' (*Lib. oct.*).

On any Thursday or Sunday afternoon, anyone who goes to the 'Corona Boreal Square' in Aravaca will find a large number of Dominican women. They get together to send letters or get news of the Dominican Republic, talk of new opportunities in domestic service and sell island products which have either been brought over or prepared here. The square on these particular days plays many roles simultaneously, although its main function is that of an immense market where products are sold and various transactions made. These include information transfer which leads to job changes, salaries in different places or decisions to stay in the same one. An analysis of the surroundings and atmosphere gives the impression that one is receding in time.

Thus we encounter the paradox represented by the arrival of foreign immigrants in contemporary Spain. On the one hand, their arrival is interpreted by some politicians (and by people in general) as representing Spain's membership of advanced capitalism, while on the other, they can be seen as a revitalization of old traditions. The meetings of Dominican women in the Aravaca square 'revive' – perhaps without wanting to – the old Spanish tradition while at the same time bringing in an element which Saskia Sassen calls the 'peripherization of the centre'. In any event, we must emphasize that the arrival of these immigrants not only revitalizes certain traditions that may appear obsolete, but also whole areas of the economy that could be considered outdated or to have disappeared. The extent to which this is due to the fact that they are absolutely predisposed to prolonged self-exploitation or attempts to find a niche in a very competitive labour market will be seen below.

The Disqualification Phenomenon and Ethnic Specialization

There is considerable difference between the immigrants' professions – what they claim to be – and their occupations in the land that receives them. In our survey made in 1994,[1] sixty previous professions or occupations were found. These varied from economists to drivers, artists to plumbers. On grouping these, the professions most often found are in agriculture (4.9 per cent), construction (4.1 per cent), mining (4.1 per cent), teaching (4.6 per cent) or sales (4.1 per cent). In addition to this enormous variety of professions, the large number of immigrants who claim to lack one is also striking (36.4 per cent). This wide range is quickly cut down if we enquire as to their present occupation in Spain. A high concentration of people of the same national origin are found in the same occupation. For example 82 per cent of the Dominicans work in domestic service, as do 61.3 per cent of the women from the Philippines, 59.8 per cent of Poles and 43.8 per cent of Peruvians. Cape Verdeans have a high concentration of miners (82 per cent). In agriculture the number of Moroccans (48.1 per cent) and Gambians (26.8 per cent) is also noteworthy. In addition one should mention the construction trades where 22.8 per cent of Poles work alongside 15.9 per cent of Gambians and 11.9 per cent of Moroccans.

Two phenomena appear that are worth analyzing. On comparing the different professions with their present occupations, one finds a clear maladjustment between one and the other. As stated above, the professions claimed were around sixty in number. A comparison with the jobs held in Spain can be reduced to the categories of domestic and agricultural work, travelling sales, construction, and four or five professions which can be classified as trades. Two properties seem to be attached to this phenomenon: a great reduction in the variety of the immigrants' professions; and that the workers are mostly non-specialized, doing generalist work in a reduced niche. The two together make for a typical disqualification phenomenon.

Thus a massive process of disqualification is under way. A great part of the immigrants' acquired abilities are unused and therefore lost. This appears to confirm Braverman's (1994) thesis, but the reasons for this are the opposite to those which Braverman underlines. Instead of producing greater specialization and subdivision of tasks, there is a conversion of workers into generalists, causing them to lose all the qualifications and special skills they brought with them.

The second important characteristic is that within this reduced job spectrum there is a concentration of each national group in a particular type of job. This means that the groups are not equally divided between different types of work; nor are they highly diversified – just very restricted in number. This could be designated in pretentious terms as the ethnic division of labour occurring at various levels. It could also be designated, although somewhat confusingly, as a specialization of each immigrant group in particular activities. This is frequent throughout history and is so evident in the Spanish case that anyone might ask why Madrid has so many taxi-drivers from Sanabria (Zamora).

This concentration of diverse groups – this narrow spectrum of activities – is due to the very narrow job possibilities open to them. However this concentration also has much to do with the recruitment system. In the same way that one can broadly study the importance of migratory networks in the emigration layout, one must state that these networks play a fundamental role in finding work, particularly for immigrants. It is particularly interesting to study the problem of searching for and getting a job.

Networks and the Labour Market

Starting from the broad notion of a network given by Mitchell (1969), we can think of it as a specific group of connections or relationships between a defined complex of people, with the added characteristic that these connections can be used to interpret the social behaviour of those implicated. Also one can underline the central idea that the primary element flowing through this network is communication. This circulation of information between individuals serves, amongst other things, to establish social norms and create a certain consensus (or otherwise). On the other hand, there is the instrumental aspect dealing with the flow of goods and services rather than information.

From these considerations we could talk of a labour network. To understand this, some analysis of the Dominican concentration in the Corona Boreal Square is necessary. Amongst the women who meet there, the majority work in the neighbouring areas and originate from a particular area in the south-east of the Dominican Republic called 'Vicente Noble'. From a structural viewpoint one could easily determine that some of those present are not related through kinship ties but the structural basis for their relationship is having the same place of origin. A study of the interactive aspects soon brings one to understand that through these relationships and connections a considerable amount of information flows with regard to salaries, household/family qualities and jobs available. In addition, there is also contact between potential employers and future employees through third parties who are also employees. The observable reality is that this is a 'job fair', located in a particular place, where the employers are not present but are represented by their employees, who put potential new employees in contact with them. What makes this all possible is their common origin. This structures both supply and demand.

As this brief description shows, the labour market, among other things, is a structured one, at least in this central aspect. Marc Granovetter, in his classic work of 1973, observed that a distinction can be made between strong and weak ties in such networks. The strong ones are those established between people whose links are more intense and regular, while the weak ones are established between those whose interaction is more irregular and distant. Weak links are very important because through them much information flows. Information quantity is based on its novelty or the expected or unexpected nature of the message received. This implies that the information transmitted through the weak links is newer and more unexpected. Thus more information is transmitted than through stronger links. From the viewpoint of finding work, this is very important since finding work is determined by information.

In this case the connection is a weak one in principle, being just from the same country or locality. This is activated by the meetings in the square. It is through these links which the Mexicans call *paisanaje* that much information circulates putting future employees in touch with employers. This is why there is a high ethnic concentration of people in particular jobs. But there is still more: in contrast with the classical concept that weak links generate alienation (Wirth 1938), Granovetter sees them as being indispensable for the opportunities offered to individuals and hence their integration into communities. Strong links or connections lead to greater fragmentation. On the basis of this case, the weak links are exclusively based on locality or national origin. They are central to transmitting information regarding job opportunities and give considerable cohesion since they are based on common elements of a general nature. More individualized links lead to more divisive phenomena. The origin of the force of a weak link, the strength of sharing a homeland, can be explained by the above.

It must also be emphasized, although this will be re-examined below, that the channelling of job offers through the ethnic networks are, in the last instance, the structuring of the job market through a network basically composed of group members already doing this type of work.

This has three important consequences. The first consists of the basis of labour relations being the common place of origin. This brings workers from the same place to the same type of jobs, be they in agriculture, domestic service or travelling sales.

The second consequence is much more important in that the concentration of workers from the same place makes for what could be called a 'pseudo-internal' job market. The creation of this market, based on workers recruited from the same place of origin can in fact exclude other workers, including natives. This is very important to bear in mind when analyzing job market competition. It is sometimes affirmed that immigrants do not compete in the job market because they take jobs that the natives do not want. One must emphasize that sometimes the creation of such a pseudo-internal job market serves, in fact, to exclude the native population from certain types of jobs. This is not surprising since the job market seriously deviates from the formal stipulations of neo-classical market analysis.

The third observation is a general one, derived from the first two. There are authors who rightly establish a distinction between the network which recruits workers (consisting of the means used by employers to recruit workers) and the network of supply through which these workers offer their services. Granovetter and Tilly (1988) affirm that there are two important reasons for which the distinction between networks of demand and supply are important. First, the network of supply varies from the point of view of age, sex, race, national origin or citizenship. Depending on the articulation with demand, networks have important effects on worker recruitment to particular posts. Secondly, if good results are obtained by those who control the recruitment network, established linkages tend to be self-reproducing. Certain characteristics of the migrant populations, which observers consider to be ethnic characteristics, in fact emerge from joining these networks.

'Push' or 'Pull'?

The factors which make up 'push' and 'pull' are fairly diffuse. There has been continuous criticism of the push and pull theories: although it is easy to compile a motivation list and present it as a theory of migration, this type of analysis does not resolve the fundamental question as to why, in spite of individual idiosyncracies and the most varied motives, population movements of known magnitude and direction are produced with predictable regularity over long periods of time (Portes 1981).

This unjust criticism reduces the push-pull theories to a sort of inventory of idiosyncratic motives for emigration. From the labour point of view, one could state that those who basically defend the attraction effect, emphasize unsatisfied demand for manual labour in the receiving countries; while the defenders of the push factor affirm that the migratory phenomenon occurs independently of the labour demands of the receiving countries. Defending one viewpoint or the other has consequences regarding the role of the immigrant labour force. In the first case, it is thought that immigrants play a complementary role with respect to the native population, while in the second there is competition between them. We believe that this dichotomy is useful because it can helps to clarify many aspects of immigration.

However, the situation cannot be so dichotomous because the job market is not homogeneous, nor does the possibility for perfect interchange exist between native and immigrant labour. It is important to clarify the situation described as being one which cannot be analyzed thoroughly through the imagery of attraction and expulsion. When a migrant labour network appears, such as that between Spain and the Dominican Republic, one should talk of a chain of work more than the factors of attraction and expulsion which are obviously present. In this context one should refer to the similarity to what has been described by Hopkins and Wallerstein (1986) as 'commodity chains', which they define as a 'job network and production processes whose final product is a finished commodity'. This is a job network that enables people to circulate from a more peripheral area to one that is less so, in order to produce some type of goods or services. If we think of this network as a chain, it plays an active role at the two extremes of the process. The place of origin favours circulation and mobility of the work force, while the place of arrival constitutes the centre of contact between supply and demand.

Some other important aspects have also to be underlined. First, this chain mobilizes the labour force at its origin. Secondly, not only does it play an active role in the acceptance of a job offer but it creates or opens up new job possibilities on arrival. Thirdly, this could be a monopolizing force in particular local job markets. These observations are perfectly applicable to the Dominican women and to their situation as domestic workers in certain areas such as the north-east of Madrid. Yet they cannot be applied to the migratory process of other collectives. What does seem clear however, is that there are many cases of 'ethnic concentration' in particular jobs, although for very varied reasons. Our observations explain the concentration of people of the same geographic origin in particular jobs along with the type of jobs, although in no way is this solely explicable by the network of relationships. Immigrants occupy a highly restricted niche within the job framework. Not only is it restricted but also appears to be degrading work, poorly paid under precarious and bad conditions.

The Dual Labour Market Hypothesis

This last observation introduced an important problem which will be discussed in the following pages, namely the dual job market – its segmentation or division. Although the three represent descriptions of relatively different phenomena, they can be initially considered synonymous in order to clarify a problem which often is not taken into account. The theory of the dual job market is basically an attempt to convert certain psycho-social elements into ones that are endogenous to the economic system (Piore 1974). In the neo-classical economy, individuals have preferences that are considered exogenous to the economic system and that change slowly, if at all. By contrast, Piore's doctrine defends the idea that certain work habits depend on the type of work accomplished (Doeringer and Piore 1971).

The theory of dualism in the labour market postulates that this is not a continuous phenomenon but contains two segments. These are institutionally based. At first the primary and secondary labour markets must be related to certain behavioural traits that are required and simultaneously transformed by the job market segment that these workers are in. Later this insistence on behavioral traits is abandoned. This dualism is no fetish. It is a way to simplify job market discontinuity and the acceptance of many more differences in the types of jobs and businesses does run counter to the postulates of dualism theories. One must also emphasize an aspect that Piore (1971) insists on from the start. He claims that the distinction between primary and secondary sectors is not necessarily associated with particular firms. In some, where the majority of the jobs have characteristics of primary ones and are full of stable workers, there are sections or departments with inferior job opportunities accommodating an unstable or temporary labour force. Often in central firms there are parts where people work with low pay, no job security etc. and there are also peripheral firms where part of the workers are in the primary job sector.

Considering the dualism theory or job market segmentation, in vulgar fashion it is affirmed that a division exists between the two types of work: one which is well paid and the other less so. Undoubtedly the greater part of the immigrant population works in poorly paid jobs. However, using other criteria to distinguish different segments of the job market such as security and job stability in contrast with seasonality and instability, the problems get more complicated. Observing the jobs that many immigrants to Spain perform, one realizes that many Moroccans work in agriculture where the most important problem is seasonality. However there are also Dominican women working as interns in domestic service where their stability is total and hence where jobless periods, even between jobs, are practically nonexistent.

According to Piore, job stability and security is one of the basic criteria for distinguishing between the primary and secondary job markets. However when considering agricultural and domestic work which, as is known, is often where immigrants are employed, one realizes that domestic work represents an extreme in job stability, which is almost total. Agricultural work has gradations from growing vegetables in El Ejido or Roquetas de Mar, where the seasonality is small, with only a couple of inactive months, to migrant agricultural labour in different areas of the peninsula where the workers collect olives in Jaen, fruit in Lerida or saffron in La Mancha. Here the instability is much greater although the salaries are considerably higher. A simple observation indicates that the dual job market idea is not easily applicable here and from the viewpoint of its first scientific presentation, the criteria for distinguishing one segment from the other are not always clear. If this were so, the dualism or segmentation hypothesis would undoubtedly have to be abandoned.

In any event, we do not believe that it should be abandoned, but it is evidently important to understand what could be learned from applying it to the problems currently being analyzed. The first and fundamental consideration should be the consequences that can be deduced from applying this hypothesis, or, stated another way, what are the implications of this theory?

Let us first define a segment as a 'subgroup or segment of workers and jobs among which the determinants of compensation in the job market and mechanisms of asignation within it have similar characteristics' (Mazany, Apostle and Clairmont 1986). The problem of understanding the existence and function of the diverse segments can be considerably simplified if one considers that in each of them there is a clear difference in rules and procedures according to which a job is assigned a price. These rules and procedures result in lower labour costs in the secondary job market than in the primary one. In addition, the dual market theory proposes that certain barriers exist that impede or make it more difficult for an objectively-qualified labour force in the secondary sector to obtain a job in the primary sector competing with those of equivalent qualifications (Morrison 1992). What has just been stated can be expressed in a simpler, although less precise, way by saying that the number of jobs available in the primary sector is limited with respect to the supply of qualified workers. This brings a rationing of offers and this in turn, a form of discrimination according to race, gender etc. which are used as discriminatory elements to decide who can and cannot accede to jobs in the primary sector. In fact in one of the first texts analyzing job market segmentation (Reich, Gordon and Edwards 1973), the authors affirm that secondary jobs are basically (although not exclusively) occupied by minorities, women and young people.

When this viewpoint is applied to the distinction between natives and immigrants within the job market, we find that the presence of immigrants in the labour market does not cause a great displacement of natives because they accept a different group of jobs – those which the natives refuse (Piore 1979). It is important to state however that although immigrant workers are situated in the secondary job market, this does not imply that they do not compete with natives for this type of work. Enrico Pugliese (1993) explains this phenomenon well when he affirms that the majority of immigrants work in secondary jobs. This is more evident now than in the past. However the lack of preference by the local and national labour force for this type of jobs does not imply rejection. The presence of immigrant labour cannot be considered as an indicator of unsatisfied demand for work, even in the secondary job market.

At certain points in time, employers exploit race; at others, ethnicity and at yet others, gender, in order to divide the workers. This does not imply that there is no competition between groups for the same jobs. In other cases, when the demand is cyclic, seasonal or unstable, production in a monopolistic setting is revealed to be inadequate. Little by little, more and more of certain products are subcontracted or exported to smaller firms, which are more competitive and less capital intensive in the industrial periphery.

This last observation can be perfectly understood as labour market segmentation, which is often made up of more than two segments. This can sometimes be a way to make the division of labour more concrete as Piore supposes, and, more frequently, is an employer-strategy to divide workers and reduce labour costs. The dividing line can be established in many ways – along sex, race or nationality – or include the 'construction of skills' needed to carry out a job which could serve to create segmentation phenomena whose sole function is to lower costs and divide workers. The constitution of firms as central and peripheral businesses along with the phenomenon of subcontracts is an omnipresent possibility since the origin of capitalism. All these dividing lines could be activated or deactivated at determined points in history and for each particular case. One thus realizes the structural reasons and strategies for these divisions. However much one may insist on 'human capital' in assigning jobs and work to one segment or the other, one must never forget that always and under all circumstances 'the number of jobs available in the primary sector is limited with respect to the supply of qualified work' (Morrison, 1990). Hence the assignation of jobs to one or the other sector is mostly arbitrary.

We believe anyway that the fundamental problem at present is to establish whether the hypothesis of the dual or segmented job market serves to describe the labour situation of immigrant workers with respect to natives. In order to elucidate these problems, let us briefly analyze the activity sectors which primarily employ the immigrants being studied. These are construction, domestic service and agriculture. This brief study could establish a typology of groups and activities. Some of these sectors are analyzed more carefully than others, because the problems presented seem to be more interesting.

THE CONSTRUCTION INDUSTRY

Amongst the immigrants interviewed, 10 per cent work in construction. If we add those who frequently work in related professions (guilds or trades), then we have another 7 per cent who also work in this area. It can be argued that much of the construction sector belongs to the secondary job market. However, it is highly fragmented internally. According to a recent SEOPAN report (1992), there is a radical change in the organization of the market. The big firms tend to become managing outfits providing economic and legal expertise, design and knowhow, subcontracting the execution, labour costs, social security and so on to smaller firms.

Here we find a clear profile of a dualistic structure in the construction industry. This is demonstrated by the gradual disappearance of the medium-sized industries and the constitution of two opposing poles. At one end are the big industries that contract major work, offering technology, financing, management, conceptualization and design. At the opposite pole are the firms or businesses that carry out the work – what one may bluntly but usefully describe as the 'manual labour'. The latter subcontract this from the big companies. This phenomenon has been long described by many authors but perhaps the clearest description is that of Reich, Gordon and Edwards (1973).

This description clearly corresponds to the dual structure of firms, considered a monopolistic environment alongside small, more competitive ones, which subcontract and carry out some construction projects. Job dualism or segmentation exists with a stable market sector (clearly defined jobs and more or less clear systems of promotion) contrasting with the other sector (unstable, poorly paid jobs and a randomized promotion structure). In the case of construction in Spain, not only is there a polarization or segmentation of jobs and businesses, but there is a clear distinction between big companies that are more or less converted into centres of finance, design and project conception as opposed to small firms that subcontract manual work. The distinction is even greater between conceiving and directing projects carried out by particular companies and the smaller ones carrying out subcontract work.

There is a very high accident rate in the construction sector: as Roa Baltar observed (1994: 29), 'On average in the construction trade, 2.24 times more accidents occur than in the rest of industry'. In the 1994 Senate report on construction worker accidents, Mariano Aisa Fernández, (the SEOPAN President), affirmed that, in his opinion, the increase in accident frequency since 1985-1986 is partly due to 500,000 new workers who joined the labour force from other sectors and had no previous construction experience. Presumably these are workers in the small companies – increasingly unqualified and inexperienced. This is a longstanding phenomenon referred to in earlier observations of the Madrid Community Office of Economic Planning report (CAM 1988), which stated that the construction sector has a lower level of professional qualifications than the national average.

The distinction between large and small companies brings with it a job setting in which requalification occurs in one, while in the other there is a continued process of disqualification. Growth is towards ever greater externalization of work by 'management firms' and continuous subcontracting of activities to smaller and smaller firms. The above-mentioned Senate report analyzes the problem of the subcontracting accurately, when they affirm that among 250,000 Spanish construction firms, the 50 largest cover 30 per cent of the sector leaving the other 70 per cent to an enormous number of other companies. This gives rise mainly to subcontracts and even subcontracting subcontracts, as can be observed in this 70 per cent. This continuous atomization is reinforced by the phenomenon of self-employed workers who are called 'pseudo-autonomous' or falsely autonomous. They consist of workers who are subcontracted as if they were self-employed to save social costs for the company. An example follows which clearly shows how this works. In 1980 the increase in construction jobs was 835,000 people i.e. 81.9 per cent of the people employed in this sector. In 1985 this figure was reduced to 534,600 implying a 36 per cent reduction in the number of paid workers who in the same year went on to represent 71.6 per cent of the workforce. Most of those who disappeared were self-employed.

The Senate report affirms that 28 per cent of fatal accidents originate from inadequate job organization before execution, which could be avoided if jobs were adequately organized from a security standpoint by eliminating simultaneous incompatible activities like soldering, painting, using organic solvents or by co-ordinating those who intervene in these before and at the start of the project, among other measures.

The Senate document ascribes the high accident level to the lack of horizontal co-ordination between various trades and subcontractors. While soldering is going on, painting or the use of organic solvents with the concomittant risks of fire and explosion may continue. Not only is there a lack of horizontal co-ordination, as seen above, but the conception, organization, financing and carrying out of projects are also vertically disconnected.

The total separation between project design and execution that results in these accident figures clearly involves carrying out what Braverman calls the second principle of scientific organization, Taylorism, which, according to him, should denominate the principle of separating project design and execution, rather than the commoner definition of mental and manual work separation. Here we not only find separation within the firm itself, in which there is internal division between managers and manual workers, but rather a division between different firms, some taking care of management and design whilst others subcontract the tasks to be carried out.

The second phenomenon, described as horizontal disintegration, consists of each task being carried out independently of the others with no co-ordination between them. Often, activities that are incompatible from the viewpoint of worker safety are carried out simultaneously. This increases the number of accidents and reflects the first principle of the scientific organization of work which according to Braverman represents the dissociation of the work process from worker capacity. This work process is independent of workers' traditional knowledge. Thus nothing depends on the skills of the worker but only on organization or management practices. When this has nothing to do with the organization of the work process, accidents occur.

There is a third element to be underlined: worker disqualification. The SEOPAN president thinks that the increase in accident frequency since the mid-1980s is partly due to the labour reactivation in the construction sector incorporating half a million new inexperienced workers. It is affirmed in conclusion that the lack of professional training in construction, with a high proportion of unqualified workers, is one of the main problems. Braverman also discusses continuous worker disqualification within capitalism. Although this viewpoint has been criticized by authors such as Gordon, Edwards and Reich (1982), we believe that their basic idea describes what has occurred in the construction trade. In capitalist evolution, qualification requirements have become polarized with a highly qualified minority and a mass of workers whose qualification requirements have been significantly reduced. In this case, job qualification is so much reduced that while in other industries a worker knows from day to day what he may do (and thus get accustomed to it), in construction, work depends on climate. A worker may find himself doing many different things in one day – from manning a pneumatic drill to digging a trench and two hours later carrying building materials up to the tenth floor. What in this text is termed 'impossible to get accustomed to', signifies the impossibility of getting on-the-job training. This is due to complete job instability and constant changes of task.

The reason for such a situation, in which one may even talk of disorganization in the work process, is to be found in the total submission of the productive process to external market forces. This explains the importance of the immigrant workers in this activity. They are always contracted for a short time, often a week and sometimes on a day-to-day basis – although we have not found cases of wage discrimination due to their being immigrants. They are simply available manual labourers who can be contracted when there is demand. With declining demand, or the dictates of needs and climatic conditions, these workers do not work. The nature of the 'cheap manual labour reserve' can be understood by the following example. An architect working in the hilly area north of Madrid claims that in five minutes he can find 100 Moroccans to work for just a day. Here the immigrants occupy the secondary job market, although not as in Piore's conception. The duality stems from the segmentation of the companies into those which conceive and design projects and firms or individuals who subcontract out some of the work. The immigrants are in the second category, with unstable labour conditions determined by transitory production needs. The population involved in this shows great instability and geographic mobility.

DOMESTIC SERVICE

'Live in' domestic service, i.e. with the employee living in the employer's home, is the basic activity of the Dominican women, along with Filipinas, Peruvians, Moroccans and Poles. Immigration changes this type of activity, which until the 1960s was the mainstay of young Spanish women who had migrated from their villages to Madrid.

The first characteristic of these workers is their capacity to save. Although salaries are low, around 70,000 pesetas a month or even less (in 1994), employees do have their need for room and board covered.

The majority of the Dominicans are married, but internal domestic service impedes their coming to Spain with their spouses and children. At first their savings are remitted to pay for the trip. They have to pay out a lot and the agreement is often that whoever arranged the trip and the job keeps much of the wage. Little by little, money gets sent to the family who stayed behind, either to maintain the children or buy a house or a bit of land. Later they arrange to pay for the trip over for a daughter or some other female relative, thus creating a migrant chain. Gradually part of their savings remain, although they still send some to their land of origin, with which it seems that their emigration takes on a more definitive character. This capacity to save is still more clearly manifested in comparing the Cape Verdian miners with their female compatriots in domestic service. It is noteworthy that although the salary difference between miners and domestic workers is immense (often a five- or six-fold difference), the women save and send home more to their families than do the men.

It is infrequent that the husbands come with their wives, for reasons that have little to do with the composition or organization of the domestic unit, nor with the scarcity of funds for the trip over. This has more to do with the type of domestic intern work which normally does not admit a couple. In fact when husbands do come, it makes it impossible to work in homes and they then need to find a home of their own thus considerably diminishing their resources. In this overview, two elements play a central role and are perhaps not taken into account. One may have the impression that the arrival of immigrant women and their going into domestic service result from personal choice. Nothing could be further from the truth. When it is understood that these are coloured immigrant women who do not have many other job possibilities open to them, one can understand that this also represents a handicap in the later evolution of their employment.

In any event the character of their work as internal domestics has important consequences for understanding the mechanics of the migratory process. Analyzing the migration of Cape Verdeans to the Bierzo region, one encounters the fascinating phenomenon of the separate migration of sexes. The men come mainly to work in the mines while their womenfolk migrate on their own to Madrid to work in domestic service and later, they meet in particular places of leisure and diversion in the capital on weekends. In the case of the Dominicans the process differs in that their families remain in the Dominican Republic.

The elements offered here could provide a context but do not seem to be of much help in understanding the type of activity carried out by immigrants within the job market. The first basic distinction to be established is between internally or externally employed workers. Everyone knows what this means. The former live in the employer's home and the latter outside. There is a clear salary difference. Interns are paid monthly while external workers' salaries are calculated on an hourly basis.

Their work conditions also differ considerably so they will be considered separately. Living in has the immediate consequence of the number of hours they must spend in the workplace. It is striking that in the survey the Dominicans answer that the number of hours worked averages 11.9 per day. Considering that 84.4 per cent of them work as interns in domestic service, what clearly shows up here is an enormous increase in the number of working hours. We know that this is not overtime but what is legislated as 'hours of presence'. This designation of time agreed to by the employer and employee as 'not being dedicated to habitual domestic tasks but to jobs requiring little effort such as opening the door, answering the telephone, etc' is purely euphemistic. Since it is difficult to determine what represents greater or less effort, the result, according to the workers themselves, is that the hours of presence are just more working hours which prolong the working day, sometimes even up to 16 hours – a characteristic of domestic labour throughout history. Ten and 12-hour workdays are not something of the distant past for internal domestics. This clarifies the comparative differences between internal and external work perfectly: namely lower pay and longer working hours than in external domestic service.

One noteworthy point is that the work of the interns represents an extreme of maximum stability. They work all year round, change jobs very little except at the beginning, and, most important of all, when they leave one house they immediately find another. However, the external domestic workers have a highly seasonal job, change employers often and have jobless periods in between. From this point of view there is an important difference between the two types of domestic service and if we make the distinction by the criterion of stability, (Piore's central distinction), then it can be affirmed that internal domestic work belongs to the primary job market sector and external work to the secondary one. This is absurd, but the absurdity is due to poor criteria in distinguishing primary and secondary markets with particular respect to job stability/instability.

What must be emphasized is the total absence of native women in internal domestic service, although this used to be extensive among Spanish women. However what occurs with the immigrants is not the same, since this was a European phenomenon from the beginning of industrialization. The internal domestics were young unmarried women from rural areas who worked as domestics until they married or found a better job. In the Dominican case, these women are married before they come and it is possible that domestic service becomes their permanent occupation.

In external domestic service, two population groups coincide in the same activity: natives and immigrants. Salaries are higher, although instability and saving capacity differ. In any event, attempting to study the dichotomy between the primary and secondary job market is not of much use in interpreting the evolution of domestic service – particularly with respect to the immigrant population.

AGRICULTURE

It is evident that in the case of the agricultural workers in El Ejido and Alicante and other places referred to, the foreign workers are clearly in the secondary job market sector. This is manifested by the temporary nature of the activities and by the fact that, independently of crisis or growth periods, agricultural work is seasonal. There are periods of abundant work such as harvest time and others where there is no work and the workers are jobless. Thus these migrants make up an 'army of reserve manual labour' that is always available and can be employed or left alone, as convenient.

The situation of the immigrant agricultural workers in the secondary job market stems from the seasonal character of agricultural work. We might even say that the distinction between agricultural workers who have a more or less fixed status and temporary workers should be abandoned. Really, all agricultural workers are temporary. This will be proved below when particular cases are analyzed but this characteristic instability is the basic diacritical sign to distinguish between primary or secondary job markets, according to Piore.

Normally the great northerly migrations in Europe are thought to have been directed towards industry. Now that immigration has begun towards southern Europe and is more towards agriculture, it is assumed that it is because these are more agricultural countries, or because this is surplus immigration at a time of economic recession. In fact, in Europe as in the USA, agriculture has always been a fundamental attractant for the immigrant population. Even in countries like Germany, with an enormous industrial component, immigration towards agriculture has played a central role. As has been well-demonstrated by Hollifield (1992), the sector of the German economy which in the 1950s exerted most pressure to admit more foreign immigrants was agriculture. German farmers fought for them, as did the French. They insisted that, with the idea of seasonal admission, this was limited to certain periods of the year. Thus the *Gastarbeiter* programmes were created insisting on a host and a limited period of stay for seasonally imported labour.

In the French case, constant pressure for this has been exerted up until the present. This indicates two important points: first that the idea of immigrants being first and foremost required for industry is false. Secondly, that agricultural immigration has been the most consistent and long-lasting phenomenon in European history to date. For these reasons, to consider this a secondary phenomenon is both empirically and theoretically mistaken, as will be discussed below.

It must also be emphasized from the start that agriculture plays a central role in the arrival of the immigrants. The origin of the first Moroccan immigrants to places like El Ejido between 1985 and 1989 must not be sought in Morocco itself, but in France, where they worked mainly in seasonal agriculture. They came to El Ejido on being expelled from France; others came for a period and remained there, while still others on holiday heard that there was work available without too much police control. Hence their arrival in such places was just another stage in the nomadic process of spatial displacement, the search for temporary work which later became something more or less stable. The spatial displacements of the immigrant agricultural workers have consequences with respect to their settlement. In Murcia or Almeria the Moroccan workers began as temporary workers for a certain time.

Work in the greenhouses of Almeria and in places like Murcia, the lower Segura plain or the Maresme are characterized by long working seasons. Work in El Ejido can be considered the most representative of these in that it lasts from September to May or June. Although even in this case and supposing one works daily – which is usually not the case – it is seasonal work. For this reason, almost all agricultural work is temporary. In areas where the season lasts longer, there are very few workers for the same employer. They often change, even from day to day. It is also true that there are workers with longer term contracts of about six months. They must then live on the estates next to the greenhouses or in the storehouses where the tools are kept. The worker thus has two different functions: worker and caretaker. In Almeria there is not much worker circulation within the province, while in Murcia and Alicante workers often move around to find work.

Among the workers who remain more or less established in a particular place, there are four or five months of the year during which they do not work there. In this case, those whose status is legal either go home or emigrate to other parts of the country to work for shorter seasons. Those who are illegal do not return home, but look for other work or remain jobless there. The seasonal character of agricultural work along with the jobless periods is clearly demonstrated in the survey where the Moroccans, half of whom work in agriculture, have only 32 per cent of these workers employed all year, while the Dominicans in domestic service have a very different situation, with 71.3 per cent employed all year round.

Much temporary work lasts two or three months at the most. What makes some jobs last longer is if all the agricultural activities are carried out; harvesting alone does not take long. Salaries are higher in the latter case. It is also noteworthy that while in the greenhouses (where mostly immigrants work) the proprietors may work alongside them, in many areas, such as Murcia or Alicante or in the Maresme, the temporary work is done by native day-workers alongside immigrants. Comparing the situation of more permanent agricultural work, as in the greenhouses of Almeria, in Murcia or Alicante or in the Maresme, with what occurs with temporary work where the workers range further afield, one finds similarities with what occurs in internal and external domestic service. The former is more stable but, with lower pay, is entirely in the hands of foreign women, while both natives and immigrants work externally with better pay although greater instability.

Similarly in agriculture, work in the more permanent jobs is by the proprietors and their relatives, either together with immigrants or by immigrants alone, while the temporary jobs are taken by both native and immigrant day-workers. The State Federation of Agricultural workers of the Comisiones Obreras trade union reports that 150–200,000 Spaniards work as temporary day-workers (Report, Federacion Estatal del Campo de Comisiones Obreras 1993), which implies that 14 per cent of the working population is involved at least for some periods in such activities. Their figures for the volume of immigrants is 40,000. Thus the majority are Spaniards.

There is however a clear difference between agricultural and domestic work. The latter is so compartmentalized that practically no one works partially as interns and later as externs or vice versa. In the first category there is often a worker who spends a particular period in one type of agricultural area on a more permanent basis and later moves to an area of temporary work. This indicates, as stated earlier, that agricultural work is always seasonal. In any case, one may affirm that the immigrant workers seem to prefer work with a certain degree of stability and are ready to compromise on lower pay while the native populace hold job stability in lower esteem, will not accept this sort of compromise, and are more interested in higher salaries. This observation appears to tie in with the data but does throw out the classification and established criteria that distinguish the primary and secondary job markets. From this point of view we consider that the dichotomy is not too useful to describe the Spanish data.

The mechanisms producing work in more stable work areas are well studied; however, temporary work is less so and for this reason a few observations are in order.

The most important temporary work activities are:

- collecting olives in Jaen,
- asparagus in Navarre and the Rioja,
- potatoes in the Rioja and Navarre,
- strawberries in Huelva,
- fruit picking in Lerida and Saragossa,

- grape harvest in the Penedes, and
- tomatoes in Murcia and Alicante.

There are other activities which at present seem to have less importance in numerical terms, such as asparagus and cherry picking in Caceres, saffron in La Mancha etc. It is also important to note that these temporary worker migrations have been going on from time immemorial between different areas of the Peninsula. For example, the Galician emigration to Castille for harvesting, the longest being to Andalusia through Portugal, which was, in this sense, international migration. This however was largely internal migration, in that it was from certain provinces to others which is, in this sense, similar to the Andalusians going to the Penedes for the grape harvest or the gypsies of Leon going to the Rioja to collect potatoes. It is often forgotten that this has been continuous through history.

A single job market existed in many parts of Europe long before the term was invented. In creating this transnational job market, temporary agricultural work plays a central role. Long-term observation shows that this has lasted throughout history, although the populations have changed. In the seventeenth and eighteenth centuries, the French came to Catalonia or Aragon or Madrid, while in the twentieth century it was the Spaniards who went to France or the Moroccans, Algerians or Portuguese to the Rioja or to Lerida.

The role of temporary agricultural work in constituting a transnational job market and emigration can be understood if one observes that at the same time that Moroccans work picking pears in Lerida, there are 12,000 Spaniards who go to work in France during the grape harvest. At the same time that Moroccans and Andalusians go to pick strawberries in Huelva, the Spaniards have recently started to go to Belgium and do the same in an organized fashion. To all these elements must be added the fact, which may be disputed, that Moroccan emigration to some areas like the Maresme or El Ejido, began as an itinerant movement of temporary agricultural workers. Within this, one must include the part that is not carried out in Spain but is located in France. All this permits one to comprehend the economic and cultural importance of temporary agricultural work.

However, more data can be added. First, this is the work in which most immigrant groups are implicated. With this it is not claimed that the largest numbers of immigrants are working in this sector, but that it is the work which employs the biggest variety of nationalities. In addition to

Moroccans and Algerians, there are important numbers of Portuguese, Gambians and Senegalese, Latin Americans, Russians, Poles and Rumanians. Even in the French grape harvests, in addition to Spaniards, Moroccans and other groups, considerable numbers of Polish workers have started to arrive. Their varied national origins correspond to the varied regional origins within Spain. In the same way that the Andalusians go to Lerida or the Penedes, gypsies from Catalonia can go to the Rioja.

Looking at the conditions and work organization, it can be said that there is considerable variation from place to place. It is unusual for a job contract to be made in advance, and more often there is nothing in writing. The manual labour recruiting systems vary – from the 'Penedes Winegrowers Association' sending out some of its members to contract workers in the province of Cordoba, to those who came one year and promised to return, to those who come to try their luck.

In general, wage discrimination exists and the immigrants are paid 25–30 per cent less than the natives (CCOO Report). It is also important to remember that housing discrimination occurs, referred to in the 1993 report and, although legislated against, non-compliance occurs in 75 per cent of the cases. The situation is also bad for the natives but there are gradations and important differences. Those encamped in Santo Domingo de la Calzada are much worse off than many immigrants to the Penedes. But here too important differences exist between natives and immigrants. The CCOO Report claims that the majority of the temporary workers are housed on the farms or in peasant homes. On visiting some of these it was found that they had reasonable hygienic and living conditions. Only some small groups of Moroccans were housed in garages or very deficient houses.

Another example – the native strawberry pickers in Huelva – are housed mainly in rented flats or houses. But if many come, they are housed in stables or barracks in very poor conditions and the immigrant situation is always the worst. 'In Palos de Moguer the general panorama is painful giving a sensation of misery, lack of hygiene, shacks and often many Moroccan workers sleeping in the greenhouses or strawberry tunnels'... As everyone knows there is an enormous difference between living in a shack or shanty and in a greenhouse. Although the owner is supposed to find decent housing for the workers, in the natives' case there is some concern in this respect which sometimes produces results. But no such preoccupation exists with respect to the immigrants so their living conditions are much worse. There is clearly a cut-off between native temporary workers' housing and that of the immigrants, which is always worse.

SOME TENTATIVE CONCLUSIONS

How useful is the labour market segmentation theory in explaining the role of immigrants in the Spanish economy? In the case of the construction sector there seems little doubt that a large part of it is a secondary sector. The radically changed structure of the industry has resulted in a dualistic industry: large hi-tech companies which control financing and design (with few immigrants) alongside many small subcontracted firms that are dependent on cheap flexible labour for their continued existence. These small firms are reliant upon (illegal) immigrant labour for their transitory production schedules; the immigrants experience job instability, required geographic mobility, usually no social benefits, and dangerous working conditions. There is no evidence of wage discrimination relative to natives.

Domestic service, as we have already commented, represents an extreme of stability in employment for those who 'live in'. However, this form of employment is no longer attractive to natives, requiring as it does, potentially unlimited working hours and the sacrifice of private life. This sector is clearly a secondary sector, with 'live-out' housekeeping as a more desirable form of employment for Spanish workers. Again, we appear to find dualism with concentration of immigrants in the secondary market.

The agricultural sector seems to be almost entirely a secondary sector, if we exclude the more permanent employment of proprietors and their families. Almost all agricultural work is temporary, although with natives working alongside immigrants. However, the apparent disinterest of natives in job stability but rather in higher wages contradicts Piore's criterion of job stability as the defining feature of secondary work. It may also be significant that it is in this sector – the only one in our study which is not dualistic – that clear wage discrimination and also housing discrimination occur *vis-à-vis* natives. A possible explanation is that Spanish workers reluctantly accept work in a secondary sector: because they view this as a temporary phenomenon, their real interest lies not in acquiring permanent agricultural work but permanent employment elsewhere. Thus a short-term approach leads to a preference for immediate higher earnings.

We have observed several patterns which require comment. First, that there is good evidence of labour market segmentation with immigrants working overwhelmingly in the secondary sectors. Secondly, that the experience and qualifications of the immigrants are of little or no relevance – the 'disqualification phenomenon'. Thirdly, that immigrants occupy a very narrow range of jobs – basically unskilled – with some patterns of ethnic specialization. (We have suggested above that network theories provide a good explanation of that phenomenon). Combining these three sorts of observation, one has to conclude that the labour market does not even approach the neo-classical model. More importantly perhaps, it seems that the real comparative advantage (relative to native workers) of all immigrant groups lies in their desperation. It is this propensity for self-exploitation – human commodities in an unregulated market – which paradoxically guarantees their employability and very survival.

NOTE

1. See below Martínez Veiga (1997).

REFERENCES

Attewell, P. (l987): 'The Deskilling Controversy', *Work and Occupations* 14/3.

Boissevain, J. (1984): 'Small Entrepreneurs in Contemporary Europe', in R. Ward and R. Jenkins (eds.), *Ethnic Communities in Business*, Cambridge: Cambridge University Press.

Bonacich, E. and J. Modell (1981): *The Economic Bases of Ethnic Solidarity*, Berkeley: University of California Press.

Braverman, H. B. (1974): 'Labour and Monopoly Capital: The Degradation of Work in the XX*th* Century', *Monthly Review Press*.

Comisión lnterministerial de Extranjería (1994): *Anuario estadístico de extranjería*, Madrid.

Diner, H.R. (1983): *Erin's Daughter in America*, Baltimore: Johns Hopkins University Press.

Doeringer P.B. and M.J. Piore (1971): *Internal Labor Markets and Manpower Analysis*, Lexington: D.C. Heath.

Epstein, A. (1969): 'The Network and Urban Social Organization', in C. Mitchell (ed.), *Social Networks in Urban Situations*, Manchester: Manchester University Press.

Federación Estatal del Campo de Comisiones Obreras (1993): *lnforme sobre el tra bajo temporero*, Madrid.

Gordon, D., R. Edwards and M. Reich (1982): *Segmented Work, Divided Workers*, Cambridge: Cambridge University Press.

Granovetter, M. (1973): 'The Strength of Weak Ties', *American Journal of Sociology*, 78.

Granovetter, M. and C. Tilly (1988): 'Inequality and Labor Processes', in N.J. Smelser (ed.), *Handbook of Sociology*, London: Sage.

Hollifield, J. (1992), *Immigrants, Markets and States*, Cambridge MA: Harvard University Press

Hopkins, T. and I. Wallerstein (1986): 'Commodity Chains in the World Economy Prior to 1800', *Review* 10/1.

Light, L. (1971): *Ethnic enterprise*, Berkeley: University of California Press.
Light, I. and E. Bonacich (l988j: *Immigrant Entrepreneurs. Koreans in Los Angeles 1965–1982*, Berkeley: University of California Press.
Littler, C. and G. Salman (1982): 'Bravermania and Beyond: Recent Theories of the Labour Process', *Sociology*, 16
Manwaryng, T. and S. Wood (1955):'The Ghost in the Labour Process', in D. Knights, M. Willmoth and D. Collinson (eds.), *Job redesign*, Aldershot: Gower.
Martínez Veiga, U. (1997): *La Integración Social de los Inmigrantes Extranjeros en España*, Madrid: Trotta (Information about the 1994 survey).
Meijide Pardo, A . (1960): *La emigración gallega intrapeninsular en el sigio XVll*, Madrid: Instituto Balmes de Sociologia.
Mitchell, C. (ed.) (1969), *Social Networks in Urban Situations*, Manchester: Manchester University Press.
Moch, J.P. (1992): *Moving Europeans. Migration in Western Europe since 1650*, Bloomington: Indiana University Press.
Morrison, P.S. (1992): 'Segmentation Theory Applied to Local, Regional and Spatial Labor Markets', *Progress in Human Geography*, 19/4.
Piore, M.J. (l971): 'The Dual Labor Market. Theory and Implications', in D.M. Gordon (ed.), *Problems in Political Economy: An Urban perspective*, Lexington: DC Heath.
Piore, M.J. (1974): 'Comment on Wachter', *Brookings Papers on Economic Activity*, 3.
Piore, M. (1979): *Birds of Passage. Migrant Labor and Industrial Societies*, Cambridge: Cambridge University Press.
Piore, M. (1980): 'Economic Fluctuation, Job Security, and Labour Market Duality', *Politics and Society*, 16.
Poitreneau, A. (1962): 'Aspects de l'émigration temporaire et saisonière du XIX siècle', *Revue d'histoire moderne et contemporaine* 9.
Portes, A. (1981): 'Modes of Structural Incorporation and Present Theories of Labor Immigration', in M. Kritz, C. Keely and S.M.Tommasi (eds.): *Global Trends in Migration*, New York: Center for Migration Studies.
Portes, A. and R. Bach (1985), *Latin Journey*, Berkeley: University of California Press.
Portes, A. and R. Manning (1986): 'The Immigrant Enclave: Theory and Examples', in J. Nagel and T. Olzak (eds.): *Competitive Ethnic Relations*, Orlando: Academic Press.
Pugliese, E. (1993): 'Restructuring of the Labor Market and the Role of Third World Migrations in Europe', *Environment and Planning* 11.
Reich, M., Gordon, D.M. and R.C. Edwards (1973): 'A Theory of Labor Market Segmentation', *American Economic Association*, 63/2.
Roa Baltar, J. (1994): 'Informe sobre siniestrabilidad laboral en el sector de la construcción en España', *BOCG Senado*, Madrid.
Rollins, J. (1985): *Between Women, Domestics and their Employers*, Philadelphia: Temple University Press.
Sarasúa, C. (1994): *Criados, nodrizas y amos*, Madrid: Siglo XXl.
Sassen, S. (1987), *The Mobility of Labor and Capital: a Study in International Investment and Labor Flow*, Cambridge: Cambridge University Press.
Srinivas, A. and M. Beteille (1964): 'Networks in Indian Social Structure', *Man*, 65.
Waidinger, R. (1993): 'The Ethnic Enclave Debate Revisited', *International Journal for Urban and Regional Research*, 13/3.
Wilson, K.L. and W.A. Martin (1982): 'Ethnic Enclaves: A Comparison of Cuban and Black Economies in Miami', *American Journal of Sociology*, 78.
Wilson, K.L. and A. Portes (1980): 'Immigrant Enclaves: an Analysis of the Labor Market Experience of Cubans in Miami', *American Journal of Sociology* 86.
Wirth, L. (l938): 'Urbanism as a Way of Life', *American Journal of Sociology*, 44.

Italian and Spanish Labour Leaders' Unconventional Immigration Policy Preferences

JULIE R. WATTS

Despite legal guarantees of workplace equality between native and immigrant workers, including equal pay for equal work, globalization and restrictive immigration policies have combined to relegate most immigrant workers to the margins of the labour market. From an ideological perspective, restrictive immigration policies that marginalize immigrant workers are unacceptable to many labour leaders, who believe that all workers should be equal regardless of their country of origin. However, ideology is not the whole story.

In this article, I explain why many Spanish and Italian labour union leaders prefer moderately open immigration policies. Moderately open immigration policies are measures that permit legal avenues for immigration through employment-based quotas and family reunification, and enhance the immigrants' legal and employment status through long-term work and residence permits and legalization of illegal immigrants. Labour leaders want to reduce illegal immigration and precarious forms of employment by way of more moderate immigration policies, which ultimately, they believe, help immigrant and native workers.

I offer ideology as one explanation, but argue that it is not a sufficient one. A more complete account of labour leaders' immigration policy preferences must address changes in the global economy since the mid-1970s. Therefore, globalization is the independent variable that explains the immigration preferences of labour unions' leaders. I define globalization as a process in which:

- labour migration is facilitated by improvements in transportation and communication technology,
- demand for immigrant labour has shifted from industries that enjoy stable employment to ones that offer more precarious forms of

employment, such as domestic service, seasonal agriculture, construction and the underground economy, and

- the growth of the underground economy and the expansion of legal and illegal immigration networks have weakened the ability of the state to control immigration flows.

Intervening between changes in the global economy and labour leaders' attitudes toward immigration policy are several domestic institutions, which help shape labour leaders' immigration preferences. First, the states' capacity to control immigration is undermined by increasing economic openness and competition.[1] Since the mid-1980s, labour leaders have increasingly doubted the efficacy of restrictive immigration policies. This is because growing economic interdependence has made communication and transportation technology more accessible to migrants, and opened developing countries' economies to greater international trade and capital flows. These trends, in turn, accentuate demand for cheap labour in receiving states and increase the supply of unemployed labour in sending states, thereby weakening the state's capacity to control immigration.

However, this was not always the case. In fact, as recently as the mid-1970s, the leadership of the French *Confédération Générale du Travail* [CGT] supported the government suspension of labour immigration. They believed that a temporary ban on new employment-based immigration was a feasible and necessary measure to get France through economic crisis. According to Gérard Chemouil, Chief of Immigration for CGT, it took 10 years for the CGT to realize that the economic crisis of the early 1970s was not short-term, and that supporting the halt to immigration contradicted CGT's efforts to help immigrant workers in France.

Secondly, the secondary and underground economies are expanding as alternatives to the highly regulated formal economy. Global economic competition from low-wage countries threatens the profitability of many labour-intensive Spanish and Italian firms. Hence, to improve their earnings, some employers have moved production to the largely unregulated secondary and underground economies, which threatens workers' wages and working conditions and the power of labour unions to regulate the labour market.

Many labour leaders believe that by imposing restrictive immigration policies, the state may actually encourage illegal immigration. Since, by definition, illegal immigrants must work in the underground economy, many Spanish and Italian labour leaders connect an increase in illegal immigration with the growth of the underground economy. Labour leaders, who fear that an expanding underground economy undercuts workers' wages and protection in the formal economy, want to bring the underground economy to the surface. Hence, they prefer policies that promote legal over clandestine immigration, specifically legalization of illegal immigrants.

Whether globalization has a direct deleterious effect on union membership is uncertain because many domestic factors intervene between expanding global competition and union density. Nevertheless, Italian and Spanish labour union leaders believe that global competition erodes traditional work relations, and, as a result, diminishes traditional sources of union membership. Hence, many labour leaders are experimenting with new programmes and institutions that appeal to new kinds of workers in unconventional work relations. Women, young people and immigrants are examples of this new, often precarious, workforce – usually employed part-time, on a temporary basis or without contract.

Consequently, I examine how union organization around the issue of immigration helps shape labour leaders policy preferences. For example, Spanish and Italian unions provide legal services to immigrants who wish to regularize their status, reunite with their family, and renew their work and residency permits. Because they provide these extensive services on the local level, the unions have become important advocates for immigrants on the national level, where they lobby for more moderate immigration policies.

The relationship between Spanish and Italian labour unions and immigration is interesting for several reasons. First, Italy and Spain are new countries of immigration, yet both have long histories of employment-based emigration. Therefore, in the 1980s when immigrants began arriving in substantial numbers, the Spanish and Italian unions already had migration experience, and thus were better prepared to address the needs of immigrants than most societal actors and government officials. As a result, the unions became leading providers of services for immigrants and leading advocates for more moderate immigration policies.

Secondly, both Italy and Spain have highly segmented labour markets and large underground economies. Also, the demand for immigrant labour is highly decentralized into small and medium size enterprises (SMEs), which makes it difficult for unions to organize immigrant workers and for the government to monitor compliance with labour laws. SMEs have become a vital part of the economy as subcontractors for large firms, as employment creators and as contributors to gross domestic product (GDP). According to 1997 OECD reports, Italian SMEs employ 43 per cent of the workforce and contribute 40 per cent of GDP. In Spain, SMEs make up 64 per cent of the workforce and 41 per cent of GDP. Hence, the demand for immigrant labour is highly decentralized and persistent.

Thirdly, the Spanish and Italian cases offer interesting comparisons of how unions approach immigrant workers and are strengthened by organizing around immigration. The Spanish unions, with the lowest membership density in Europe, have decided that affiliating immigrants is not a priority. Nevertheless, the unions have been empowered politically and organizationally by developing national networks of service agencies for immigrants. On the other hand, the Italian unions, with much higher overall membership rates, have placed more emphasis on organizing immigrants, as well as providing services to immigrants and advocating more moderate immigration policies.

IDEOLOGY AS A NECESSARY BUT INSUFFICIENT EXPLANATION

> The problem is not the immigrant worker, but the capitalist economic system that converts human beings into interchangeable and disposable pieces. We cannot unload our frustrations against the weak, but must fight for the security of all. For this we need the participation of everyone, including immigrant workers. We believe that not only would it be selfish but also self-destructive not to support immigration under the pretext that we already have enough problems in Spain. (Comisiones Obreras 1995).

For many labour leaders, the belief that immigrants are part of an international class struggle makes restrictive immigration policies unacceptable and helps form the philosophical foundation for their preferences for moderately open immigration policies. However, these same labour leaders argue that an exclusively ideological argument is not central to their immigration policy preferences. According to Victor Gomez, a lawyer with CCOO, the philosophy that all workers are equal regardless of their country of origin is important to CCOO's immigration preferences, but not as relevant as economic, institutional and organizational explanations.

Moreover, based on a purely ideological explanation, we would not expect a union founded on the principles of anti-communism, Catholicism, and the rejection of class conflict, such as *Confederazione Italiana Sindicati Lavoratori* [CISL], to be a leading immigrant organization in Italy. Consistently, CISL has supported moderately open immigration policies, including a regular legalization process for illegal immigrants and more expansive quotas. CISL's leadership bases its support for moderately open immigration policies on the belief that immigration to Italy is a new and irreversible phenomenon. Consequently, CISL's leadership believes that Italians and immigrants should have equal social, economic and political rights, as well as access to union membership. CISL has the largest immigrant membership in Italy with 70,000 immigrant members.

To better understand labour leaders' stance on immigration, it is necessary to discuss how globalization has hindered states' capacity to control immigration effectively, stimulated the growth of the underground economy and changed the dynamics of labour union organization and membership.

LABOUR LEADERS DOUBT STATE CAPACITY TO CONTROL IMMIGRATION

> Italian immigration law is one of the most restrictive in Europe on controlling flows. It is almost impossible to enter Italy legally, but the application of the law is very poor (Angelo Massetti, International Department, *Unione Italiana del Lavoro* [UIL]).

The efficient functioning of the market requires free international exchange of goods, money and people, which often challenges the state's capacity to control national economic policy, labour markets and borders. On the other hand, states often interfere with the market to promote the national interest through protectionist trade, investment and immigration policies.

During much of the nineteenth century the market functioned with little state interference. For example, passports and work permits were not required for migration within Europe. However, protectionism, war and depression prevailed during the first half of the twentieth century, effectively closing international markets. Unlike the free market period that preceded the First World War, today's global marketplace is more inclusive and moving at a quicker technological pace. More developed and developing states participate in the global market. Globalization is being driven by rapid changes in technology, such as cheap and efficient communication networks that allow firms to locate different parts of the production process in different countries. More accessible communication technology also facilitates trade in services reducing the need for personal contact between producers and consumers.

However, the global market for labour is relatively underdeveloped compared to the global markets for goods, services and money. In developing countries the encroaching global market has helped stimulate migration, but states still largely influence migration patterns through rules governing entry and exit. Unlike free trade, which is built on firm international institutional foundations, a comprehensive international regime for migration has not developed. Until the recent decision by the member states of the European Union to co-ordinate immigration policy, states found it more effective to impose immigration policies unilaterally than to co-ordinate them at an international level.[2]

Despite the resilience of state sovereignty over the free movement of people, many government officials in receiving states are concerned about an 'immigration control crisis' and have less confidence in their ability to effectively regulate immigration flows and the employment of illegal workers than they did 15 years ago.[3] Cornelius, Hollifield and Miller (1994) articulate the conflict between states and the market in terms of migration as a 'gap' between policies to control immigration and immigration outcomes. This gap between policies and outcomes is due to pressures emanating from outside the state, such as the expansion of transnational migration networks aided by advances in, and greater access to, communication and transportation technology. When states restrict labour migration, these networks help to sustain flows through family reunification and illegal immigration. A second exogenous factor is increasing economic openness among developing countries, which in the short-run accentuates social and economic imbalances and encourages emigration.

Spanish and Italian labour leaders are cognizant of the difficulties which states have in controlling immigration. For example, under Spain's first immigration law, the 1985 *Ley Organica sobre Derechos y Libertades de los Extranjeros en España* [Organic Law on the Rights and Freedoms of Aliens in Spain] or LOE, the majority of permits granted to non-EU immigrants have been for one year or less (see Figure 1). By limiting most permits to one year, and to jobs that Spanish workers do not want, the Spanish government has institutionalized precarious employment for the

FIGURE 1

SPANISH WORK PERMITS, 1987–1996

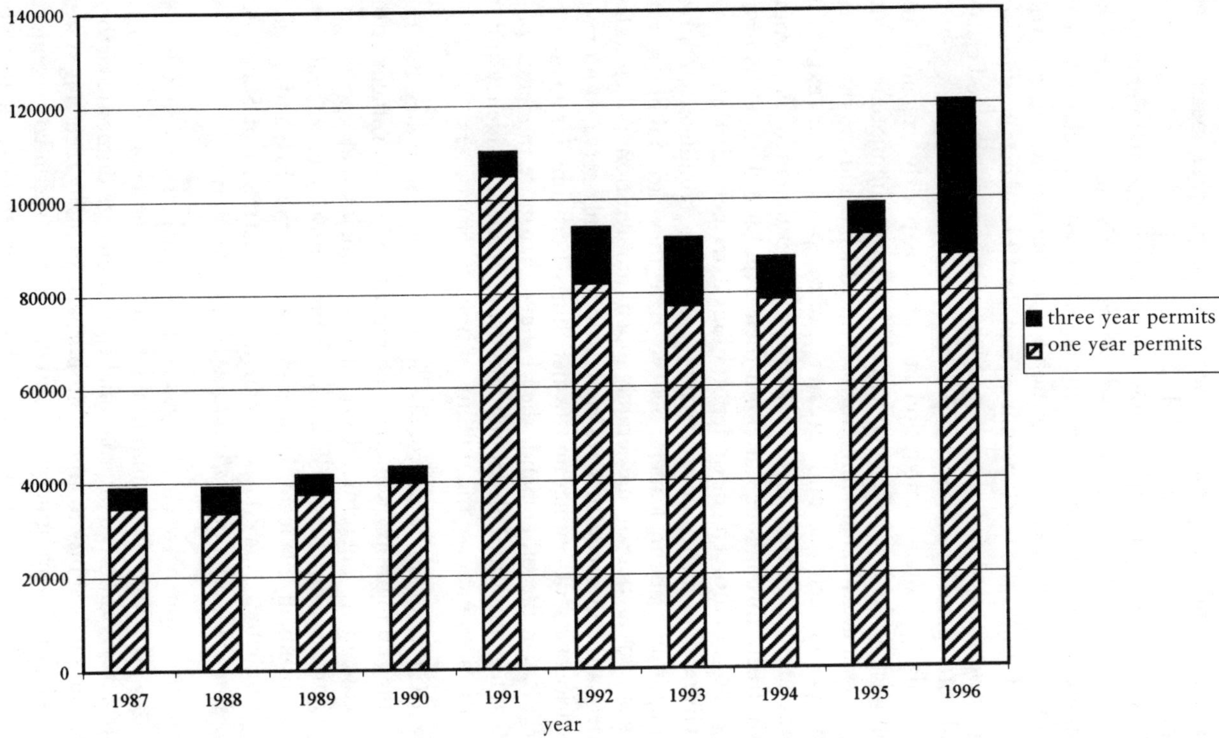

Source: *Comision Interministerial de Extranjeros* [Interministerial Commission for Foreigners], *Anuario Estadistico* [Statistical Annual], 1996.

majority of immigrant workers. In addition, the administrative difficulties and delays in renewing work permits mean that many immigrants fall into periods of illegality.

Overall, the LOE largely failed to regulate legal immigration flows. Instead, its lack of clarity and its restrictiveness have heightened immigrant insecurity and forced many immigrants into clandestine status. In response to the 1985 immigration law, labour unions began advocating for a reform of the work permit system. In 1996, a major administrative reform was passed with the input of labour unions that helped clarify and moderate Spanish immigration policy.

Similarly, Italian immigration law often is poorly executed. In fact, loopholes in the law have encouraged clandestine immigration. Until the recent change in Italian immigration law, which mandates the creation of deportation centres and greater police powers to expel illegal immigrants, deportation rules allowed undocumented immigrants to move freely throughout Italy until their expulsion date. Of course, this made police enforcement of deportations extremely difficult.

Given the difficulties faced by states in completely controlling immigration, labour leaders believe that they are taking a rational position in favour of moderately open immigration policies. Labour leaders are convinced that restrictive policies only serve to increase the precariousness of immigrants, which hurts both immigrant and native workers. On the other hand, they believe that more moderate policies, such as legalization of illegal immigrants, permanent residency and family reunification, increase the stability of immigrant workers.

> UGT does not want totally open immigration policy but realizes that immigration will continue regardless of government efforts to control it. Therefore, UGT favours policies that encourage legal immigration such as family reunification, regularization, free movement of legal immigrants within the EU and permanent residency. (Ana Maria Corral Juan, Department of Social Action, *Union General de Trabajadores* [UGT], Madrid.)

The connection between changes in the global market and increasing mobility of people is an important factor in the 'crisis of immigration control'. In addition to international constraints are domestic factors that limit the state's ability to control its borders. In many receiving states, the demand for cheap immigrant labour in the secondary economy is persistent. Employers often prefer illegal immigrants over native workers because they are willing to work for less money and in worse conditions.

Illegal economic activities are extremely difficult for the state to control because they are highly decentralized into small firms and households, and large firms can obscure illegal economic activities through subcontracting. Also, it is often not in the interests of the state to penalize employers who hire illegal immigrants, because the secondary economy makes up an increasingly large proportion of GDP and produces many intermediate goods used in the primary economy.

Reservations about the state's ability to control immigration through restrictive policies, combined with concerns about the perverse effects these policies have in marginalizing immigrants, help to shape labour leaders' immigration policy preferences. For example, recognizing that immigrants with short-term work permits often fall into periods of illegality, most labour union leaders want a simpler method for renewing permits, more long-term permits and a means for undocumented immigrants to regularize their status.

In promoting more moderate immigration policies, labour leaders run the risk of ostracizing those workers who feel threatened by immigrants. Consequently, labour leaders in Italy and Spain are trying to educate all workers about the costs of highly restrictive immigration policies, which marginalize immigrant workers, and, in turn undermine the wages and protection of all workers.

REGULATING THE UNDERGROUND ECONOMY AND ITS WORKERS

The underground economy is pervasive and growing throughout Western Europe as increasing global competition has forced employers to seek alternatives to highly regulated, inflexible labour markets. In Spain, the underground economy accounts for 25 per cent of GDP and 25 per cent of workers are engaged in underground work. Approximately 75 per cent of immigrants who come from third world countries work in Spain's underground economy.[4] In Italy, where the underground economy also makes up 25 per cent of GDP, 14 per cent of workers in the underground economy are illegal immigrants.[5]

The growth of the underground economy and its connection to illegal immigration troubles labour union leaders. Employment opportunities in the underground economy attract illegal immigrants, despite the risks of expulsion, because the immigrant faces fewer opportunities and worse living standards in his country of origin. In a recent survey published in the Moroccan weekly, *Le Journal*, nearly 90 per cent of Moroccans in their twenties said they wanted to leave. Reasons given for emigration included 'high unemployment rates, flagrant social marginalization and inequalities, which grow unceasingly'.[6]

According to research by Dell'Aringa and Neri (1987) and Djajic (1997) the presence of flexible illegal immigrant labour encourages some employers to sink capital into the underground economy, where employers can avoid the formal economy's labour regulations, taxes and high wages. Consequently, when employers transfer resources to the underground economy it hurts the wages and working conditions of all workers.

Many labour leaders concur that illegal immigration and the growth of the underground economy are positively correlated. At the same time, they realize that illegal immigration is not the cause of the underground economy. For example, the proportion of illegal immigrants employed in Spain's underground economy is only 5 per cent of the total underground workforce.

Labour leaders want to unite the underground economy with the formal economy. However, they do not want to do this by sacrificing the high wages and protections that have made formal labour markets inflexible. Instead, they would prefer to regulate the underground economy and bring its workers to the surface. One way to do this is to increase the costs and risks of employing illegal immigrants through employer sanctions. As the costs of employing illegal immigrants increase, some employers will replace illegal immigrant workers with native and legal immigrant workers. Indeed, labour leaders advocate stiffer employer sanctions, under the condition that illegal immigrants are not deported.

Another way to bring part of the underground economy to the surface is to legalize illegal immigrant workers with the requirement that they find legal employment. Once in the legal labour market, illegal immigrant workers should not be preferred over native workers because of their cost effectiveness. Most labour leaders support amnesties on the economic grounds that it helps both native and immigrants workers by regulating the underground economy.

However, by trying to regulate the underground economy through employer sanctions and legalization, labour unions create the same inflexible labour market conditions that forced employers to go underground in the first place. Hence, the unions are caught in a vicious circle, in which sanctions and legalization are only a temporary solution to deeply embedded structural problems of labour market segmentation.

The foundations for labour market segmentation were laid in the post-war period when labour unions negotiated high wages and generous benefits for workers in exchange for control over production decisions. In the late 1970s and 1980s, labour market segmentation came to fruition as a result of increasing global competition and the drive for European employers to compete with Asian and American markets.

As the period of economic growth and full employment of the 1960s gave way to recession and unemployment in the 1970s and 1980s, labour unions faced the negative effects of their trade-off with employers and the state. First, employers gained access to more flexible labour resources through reforms in the labour law. For example, in 1984, Spanish employers were given the right to hire workers on fixed-term contracts. By 1997, nearly a third of Spanish workers were on temporary contracts. Secondly, employers have found ways to circumvent labour laws and unions by creating micro-enterprises in which it is extremely difficult for unions to organize. For example, Italian labour legislation increased job security for workers in firms with more than 14 employees. As a result, in 1997, micro-enterprises made up 51 per cent of firms in Italy.[7] Finally, some employers have turned to the underground economy.

The underground economy is part of a growing secondary economy. Production is uncertain in the secondary sector due to economic fluctuations and changes in weather and tastes. Production also tends to be labour-intensive, seasonal and lacking in economies of scale. Activities that meet these criteria include agriculture, construction, restaurant and hotel services, domestic service and some labour-intensive manufacturing such as clothing. As several immigration scholars have noted, among these Portes (1978), Piore (1979) and Cheng and Bonacich (1984), the precarious status of many immigrants makes them well-suited for secondary sector jobs. For example, in Spain, nearly 7 per cent of domestic workers are immigrants and 81 per cent of female immigrants are employed in domestic service. Among 424 immigrant domestic workers surveyed in Madrid and Barcelona by the Spanish research unit *Colectivo Ioé,* 10 per cent had a permanent contract, 10 per cent had temporary contracts and 80 per cent did not have any written contract.

The secondary economy is less regulated than the primary or formal economy because firms are smaller and more decentralized, making their activities more difficult to monitor and regulate. Much of the activity in the secondary economy is legal and technically covered by collective bargaining agreements, which, by Spanish and Italian labour law, include non-unionized workers and firms. However, many secondary sector employers avoid regulations by taking advantage of loopholes in labour legislation and not adhering to collective bargaining agreements. As a result, workers in the secondary economy are typically not protected by labour laws or collective bargaining agreements, nor are they unionized. Thus, workers in the secondary economy are considered 'outsiders' compared to the 'insiders' in the primary economy, who represent labour unions' core constituency.

Studies on how immigration is connected to the growth of the secondary economy and overall welfare have yielded varying results. For example, cheap immigrant workers help increase profits in labour-intensive industries by lowering labour costs. But, in the long-run, productivity suffers as employers become reliant on cheap labour and fail to mechanize production.

More important from the perspective of labour leaders is how an influx of unskilled immigrants affects the welfare of skilled and unskilled workers. When insulated by segmented labour markets, skilled workers benefit from cheap immigrant labour that produces intermediate goods at a lower cost for the primary economy. Unskilled workers' welfare may also improve as immigrants, who tend to occupy the lowest rung of the employment ladder, allow unskilled native workers to advance.

However, because production costs can be reduced by employing low-wage immigrant labour, an increase in the number of precarious immigrants may encourage firms to move some resources to the underground economy, given capital mobility across sectors. Dell'Aringa and Neri (1987) estimate that illegal immigrants receive a net wage that is 20–30 per cent lower than the legal wage for the same job, and employers who hire off-the-books can evade tax and social security payments, which in Italy amount to 50 to 60 per cent of basic pay. Therefore, precarious immigrant workers may directly lower wages and cause job losses among unskilled native workers. Or, as both Cheng and Bonacich (1984) and Dell'Aringa and Neri (1987) have argued, immigrants may indirectly compete with unskilled workers in the secondary economy through a kind of displacement-wage effect. As capital is transferred to the underground economy, where wages and working conditions are generally worse, than in the official economy, part of the legally employed workforce moves with it.

Michael Piore (1979) provides a useful description of the ultimate, potential effect of low-paid immigrants on the primary economy. He argues that when production costs in the underground economy fall significantly below legal production costs, the underground economy will not only absorb production from the secondary economy but may expand into the primary sector. Under these circumstances, the job security of even the 'insiders' in the primary sector may be threatened.

Labour union leaders realize that restricting immigration does not address the fundamental problem of segmented labour markets. In fact, by restricting legal immigration the state may encourage illegal immigration by making legal migration almost impossible. On the other hand, moderate immigration policies help to stabilize the situation of immigrants and bring them out of the underground economy.

Consequently, Spanish and Italian labour leaders have been active in lobbying for and implementing legalization programs as a means of reducing the size of the underground economy and protecting immigrant and native workers. Labour leaders believe that they can lobby for more moderate immigration policies without arousing resentment from their core constituency because labour markets are sufficiently segmented so that 'insiders' do not compete with immigrants. Amnesties have been carried out in Spain in 1985, 1991 and 1996, in which illegal immigrants could be legalized if they met certain basic criteria such as length of stay and employment. Similarly, Italy has had four amnesties in 1982, 1986, 1991 and 1995.

The connection between illegal immigration and the growth of the underground economy under conditions of highly segmented labour markets helps to explain labour leaders' preferences for moderately open immigration policies. Faced with a narrow range of policy choices of what do about illegal immigrants in the underground economy – deportation or legalization – labour leaders choose legalization.

IMMIGRANTS AS A SOURCE OF STRENGTH FOR UNIONS

Competition from low-wage countries has driven employers in high-wage countries to find ways to improve their labour market flexibility. One consequence of the search for flexibility is rising unemployment, which heightens the insecurity of workers and discourages them from joining unions. Therefore, we should expect to see a convergence of decreasing union membership in high-wage countries open to the global economy.

However, recent research by Lange and Scruggs (1998) indicates that domestic institutions intervene between global economic forces and union density rates, so that density rates across countries are in fact diverging. In countries with low-union density at the start of the 1970s membership rates have continued to decline, while unions in high-density countries have become stronger.[8]

Spain qualifies as a low union density country. Immediately after the Spanish transition to democracy in 1976, unions were legalized and unionization rates soared to 40–45 per cent of the workforce. Thereafter, unionization rates fell sharply to 20 per cent in 1982 and today are less than 10 per cent of the workforce. Italy, on the other hand, experienced a slight increase in union density between 1970 and the early 1990s. In 1970, the unionization rate in Italy was 38.5 per cent of the workforce, whereas in 1990, 39.3 per cent of the workforce was unionized.[9]

Despite diverging unionization rates, both Italian and Spanish labour leaders feel threatened by the effects of increasing global economic competition. As a result, they are searching for new forms of organization and reaching out to new kinds of workers, including immigrants. However, domestic institutions and union structures have conditioned how Italian and Spanish unions organize around immigrants. In Spain, CCOO and UGT have developed national networks of social service offices for immigrants. At the same time, labour leaders have discounted immigrant membership in the unions. Likewise, the Italian unions provide social services to immigrants. However, two of the Italian unions have also placed a great deal of emphasis on organizing immigrants through parallel unions.

The lack of associationalism in Italian and Spanish societies and their mutual histories of emigration helped shape the social service model. Between 1940 and the late 1960s, millions of Spanish and Italian workers emigrated to northern Europe and Latin America. The labour unions have supported expatriates in many ways, such as negotiating labour agreements with receiving states and assisting in the repatriation process. According to Francisco Soriano, the former Director of Immigration for CCOO, Spanish workers and labour leaders share a global perspective on immigration and are sympathetic to the plight of immigrant workers because of Spain's experience with emigration. In its first congress in 1977, CCOO created a Secretariat for Emigration, which became the Secretariat for Emigration and Immigration in 1987.

The second factor behind the development of the social service model was the void in support services for immigrants. In the mid-1980s, when immigrants first started to arrive in Spain and Italy significant numbers, few non-governmental organizations existed for them and the government was unprepared and poorly organized for addressing immigrants' needs. However, because of their experience with emigration, the Italian and Spanish unions were quickly able to fill this void. Vaifra Palanca of the Italian Ministry of Social Solidarity, confirmed that the Italian government has relied extensively on the unions to provide employment and legal services to immigrants because they were one of a few non-governmental organizations that had the resources, experience and networks to help immigrants. As a result, the Spanish and Italian unions have been one of the main beneficiaries of state funding for immigrant programmes.

In 1986, CCOO opened its first *Centro de Información para Trabajadores Extranjeros* [Information Center for Foreign Workers] or CITE, to provide legal, social and educational services to immigrants. Today, CCOO has more than 100 CITE offices throughout Spain, and UGT has established 11 *Centro Guias para Inmigrantes y Refugiados* [Advisory Centers for Immigrants and Refugees] in regions most heavily populated with immigrants. The CITE and *Centro Guia* offices provide immigrants with free legal services concerning regularization procedures, family reunification, and how to obtain work permits, residence permits and visas. They have initiated campaigns at local level to promote immigrants' rights. For example, CITE and *Centro Guia* representatives were active in the campaign to regularize immigrants in 1991. Finally, these local offices provide language and professional training to immigrants.

Similarly, Italy's largest union, *Confederazione Generale Italiana del Lavoro* [CGIL], has a national network of offices that provide legal and social services to immigrants. In 1982, CGIL established its first *Ufficio Straneri* [Foreigners Office], which helped seasonal workers from Eastern Europe. CISL and *Union Italiano de Lavoro* [UIL] also have local offices dedicated to helping immigrants.

However, unique to CISL and UIL are parallel immigrant organizations. These parallel organizations differ from the social service agencies of CCOO, UGT and CGIL because they are membership organizations for immigrants, including illegal immigrants, unemployed immigrants and immigrants without a formal employment contract. CISL and UIL leaders believe that the parallel union structure better promotes organization and solidarity among immigrant workers, who have little experience with union democracy, and provides a stepping stone for immigrant membership into CISL and UIL.

In 1988, UIL formed its union for immigrant workers called *Unione Italiana Immigrati* (UNITI). UNITI's mandate is to organize immigrant workers, train immigrants in union democracy and provide legal and professional services. UNITI represents all immigrants, including those who are illegal, unemployed or working without a contract. When immigrants obtain a formal contract they can then become members of UIL. UNITI has approximately 15,000 members, concentrated in Sicily, Latium, Calabria, Veneto and Lombardy.

In 1989, CISL adopted the parallel union model with the creation of *L'Associazione Nazionale oltre le Frontiere* [ANOLF]. ANOLF's three main functions are: to provide legal, professional and educational services to immigrant workers; to promote activities in the immigrants' countries of origin; and to promote solidarity between immigrants and Italian workers through cultural and social activities. Membership in ANOLF is also open to all immigrants. ANOLF has approximately 35,000 members and total immigrant membership in CISL is 70,000. This number far outstrips immigrant membership in UIL, whose main constituency is concentrated among white-collar workers. It also surpasses CGIL's 37,000 immigrant members. CGIL, a communist-based, largely blue-collar union, rejected the parallel union structure for fear of alienating both Italian and immigrant workers by segregating their demands.

Clearly the Spanish and Italian experiences with emigration and the void in social services for immigrants have been important factors in how CCOO, UGT, CGIL, CISL and UIL have organized around the issue of immigration as social service providers. However, what explains the unique parallel union structure of CISL and UIL?

The founding principle of anti-communism shared by CISL and UIL combined with the high percentage of immigrants in Italy originating from communist and former communist countries are crucial to understanding the parallel union structure for immigrants.

In 1950, internal divisions within the communist-based CGIL led to the creation of two new unions – the exclusively Catholic CISL and the non-secular, anti-communist UIL. American labour leaders influenced the founding of CISL and UIL as part of America's Cold War initiative. CISL adopted a mix of American labour and Catholic ideas, which included a focus on plant-level negotiations and working with management to industrialize and modernize the Italian economy. The Catholic influence was to reject the notion of class conflict and accept the idea of guided capitalism. UIL, the weakest of the three unions, attracted republicans and socialists who refused to join a union dominated by Catholics. The UIL has also followed a similar strategy of anti-communism and decentralized bargaining.

Because many immigrants in Italy originate from former communist countries,[10] the leaders of CISL and UIL believe that the parallel union structure better orients immigrants to union democracy and better prepares them for membership in CISL and UIL. Also contributing to the development of parallel unions are the large numbers of illegal immigrant workers who could not otherwise join a union. To join one of the three main unions, CGIL, CISL or UIL, an immigrant must be legal and have a work contract. However, illegal immigrants, immigrants who do not have a formal contract and unemployed immigrants can join ANOLF and UNITI because of the way they are constituted as immigrant organizations.

For the leadership of CISL and UIL, immigrants are seen as a source of union strength as potential members. However, immigrants may help empower unions in ways other than increasing union density. Through the social service model, CCOO, CGIL and UGT have increased their breadth of services and gained access to government funding and decision-making.

Data collected by CITE offices reveals that while immigrants frequently use the services provided by the CITE, immigrant workers are not necessarily interested in joining CCOO. In 1994, there were some 101,977 legally employed immigrant workers in Spain. In that same year, 25,856 immigrants used the services of CITE offices some 60,734 times. However, in 1994 only 8,856 immigrants were members of CCOO, a unionization rate of less than 10 per cent among immigrants. In UGT, a predominantly white-collar union, immigrant unionization rates immigrants are even lower.

Spanish labour leaders attribute low membership rates to the precarious, often illegal, short-term work done by most immigrants, and the institutionalized irregularity built into the system of short-term work and residence permits. However, affiliating immigrant workers is not the main goal of the Spanish unions, whose overall membership rates are among the lowest in Europe. Instead, CCOO and UGT have used their networks of immigrant support services to conduct grassroots campaigns on behalf of immigrants, as well as lobby local and national government officials to reform the systems for legalization, permit renewals and family reunification.

Consequently, by filling the void in social, legal and employment services for immigrants CCOO and UGT have become authorities on immigration and have influenced immigration policy. For example, recognizing that the Spanish unions had expertise in immigration issues, President Gonzalez promised that any reform of the immigration law would include input by the unions and non-governmental organizations.[11] In 1995, in fact, the government held an immigration conference in which unions played a leading role. The unions achieved many of their goals in the 1996 immigration reform, including more liberal family reunification policies, an extension of work and residence permits and an amnesty for undocumented immigrants.

At an October 1997 meeting of Spain's Forum for the Integration of Immigrants, attended by non-governmental organizations, immigrant associations, employers and government officials, the unions dominated discussions concerning the quota for 1997 and reforming the quota policy. At the meeting, the UGT representative presented a proposal, written by the unions and supported by the non-governmental associations, to reform the quota policy making it easier for immigrants to come to Spain, and providing a means for undocumented immigrants already in Spain to legalize their situation. Partially as a result of union efforts, the quota for 1997 initially set at 15,000 was increased to 24,690.

In the fall of 1989, Italian labour unions worked directly with Vice President Claudio Martelli to write the new immigration law. According to Angelo Massetti of UIL, these meetings were a direct result of union protests and lobbying efforts, which forced the government to put immigration on the agenda and heed the voice of the unions.

Finally, in 1997, the Italian unions lobbied for, and got, the inclusion of a special quota in the 1998 immigration law that would allow the unions to sponsor immigrants. Under the sponsor quota, labour unions can bring immigrants to Italy if they guarantee employment and housing.

CONCLUSION

Labour unions face many challenges as a result of a more competitive global economy. For example, labour unions must confront losses in union membership due to rising unemployment rates and difficulties in organizing contingent workers in small, highly decentralized firms. One area in which unions are trying to adapt is immigration, which many labour leaders see as an inevitable consequence of globalization.

As communication and transportation technology become more accessible, globalization helps expedite and extend migration networks. More and more developing countries are opening their economies to foreign trade and investment, which in the short-run stimulates migration to developed countries. Demand for immigrant labour in the secondary and underground economies is constant and spreading as employers cut costs to compete with less-regulated and low-wage countries. As a result of these global pressures, the receiving state's ability to control immigration is threatened.

Reservations about the state's ability to control immigration through restrictive policies, combined with concerns about the perverse effects these policies have in marginalizing immigrants, help shape labour leaders' immigration policy preferences. For example, restrictions on legal immigration may encourage more illegal immigration as migrants are left with few legal options. In addition, limits on the length and renewal of work permits force immigrants into a precarious legal and economic position in which they are dependent on their employer. Consequently, most labour union leaders prefer immigration policies that stabilize the situation of immigrant workers and provide a legal channel for employment-based immigration. Ultimately, by bringing immigrants out of a situation of institutionalized precariousness through moderate immigration policies, labour leaders believe that unions, immigrants and native workers will all benefit.

NOTES

1. See Haus, L. (1995): 'Openings in the wall: transnational migrants, labour unions, and U.S. immigration policy', *International Organization*, 49/2, pp.285–313.
2. Under the Amsterdam Treaty, competency for immigration policy within the European Union will gradually be transferred from intergovernmental institutions to community institutions.
3. Cornelius, W., Hollfield, J. and Martin, P. (eds.) (1994): *Controlling Immigration*, Stanford: Stanford University Press.
4. Sole, C. (1997): 'Inmigración y Mercado de Trabajo' [Immigration and the Labour Market] Conference paper. Fundacion La Caixa-Instituto Universitario Ortega y Gasset.
5. Caritas di Roma (1997): *Immigrazione Dossier Statistico [Immigration Statistical Dossier]*, Rome: Anterem.
6. *Reuters* (17 March 1998).
7. OECD (1997): *OECD Economic Survey, Italy.*
8. See Lange, P. and Scruggs, L. (1998): 'Where Have All the Members Gone? Union Density in the Era of Globalization.' Center for German and European Studies Working Paper 1.63, University of California, Berkeley.
9. Bedani, G. (1995): *Politics and Ideology of the Italian Workers' Movement*, Oxford: Berg Publishers
10. Albanians are the second largest group of immigrants in Italy, representing 6 per cent of the immigrant population, followed by the Former Yugoslavia with 4 per cent, then Romania, China and Poland each with 3 per cent. Caritas di Roma (1997).
11. Author interview with Victor Gomez, CCOO, Madrid, 29 October 1997.

REFERENCES

Bedani, G. (1995): *Politics and Ideology of the Italian Workers' Movement*, Oxford: Berg Publishers.

Caritas di Roma (1997): *Immigrazione: Dossier Statistico [Immigration: Statistical Dossier]*, Rome: Anterem.

Cheng, L. and Bonacich, E. (1984): *Labour Immigration Under Capitalism: Asian Workers in the United States Before World War II*, Berkeley: University of California Press.

Colectivo Ioé (1991) 'Trabajadores Extranjeras de Servicio Domestico en Espana' [Foreign Domestic Service Workers in Spain], Madrid: Colectivo Ioé.

Comision Interministerial de Extranjeros [Interministerial Commission for Foreigners] (1996): *Anuario Estadistico de Extranjeria [Statistical Annual of Foreigners]* Madrid.

Comisiones Obreras (1995): 'CCOO y Inmigración' [CCOO and Immigration] *Anuario de Inmigración [Immigration Annual]*, Barcelona.

Cornelius, W., Martin, P. and Hollifield, J. (eds.) (1994): *Controlling Immigration*, Stanford: Stanford University Press.

Dell'Aringa , C. and Neri, F. (1987): 'Illegal Immigrants and the Informal Economy in Italy', *Labour*, 1, pp.107–26.

Djajic, S. (1997): 'Illegal Immigration and Resource Allocation', *International Economic Review*, 38, pp.97–117.

Haus, L. (1995): 'Openings in the Wall: transnational migrants, labour unions, and U.S. immigration policy', *International Organization*, 49/2, pp.285–313.

Lange, P. and Scruggs, L. (1998): 'Where Have All the Members Gone? Union Density in the Era of Globalization.' Center for German and European Studies Working Paper 1.63, University of California, Berkeley.

Ministerio de Trabajo y Asuntos Sociales [Ministry of Labour and Social Affairs] (1996): *Anuario de Migraciones [Migration Annual]* Madrid.

OECD (1997): *OECD Economic Survey, Italy*, Paris: OECD.

OECD (1997): *SMEs and Globalization*, Paris: OECD.

Piore, M. (1979): *Birds of Passage: Migrant Labour and Industrial Societies*, Cambridge: Cambridge University Press.

Portes, A. (1978): 'Migration and Underdevelopment', *Politics and Society*, 8, pp.1–48.

Reuters (March 17, 1998).

Solé, C. (1997): 'Inmigracion y Mercado de Trabajo.' [Immigration and the Labour Market] Conference Paper Fundacion La Caixa-Instituto Universitario Ortega y Gasset, Madrid.

Multicultural Insertions in a Small Economy: Portugal's Immigrant Communities

DAVID CORKILL and MARTIN EATON

Since the 1980s, important changes have occurred in the part played by southern Europe in the international migration system. As the Portuguese case illustrates, the changes have been far from uniform and are still incomplete. Indeed, it can be argued that Portugal represents an interesting case within contemporary international migratory movements. Traditionally ignored as a destination point by immigrants, Portugal has now developed a 'niche' role in the immigration flows into the EU, particularly from Africa and South America. In turn, this influx is strongly influenced by common language ties and existing family networks (Fonseca 1997:15). Moreover, Portugal now recruits the majority of its immigrant workers from the Portuguese-speaking African countries (PALOPs) and Brazil (Machado 1997:38). Despite variations in the relative weight of individual countries of origin, this pattern has not altered since Portugal became relatively more attractive as an entry point to the EU, and one of the 'new immigration centres' during the 1980s.

Portugal is an example of a former colonial power that has undergone a societal transformation (Rocha-Trindade 1995). Traditionally a labour exporter, it has now become a net importer of migrant labour. In turn, it has altered from a country with a relatively liberal immigration regime to the adoption of much stricter policy instruments that are more in line with its EU partners. Such a move might appear unsurprising given the strong pressure for a common immigration policy in an EU that has moved towards free circulation of labour as migratory pressures have mounted. However, it should be remembered that the immigrant numbers are very small as a percentage of the total population. Portugal, for example, has one of the lowest proportions of non-nationals (1.2 per cent) – compared to Belgium (9.1 per cent) or Germany (8.6 per cent) – in the whole of the EU (Eurostat 1997). In addition, the relatively low unemployment levels (standing at an annual average rate of 7.2 per cent in 1995 [Eurostat 1996a]) mean there is less competition between domestic and foreign workers for scarce jobs. Consequently the Portuguese government has felt little internal pressure to control immigration by introducing restrictionist policies.

IMMIGRATION INTO PORTUGAL

For much of the twentieth century Portugal experienced a net outward movement of people. Indeed, the export of labour became a 'structural and symbolic' feature of Portuguese society (Serrão 1977, Brettell 1993), reaching a peak in the early part of the 1970s under the Salazar-Caetano dictatorship. Between 1970–74, for instance, some 630,000 Portuguese nationals left the country as either legal or clandestine emigrants (Amaral 1993). The profound economic and social consequences stemming from this phenomenon were checked only when the authoritarian regime was overthrown in April 1974. Since then there has been a considerable slowdown in Portugal's out-migration rate from a figure of 4.3 in 1980 to 1.0 per thousand head of the population in 1996 (Eurostat 1998). Indeed, during the 1980s, Portugal underwent a transformation as those entering the country began to outnumber those leaving. Several factors caused this turnaround. First, thousands of Portuguese working abroad returned to their homeland (Cavaco 1995a, Machado 1997). Estimates suggest that around 300,000 have returned from their host countries in north-western Europe (Fonseca and Cavaco 1997). Second, there was a notable increase in the numbers of foreign residents settling in Portugal. Between 1975–95 the resident foreign community[1] in Portugal more than quadrupled in size. It reached almost 170,000, which represented just under 2 per cent of the national population (INE 1996). Third, during 1975, up to three-quarters of a million *retornados* [returnees] were estimated to have been repatriated from the former colonies (Lewis and Williams 1985). Fourth, at a conservative estimate there were some 60–70,000 illegal immigrants living in Portugal at the start of the 1990s (Eaton 1993). Finally, there is a much smaller, but no less important, group of asylum seekers trying to settle in the country.

According to figures provided by the *Serviço de Estrangeiros e Fronteiras* [SEF – Foreigners and Frontiers Service] the foreign population resident in Portugal between 1986–96 nearly doubled from just under 87,000 to almost 171,000. The largest growth occurred among Luso-Africans, who comprise around half the total number of immigrants, followed by, in smaller proportions, South Americans and Asians, chiefly Chinese, Indians and Pakistanis (Machado 1997). Moreover, the Chinese component is likely to continue its growth given the handover of Macau to Chinese control in 1999.

Superficially at least, Portugal's migration patterns appear to have undergone a fundamental modification from ones dominated by out-migration into those of a receiving society (Esteves 1991; Guibentif 1996). Recent figures from government agencies[2] point to this re-orientation: between 1992–95 permanent emigration[3] from Portugal fell by approximately 14,000 persons or 64 per cent. In contrast, the resident foreign population expanded by almost 47,000 over the same period (see Table 1) – a net inflow of approximately 33,000 immigrants. Moreover, the growth rate of the foreign community (currently standing at an annual rate of around 9.5 per cent) has been accelerating. Indeed, it had more than doubled by the mid-1990s and shows few signs of slowing as we move towards the new millenium.

These developments should not, however, be taken to mean that Portugal has developed characteristics similar to those pertaining to northern Europe. The transformation into a 'new immigration centre' is incomplete. As far as migration flows are concerned, Portugal retains characteristics that are common to both the centre and the periphery. It continues to receive highly qualified professionals and to export unskilled workers to the European Union, while at the same time exporting professionals to the Portuguese-speaking African countries who, in turn, provide unskilled labourers for the Portuguese labour market (Machado 1997). Another point worth noting is that the profile of the typical Portuguese emigrant is changing from unskilled to semi-skilled. This is due to the higher levels of schooling attained by the Portuguese labour force and the demands for flexible and specialized workers in the northern European labour market, although evidence to support this is hard to come by. It should not be forgotten that there are still large numbers of poorly qualified Portuguese who choose to cross the border to find work in neighbouring Spain and who travel further afield to France.

Indeed, Portugal provides an example of 'substitution immigration' with African workers replacing Portuguese workers who have left for the more developed European countries or North America. This process began in the 1960s when Cape Verdeans in particular were attracted to Portugal by the job opportunities opening up because of major changes in the country's political economy. First, the economic expansion created new jobs. Secondly, intensive emigration to northern Europe led to acute labour shortages. Thirdly, military manpower requirements stemming from the colonial wars had drained the pool of young, working age males. Labour shortages were experienced once again in the late 1980s when unskilled labour became relatively scarce as numerous physical infrastructure projects got under way in Portugal. Simultaneously, new opportunities were arising in the service industries where women, in particular, were required for domestic and other types of work (Fonseca 1997).

PORTUGAL AND SCHENGEN

Portugal is an increasingly important destination for many of the European Union's newer immigrants who, in the main, settle permanently, and in a minority of cases use the country as a 'staging post'. This is significant because Portugal is one of the signatories to the Schengen Agreement,[4] which legislates at the EU level for the free movement of persons. Immigrants who can obtain official residence documentation can, in theory, move around the Schengen area unhampered by formal passport controls. The perception is that Portugal and Spain[5] represent the relatively unprotected 'soft underbelly'. Iberia is, consequently, being used as a 'back door' for labour migrants to gain entry to the more prosperous economies in the EU. It is also being used for drug trafficking. In both cases it is a trail facilitated by Portugal's long Atlantic coastline which makes policing and detection extremely difficult. Indeed, it is a situation made worse by overlapping authorities (e.g. the Maritime Police, Customs Directorate and Tax Inspectorate), inadequate resources and a relatively lax approach to detection.

It is noteworthy that Portugal has the highest proportion in the EU of African immigrants and is close behind Spain in terms of South American immigrants. Table 1 shows that there were more than 168,000 legally resident foreigners in Portugal at the end of December 1995. By far the largest group (more than 38,000, comprising 23 per cent of the total) came from the Cape Verde Islands, followed by Brazilians (19,000 or 12 per cent), Angolans (15,800 or 9 per cent), and those from Guinea-Bissau (12,300 or 7 per cent). The inflows reflect the importance of links with Portugal's former colonies and the close linguistic and cultural ties that exist. Table 1 also shows that the foreign resident community grew by 38 per cent between 1992-95 with the highest increases recorded among immigrants from Angola and Guinea-Bissau. As a result, immigrants from

Africa constitute around 0.8 per cent of the total Portuguese population, of whom almost half (48 per cent) originated in the Cape Verde Islands.

TABLE 1

CHANGES IN THE NUMBERS OF LEGALLY RESIDENT FOREIGNERS IN PORTUGAL 1989–1995

	Total			**Change** (Number and %)
Country of Origin	1989	1992	1995	1992–1995
Cape Verde Islands	7,972	31,127	38,746	7,619 +24%
Angola	4,842	6,601	15,829	9,288+140%
Guinea-Bissau	3,447	5,808	12,291	6,483+112%
Mozambique	2,980	3,574	4,368	794 +22%
São Tomé and Príncipe	1,873	2,519	4,082	1,563 +62%
Other African Countries	1,675	2,408	3,915	1,507 +63%
United Kingdom	7,761	9,284	11,486	2,202 +24%
Spain	7,294	7,734	8,887	1,153 +15%
Germany	4,482	5,404	7,426	2,022 +37%
France	3,019	3,674	4,743	1,069 +29%
The Netherlands	1,670	2,010	2,736	726 +36%
Other European Countries	5,021	5,390	9,589	4,199 +78%
Brazil	10,520	14,048	19,901	5,853 +42%
Venezuela	4,886	4,910	4,554	-356 -7%
Other Central/South American	532	1,002	1,412	410 +41%
United States of America	6,438	7,321	8,484	1,163 +16%
Canada	2,092	2,109	2,369	260 +12%
Asian Countries	3,741	4,769	6,730	1,961 +41%
Oceanic Countries	347	391	490	99 +25%
Total for Portugal	101,011	121,513	168,316	46,803 +38%

Sources: INE 1990; INE 1996

The European Union has remained an important migrant source with 25 per cent of the total number registered. In turn, there were some 11,500 British immigrants resident in 1995, along with growing numbers from Germany, the Netherlands, and France. The northern Europeans who settle in Portugal fall into two categories. First, there are professional and semi-skilled workers reflecting the growing internationalization of the industrial and service economies in Portugal (Williams 1992, Corkill 1997). Secondly, there are those emigrating after retirement, whose target destination is primarily the Algarve (Williams *et al.* 1997). Along with Europeans, there has also been an expansion in the number of South Americans entering the country. Strong two-way migration trails have traditionally existed between Brazil and Portugal. In the second half of the 1980s, and in the 1990s in particular, increasing numbers of Brazilians have retraced their ancestors' steps. Table 1 shows, for example, that by 1995 the Brazilian community was almost 20,000 strong. Indeed, their numbers had grown by 42 per cent since 1992 – a faster rate than for any of the European Union immigrant nationalities.

IMMIGRANT INSERTIONS INTO THE SPATIAL ECONOMY

By the mid-1980s the Cape Verdeans were the largest foreign community in Portugal (Fonseca 1997). When they first arrived in the 1960s they filled the gap left by high outflows of young Portuguese workers. The dominance of Cape Verdeans among foreigners from the PALOPs was very marked in 1986 (more than 70 per cent), but had fallen to a little over 50 per cent a decade later (Machado 1997). These tendencies were confirmed in the residency authorization requests made by immigrants during the 1996 extraordinary legalization process. The number of immigrants from Guinea-Bissau quadrupled between 1986–91, while those from Angola tripled in the same period. In terms of a spatial breakdown for the location of the immigrant community, Table 2 shows that, in late 1995, the majority (55 per cent) had settled in and around the capital. Of the remainder, 12 per cent resided in Faro (Algarve), 9 per cent in Setúbal (south of Lisbon), and 6 per cent lived in the north-west around Oporto. The capital was home to the largest foreign group – some 25,800 Cape Verdeans. The figures reveal a very high degree of spatial concentration along the western coastal margin and towards the south – areas containing the main urban cores of (perceived) economic opportunity (Peixoto 1996). Foreign residents choose to congregate in these areas because the chances of securing employment and enjoying better living conditions are relatively much greater. The evidence supports this; between 1975–95 for example the largest increases in the overall size of the foreign resident communities were in Setúbal, Faro and Aveiro. These were precisely the *distritos* [counties] with higher than average standards of living (Cavaco 1995b). As a result, each county showed higher than average increases in the size of their foreign communities. In Setúbal, for instance, the foreign community grew twelvefold over the two decades prior to 1995 (INE 1996). In part, this was due to its position in Portugal's growing industrialization process which was foreign investment-driven (Ferrão and Vale 1995). It also reflects Setúbal's role in the suburban expansion of Lisbon towards the southern bank of the River Tagus.

TABLE 2
SPATIAL BREAKDOWN OF LEGALLY RESIDENT FOREIGNERS IN PORTUGAL. DECEMBER 1995

County	Total	European	African	North Amer.	Cen/S. Amer.	Asian	Ocean.
Aveiro	6,904	888	970	823	4,098	111	12
Beja	564	404	95	16	46	3	-
Braga	2,588	824	530	156	1,002	69	5
Braganza	241	74	89	11	56	8	-
Cast. Branco	570	209	140	56	134	28	3
Coimbra	4,076	1,233	1,292	309	1,067	147	27
Evora	742	413	207	24	76	17	5
Faro	20,946	11,414	6,349	843	1,386	745	169
Guarda	672	166	115	218	165	7	-
Leiria	2,215	668	585	440	478	34	2
Lisbon	92,441	20,016	53,175	4,643	9,585	4,663	188
Portalegre	466	264	144	14	37	6	1
Oporto	10,355	3,513	2,184	381	3,817	433	16
Santarem	1,158	397	448	132	139	34	8
Setubal	15,531	2,040	11,980	223	884	347	31
Viana do Cast.	1,221	506	122	263	307	19	3
Vila Real	736	126	138	112	356	3	-
Viseu	1,268	199	174	178	689	24	3
Azores	2,834	451	322	1,907	129	16	5
Madeira	2,662	936	172	104	1,416	16	12
Portugal	168,316	44,867	79,231	10,853	25,867	6,730	490

Source: INE 1996

Apart from these general patterns, there are also several very close spatial relationships between certain areas and nationalities. These types of immigrant enclaves are usually found on a small regional scale and are related to some historical and/or traditional migration trail. A primary example involves Venezuelan immigrants in Madeira who number 1,156 or 43 per cent of all foreign residents on the island. Their presence is a legacy of the oil industry boom in the 1960s when upwards of 190,000 Madeirans emigrated to Venezuela (Farrow and Farrow 1987). Since then, classic two way migration channels have been established and hundreds of Venezuelans with Portuguese ancestry have 'returned' to the region (Lewis and Williams 1994). Similarly, there are upwards of 1,190 residents of US origin (comprising 42 per cent of the foreign community on the archipelago) now settled in the Azores. Many are employed at the island's US air base where they work as military or support personnel. Finally, there is a small but growing Asian community in Lisbon. The

4,600 strong group is largely of Indian, Macanese or Chinese extraction and many are engaged in entrepreneurial ventures, including small-scale commercial, service and manufacturing activities (Malheiros 1996).

IMMIGRANTS AND THE LABOUR MARKET

Undoubtedly Portugal has become an increasingly attractive destination for migrants. From the mid-1960s when the economy began to open up and hundreds of thousands of Portuguese emigrated, employment opportunities were created for African workers. This process of 'substitution immigration' led to the establishment of important migration channels. The inflows were augmented by 'refugee migration' during the 1970s when around 600–750,000 *retornados* entered the country following the outbreak of civil wars in the former African colonies. The more typical 'economic migration' patterns become predominant only from the late 1980s when the economy – stimulated by European integration, political stability, a favourable external environment and inflows of structural funds and direct foreign investment – began to show strong growth. It is also worth noting that as unemployment levels were low, Portugal might have seemed preferable to other European destinations with higher levels of joblessness. However, there is little evidence that immigrants were deliberately targeting Portugal because jobs were relatively easier to come by.

There are a number of reasons why employment opportunities for immigrants broadened during the late 1980s and early 1990s. First, civil construction and public works programmes expanded significantly from the mid-1980s to such an extent that the sector became structurally dependent on immigrant labour. This dependency was reinforced by the substantial investment during the 1990s in such projects as Expo-98, the new Vasco da Gama bridge, Lisbon's metropolitan underground extensions etc. Secondly, the lack of effective controls and relative ease of entry encouraged immigration. As frontier controls were tightened elsewhere in Europe the countries of southern Europe became preferred destinations for would-be immigrants. Thirdly, the number of illegal immigrants increased substantially. Finally, the continued opening of the Portuguese economy and the inflow of foreign investment in particular, generated opportunities for qualified professionals to work in Portugal on fixed term contracts. This type of immigration began in the 1960s, dipped in the 1970s, but accelerated once again from the 1980s (Machado 1997).

The picture is further complicated when evidence provided by Machado (1997) is taken into account. It had been assumed, based on the Cape Verdean case, that immigrants from the former African colonies were predominantly unqualified and unskilled. Machado's study of immigrants from Guinea-Bissau demonstrates that in many cases their education levels are quite high (they included teachers as well as scientific and technical staff). It is, therefore, wrong to assume that those working in the construction industry are almost all poorly educated. However, it is not known whether a similar picture applies to the Angolans or to the most recent immigrants from the Cape Verde islands.

ILLEGAL IMMIGRATION

It is estimated that between 150–300,000 illegal immigrants enter the EU each year and the cumulative total is thought to be in the region of five million. Illegals arrive with the help of organized networks, often carry false documentation or simply enter as tourists and stay on when their visa expires (Champion 1998; King 1996, 1998). As part of southern Europe, Portugal is on the immigration 'front line'. This is because of its proximity to the Mediterranean basin and North Africa where demographic pressures are acute and migratory potentials are at their strongest. It is estimated, for example, that in the Maghreb and other parts of Africa demographic density will double in the next 25 years. Indeed, unless measures are taken by the four 'southern flank' countries (Portugal, Spain, Italy and Greece) as many as three million clandestines could enter the EU through the 'back door' (Doomerink 1997).

Notwithstanding fears about uncontrolled immigration, it has to be recognized that illegal immigrants are actually an important and flexible addition to Portugal's labour market. Many lusophone African immigrants have left their homelands because of ethnic conflict, civil war and poverty (Brookshaw 1992). Most are unskilled, manual workers who enter Portugal's burgeoning informal sector (Miguelez-Lobo 1990, Mingione 1995, Williams and Windebank 1995, Baganha 1998). They find employment in the construction, tourism and service sectors (Campani 1993). Many live in illegally constructed shanty towns in and around Lisbon, enduring substandard living conditions (Newbery 1994, Eaton 1996).

In spite of the general amnesties granted in 1992/93, and again in 1996, not all illegals registered with the Portuguese authorities. The principal reason for their reluctance was that official recognition would quickly prejudice the comparative advantage that their cheap labour brings to employers. A residence permit makes them liable for tax and their employer for social security payments, which immediately renders them less attractive as employees. There is evidence that illegals are exploited in terms of their access to, and use of, social benefits such as housing and education (Eaton 1998). There is also a suggestion that the judicial system does, on occasion, discriminate against foreigners (Baganha 1996). However, we should not lose sight of the fact that many clandestine immigrants tacitly accept their precarious situation because their earnings, which may be low in EU and Portuguese terms, are much higher than they might expect in their country of origin.

REFUGEES AND THE ASYLUM LAW

In 1993 the President, Mário Soares (himself a political exile during the dictatorship), used his presidential prerogative to veto new asylum legislation on humanitarian grounds. The liberal *Regime Legal do Direito de Asilo e Estatuto de Refugiado* – Legal Regime on Asylum Rights and the Refugee Statute – was to be replaced by a much tighter scheme. The new scheme would provide only temporary protection for refugees from war and similar situations. An altered version of the initial legislation later entered legal circles as the *Lei de Asilo* – Asylum Law (Corkill 1996). The Social Democrat (PSD) government justified the changes on the grounds, first, that Portuguese immigration law needed to be brought more into line with EU practice. Secondly, they argued that the security of Portugal's citizens was at stake. Finally, they claimed that those most affected would be limited to the marginal cases rejected by other European countries but hoping to take advantage of Portugal's benevolent legislation on asylum.

Significantly, the attempt to introduce the 1993 Asylum Law was an example of how European pressures are influencing and shaping Portuguese legislation. Concern at the escalation of asylum requests in the early 1990s had prompted demands for tighter controls, particularly with regard to *refugiados em órbita*. These were refugees rejected by one country after another. They are also migrants who frequently change their names, obtain false documentation and, aided by bureaucratic and procedural delays, have managed to remain within the EU for extended periods. A further aim was to deny or limit immigrants' access to social welfare benefits. The new regulations provoked an angry response from organizations representing immigrants from the PALOPs. They objected to being categorized as 'foreigners' particularly when many could more appropriately be termed Luso-Africans (Machado 1994). Immigrant organizations also predicted that the measure would not alleviate but actually increase social tensions within the country (Kobayashi 1998).

The new legislation did, however, have an immediate impact. Requests to the Portuguese authorities by asylum-seekers fell dramatically in 1994 to a little more than a third of the 1993 total – only 614 compared to 1,659. In relative terms, this was a mere fraction of the 12,600 requests made in Spain or 325,000 in Germany (Eurostat 1994). In 1995, 457 foreigners requested asylum in Portugal of whom 49 were given permission to stay. In the following year, asylum applications dipped still lower to 269 (Eurostat 1998). Further controversy arose in 1997 when the authorities established detention centres for foreigners awaiting expulsion from the country. Designated as 'temporary installations' and operated under the auspices of the SEF, they were set up in several locations. These included Lisbon international airport, near the Spanish border at Vila Formosa and in a number of Lisbon suburbs. Again, the establishment of these types of detention centre followed similar developments in other EU countries such as Italy and Belgium (Endean 1998).

RACISM AND THE IMMIGRANT'S 'SOCIAL IMAGE'

As we have seen, immigration issues have raised awkward questions about Portuguese attitudes to race and challenged many of their national self-perceptions. The idea of racial tolerance is deeply rooted in Portugal's imperial past. The Salazar regime, for instance, latched onto Gilberto Freyre's propounding of luso-tropicalism to justify the retention of the colonial territories. Through a combination of the 'civilizing' mission and the designation of Angola, Mozambique, Guinea-Bissau, and the West African islands as 'overseas provinces' in the 1960s, the dictatorial regime attempted to maintain its empire. Its relative success meant that control was retained well into the post-colonial era, and long after other European powers had granted independence to their imperial possessions.

Attitudes inherited from the Salazar era find an echo in the popular contention that racism either does not exist or (at worst) is less pervasive among southern Europeans. Some comfort is taken from the notion that it is among northern Europeans that racism flourishes. In Portugal's case, the self-perception began to be undermined following the start of racist incidents in 1989. Clashes between immigrants and local youths also took place in Setúbal in 1993. The myth of multiculturalism was undermined still further in June 1995 with a serious racial attack in Lisbon's *bairro alto* district. A skirmish led to the murder of a young Cape Verdean (in possession of Portuguese citizenship and with two years' military service) who was beaten to death by a gang of 'skinheads'. The local police (said to be 'awaiting re-inforcements') were accused of arriving at the scene two hours after the murder had occurred. The incident was followed by reprisal attacks as violence erupted onto streets of the capital. Subsequent arrests (up to 20 individuals were charged with attempted murder and affray) did, however, serve to keep the situation under a measure of control. Moreover, a well-attended anti-racism march reflected the general public's response to the events, which President Soares encapsulated when he referred to Portugal's 'tradition' and 'respect' for Africans.

The prominence of immigration issues prompted the Socialist (PS) government elected in 1995 to close some of the legal loopholes relating especially to Cape Verdeans working in Portugal. On his first African visit upon becoming Prime Minister, António Guterres resolved the question of illegal workers from Cape Verde who were covered by temporary visas. In talks with his opposite number, Carlos Veiga, it was agreed that the worker must return to his/her country of origin once the visa had expired. In spite of this agreement, it is interesting to note that whenever race and immigration emerge as issues then the political consequences have been very limited. For example, parties that might be expected to make political capital by 'playing the race card' have figured only marginally in the country's politics since the 1974 revolution. A general rejection of the far Right means that the political vehicles for the articulation of xenophobic, anti-immigrant propaganda have not emerged in Portugal.

This general benevolence was also reflected in a survey of public attitudes conducted by the *Universidade Católica* for newspaper *Público* and *TVI* in August 1995. The inquiry found that more than 80 per cent of those interviewed did not consider themselves to be racist (Anon.1995). The survey also revealed antipathy towards gypsies and some resentment over housing problems. While more than 40 per cent believed that immigrants brought economic benefits, most of the respondents did not wish to live in neighbourhoods containing large numbers of foreigners because of fears about their behaviour. However, subsequent surveys (published in the press (e.g. *Público*, *Expresso* and

Diário de Notícias) exposed only weak links between immigrants and criminality. Moreover, there was little stereotyping of people of African origin as delinquents. Interestingly, it was gypsies (again) and immigrants from neighbouring Spain who were predominantly associated with drugs and other related criminal activities.

The 'social image' most closely associated with immigrants from the PALOPs was one of illegal employment (Baganha 1996). Among the Portuguese people, black youth are perceived not as 'job stealers' but as reminders of 1975. As we have said, this was a time when Portugal surrendered its empire and up to three-quarters of a million refugees, including many black Luso-Africans, arrived back in the country. It was significant that attempts by the state secret service (SIS) and some politicians to construct a negative image of immigrant youth failed. Once again, their efforts to brand 'black gangs' as enemies of social peace and stability did not find an echo in the wider Portuguese society.

In recent years, Portugal has therefore appeared to be out of step with countries like France and Germany in its public attitudes to immigrants. However, the danger still exists that immigrants could become the scapegoats for a range of social and political ills. Indeed, as we have seen, the link is beginning to be made with drugs and crime. What little evidence there is, appears to confirm that racism does exist not far below the surface of Portugal's public consciousness. However, it is certainly not as overt as elsewhere in the EU and has yet to find major political expression.

REGULARIZATION AND INTEGRATION INTO PORTUGUESE SOCIETY

It is uncertain how many undocumented migrants there are in Portugal. As we have mentioned, efforts were made from the early 1990s to regularize their position through the granting of amnesties. Illegal immigrants were given two chances to obtain the necessary documents allowing them officially to live and work in the country. Under the first extraordinary legalization programme in 1992–93 (Decree Law 212/92) some 38,365 had their status legalized (Kobayashi 1998). However, it became clear that, for reasons stated earlier, many thousands more failed to respond. This made it difficult for the government to monitor foreigners and to enforce their border controls. On a second occasion, therefore, immigrants from the former African colonies together with Brazilian nationals were offered an opportunity to qualify if they were residents in the country before 30 November 1995. This second legalization process took place in 1996 and identified some 40,000 irregular migrants, of whom all but 5,000 were accepted. SEF figures revealed that the majority were Africans with over one quarter from Angola, almost 20 per cent from Cape Verde and 15 per cent from Guinea-Bissau. Other important source regions included South East Asia, the Indian subcontinent and Brazil (Malheiros 1998). Regularization was, therefore, a very important factor in the 52 per cent recorded growth in foreign residents from 1991–97 (Barreto 1997, Pinto 1997).

Many of the immigrants who successfully gained official recognition in the 1990s were already partially integrated into Portuguese society. They were, for example, employed in the informal sector of the Portuguese labour market. However, and while there is a suggestion that the public condones their existence, such a clandestine situation is no longer acceptable to the European Commission. One of the ways in which the employment of illegal immigrants can be tackled is by the authorities taking strong legal action against employers who, in the past, have been merely subject to fines. Progress in this direction was not, however, helped when national labour shortages were exacerbated by the massive public works projects underway in Lisbon during 1998. In addition, the widespread use of contractors and subcontractors meant that detecting irregular workers was extremely difficult. Moreover, the organizations charged with detecting illegal immigrants in the Portuguese labour market have themselves been the subject of irregularities. The *Inspecção-Geral do Trabalho* [Inspectorate General for Employment or IGT] has on occasion been accused of corruption and a lack of investigative rigour (Eaton and Silva 1998). It is not surprising, therefore, that their indirect ignorance of the process has failed to eradicate the issue of clandestine workers.

The Catholic church has taken a keen interest in the precarious living conditions endured by many undocumented African immigrants. Indeed, they have urged the relevant authorities to administer civilized treatment and adopt humane solutions. Portugal's Bishops' Conference [*Conferência Episcopal Portuguesa* or CEP] has been particularly vocal. They called for the legalization of clandestine immigrants, allowing them to be re-united with their families, and urged that they be given more time to complete the necessary formalities. One of the documents put before the bishops by the *Comissão Episcopal das Migrações e Turismo* [Bishops' Commission for Migration and Tourism] criticized the 'inadequate structures' available to receive immigrants. They also commented that 'recent laws on immigration and refugees (were) very restrictive and very much in line with the most severe positions held by some EU countries'. The Commission pressed for a new legalization process to put an end to the immigrants' marginal status. They focused upon the immigrant living in a shanty town who may not be able to obtain a residence permit. On occasions, this was because the local *junta da freguesia* [parish council] would be unwilling to provide the necessary papers to facilitate the residence process. Councils were sometimes reluctant because they did not want to draw attention to their *bairros de lata* [shanty towns], and, as a result, many immigrants were left in limbo. They could not show prospective employers any legal identification and many were subsequently marginalized in the twilight zone afforded by the informal economy.

One proposal put forward by the Council for Immigrant Communities and Ethnic Minorities was for all immigrants to be informed of their rights to vote in political elections and then be encouraged to do so (Eaton 1994). Immersion in the democratic process was thought to be an initial means of helping immigrants to feel involved in their community. It was also felt that, given time, they would assist in the political and practical solutions to local developmental problems. The limited available evidence suggests, however, that there are only low levels of involvement in Portuguese politics by foreign residents (Fonseca 1997). At present, only EU citizens and citizens of the countries with which Portugal has reciprocal treaties can vote in local (but not national elections). Reciprocity exists only with Brazil, Israel, Norway and the Cape Verde islands. It was reported that in the most recent local elections (December 1997) less than 10 per cent of foreigners who were entitled to vote actually registered to do so (Martins 1997). Reasons given by the media for their general reluctance ranged from apathy and unfamiliarity with the system to speculation that their residence documentation might not be in order (Port 1997).

Among the mainstream parties and a minority of independent fringe candidates, just three foreign residents stood for the elections. These included a British person, a Swede and a German. The British candidate stood in Carvoeiro (in the Algarve) on a Socialist ticket with the intention of gathering the large local expatriate vote. However, after losing by just 42 votes, the candidate subsequently blamed his defeat on a lack of support from the PS. He also described foreign participation in the voting as 'pathetic' (Anon. 1997). On this relatively informal basis, it does appear, therefore, that the immigrant's role in Portuguese politics is not being taken seriously. In the local areas where immigrants have a significant presence, one would expect them to become more politicized. On a more encouraging note, however, the existence of immigrant associations helped to politicize questions of immigration. It is no longer possible to ignore the growth of immigrant communities and their geographical concentration is helping to raise their profile. Indeed, the government acknowledged the need to encourage social integration by appointing a High Commission for immigration and ethnic minorities in 1996. Its role was to develop programmes to rehouse immigrant families and improve their access to services (Fonseca 1997).

CONCLUSION

Immigration is now a fundamental process affecting the socio-economic development of Portugal. A foreign community in excess of 168,000 individuals may represent less than 2 per cent of the national population; however, their significance at the local level often transcends their minority status. Many immigrants gather in shanty towns around Lisbon and both their image and presence is a vivid reminder of Portugal's troubled colonial heritage. In these situations, the general feeling of ethnic tolerance among Portuguese nationals may (on an admittedly small number of occasions) change to racist abuse and discrimination. The potential for conflict does, therefore, exist and is most likely to be found at the interfaces with areas of social deprivation. To control the situation, the Portuguese authorities initially took a soft line. Deportations, for example, were low with just 166 in 1993 (Baldwin-Edwards 1997), and regularization of existing illegals became the desired norm. General amnesties offered to illegals in 1992/93, and again in 1996, resulted in a measure of success. However, the cosmetic effects of these exercises were such that they satisfied the authorities and the public at large. Again, the impression was that immigration was under control and that the twin processes of assimilation and multiculturalism were continuing apace.

It appears likely that Portugal will impose more restrictive immigration policies in future. In part, this will help satisfy EC demands for tougher control. In so doing it will maintain the high level of development funds channelled into the country. Immigration (both legal and clandestine) will, however, continue to be a significant feature of the national labour market. Indeed, it will probably remain the backbone of Portugal's informal economy. In addition, as the general workforce undergoes skills upgrading and training, so the immigrant will face possible exclusion on the grounds of qualifications. On the other hand, changing working practices, including flexible contracts, will suit the minimally qualified worker. Much will depend on whether the state is prepared to turn a blind eye or, encouraged by the European Commission, try to crack down on the informal sector. The structure of the labour market and the comparative advantage (over other EU members) derived from the immigrants points to the former.

Whatever the outcome, it is clear that the foreign resident and the illegal immigrant will play an increasingly important role in Portuguese society. In the past two decades, Luso-Africans, South Americans and Europeans have all contributed to the growing internationalization process within the country. They are prevalent in both the formal and informal economies and are engaged in important professional and manual working sections of the labour market. Their contributions may only scrape the surface of general consciousness in Portugal, but their involvement is a key factor shaping the country's socio-economic development. The immigrant's role cannot, therefore, be underestimated or ignored. Immigration is an intractable issue for Portugal. The country has a lot to gain from the physical contributions of its foreign workers; equally it has a lot to lose were they to be denied full integration into society. Moreover, if current rates of growth are maintained (or even accelerate with an expected influx of Macanese in 1999) then the foreign minority population in Portugal will double in size by around the year 2002. Consequently, the next few years will be defining points in Portugal's attempts to become a successful, modern, cosmopolitan and multicultural society.

NOTES

1. A legalized foreign resident (LFR) is 'an individual of non-Portuguese nationality to whom has been granted a residence permit by the official government authority' (INE 1996). To obtain a permit, one has to satisfy three criteria: to have been resident in Portugal for six years; be in employment and be judged 'socially acceptable' by the SEF. The numbers recorded as LFR's includes first destination immigrants, their spouses and dependents.
2. There are some errors and problems with the comparability of figures derived by different government agencies. In the case of migration there are two sources – the Portuguese National Statistics Institute (INE) for the emigration statistics and the Foreigners and Frontiers Service (SEF) for immigration data – see Machado (1997) for details of these problems.
3. Permanent emigration is defined as for a period greater than one year. However, large numbers of Portuguese emigrants classify themselves as temporary migrants, but remain illegally (and 'permanently') in their host destinations (Baganha 1993).
4. The Schengen Agreement is an EU accord allowing for free movement of people among

the signatory countries-Belgium, France, Germany, Luxembourg, the Netherlands, Italy, Spain and Portugal (see Convey and Kupiszewski 1995; Baldwin-Edwards 1997 for details).

5. Spain is a major 'gateway' into the EU for illegal immigrants arriving principally from North Africa and Morocco in particular (Pumares 1998). While the numbers are considerably larger – by about 7:1 (Eurostat 1996b) than for Portugal, the general trend is remarkably similar. Spain too, has been transformed from a labour exporter into a country of net in-migration (Driessen 1996).

REFERENCES

Amaral, J.F. do (1993): 'Portugal and the Free Movement of Labour', in Lopes, J. da Silva (ed.) *Portugal and EC Membership Evaluated*, London: Pinter, pp.240–46.

Anon, 'One in two think there are too many immigrants', *Anglo-Portuguese News*, 18 Dec. 1995.

Anon 'Four in ten don't vote: giants swallow the minnows', *Anglo-Portuguese News*, 18 Dec. 1997.

Baganha, M.I. (1993): 'Principais características e tendências da emigração portuguesa', in; *Estruturas Sociais e Desenvolvimento. Actas do 2 Congreso Português de Sociologia*, vol. 1, Lisbon: APS/Editorial Fragmentos.

Baganha, M.I. (1996): *Immigrant Insertion in the Informal Economy: The Portuguese Case.* First Report for TSER Programme, CE/DG XII-Science, Research and Development Project: Migrants' Insertion in the Informal Economy, Deviant Behaviour and the Impact on Receiving Societies, University of Parma. mimeo.

Baganha, M.I. (1998): 'Immigrant Involvement in the Informal Economy: the Portuguese Case', *Journal of Ethnic and Migration Studies,* 24/2, pp.367–85.

Baldwin-Edwards, M. (1997): 'The Emerging European Immigration Regime: Some Reflections on Implications for Southern Europe', *Journal of Common Market Studies*, 35/4, pp.497–519.

Barreto, A. (org.) (1997): *A Situação Social em Portugal 1960–1995*, Lisbon: ICS.

Brettell, C.B. (1993): 'The Emigrant, the Nation, and the State in the Nineteenth and Twentieth Century Portugal: an Anthropological Approach', *Portuguese Studies Review*, 2/2, pp.51–65.

Brookshaw, D. (1992): 'Islands Apart: Tradition and Transition', *Index on Censorship*, 6, pp.13–14.

Campani, G. (1993): 'Immigration and Racism in Southern Europe: the Italian Case', *Ethnic and Racial Studies*, 16/3, pp.507–35.

Cavaco, C. (1995a): 'A Place in the Sun; Return Migration and Rural Change in Portugal', in: King, R. (ed.) *Mass Migration in Europe*, Chichester: Wiley.

Cavaco, C. (1995b): 'Tourism in Portugal: Diversity, Diffusion and Regional and Local Development', *Tijdschrift voor Economische en Sociale Geografie*, 86/1, pp.64–71.

Champion, T. (1998): 'Demography', in: T. Unwin (ed.) *A European Geography*, Harlow: Longman, pp.241–59.

Convey, A. and Kupiszewski, M. (1995): 'Keeping up with Schengen: Migration and Policy in the European Union', *International Migration Review*, 29/ 4, pp.939–63.

Corkill, D. (1996): 'Multiple National Identities, Immigration and Racism in Spain and Portugal', in B. Jenkins and S.A. Sofos (eds.) *Nation and Identity in Contemporary Europe*, London: Routledge, pp.155–71.

Corkill, D. (1997): 'Interpreting cavaquismo: the Cavaco Silva Decade in Portugal', *International Journal of Iberian Studies*, 2/2, pp.80–88.

Doomerink, J. (1997): 'Current Migration to Europe', *Tijdschrift voor Economische en Sociale Geografie*, 88/3, pp.284–90.

Driessen, H. (1996): 'At the Edge of Europe: Crossing and Marking the Mediterranean Divide'. In L. O'Dowd and T.M. Wilson (eds.) *Borders, Nations and States: Frontiers of Sovereignty in the New Europe*, Avebury, Aldershot.

Eaton, D. 'All Ethnic Groups should be Allowed to Vote', *Anglo-Portuguese News*, 1 Dec. 1994.

Eaton, M. (1993): 'Foreign Residents and Illegal Immigrants: os negros em Portugal'. *Ethnic and Racial Studies*, 16/3, pp.536–62.

Eaton, M. (1996): 'Résidents étrangers et immigrés en situation irrégilière au Portugal', *Revue Européenne des Migrations Internationales*, 12/1, pp.203–212.

Eaton, M. (1998): 'Foreign Residents and Illegal Immigrants in Portugal', *International Journal of Intercultural Relations*, 22/1, pp.49–66.

Eaton, M. and Silva, C.P. (1998): 'Portuguese Child Labour: Manufacturing for Change or Continuing Exploitation in the Textiles Industry?, *Childhood*, 5/3, pp.325–43.

Endean, C. 'No Warm Welcome in the new Europe', *The European*, 3–9 Aug. 1998.

Esteves, M.C. ed. (1991): *Portugal. País do Imigração*, Lisbon: IED.

Eurostat (1994): *Asylum Seekers and Refugees in the EC. A Statistical Report*, Luxembourg: Eurostat.

Eurostat (1996a): 'Unemployment', *Theme 3: Population and Social Conditions, Series B: short Term Statistics*, No.1, p.10.

Eurostat (1996b): *Statistics in Focus: Population and Social Conditions, Migration*, Luxembourg: Eurostat.

Eurostat (1997): *Eurostat Yearbook 1997: a Statistical Eye on Europe, 1986–1996*, Luxembourg: Eurostat.

Eurostat (1998): *Statistics in Focus: Population and Social Conditions*, No.9.

Farrow, J. and Farrow, S. (1987): *Madeira: the Complete Guide*, London: Hale.

Ferrão, J. and Vale, M. (1995): 'Multi-Purpose Vehicles, a New Opportunity for the Periphery? Lessons from the Ford/VW project (Portugal)', in: Hudson, R. and Schamp, E. W. (eds) Towards a New Map of Automobile Manufacturing in Europe?, Strasbourg: European Science Foundation.

Fonseca, M.L. 'The Geography of Recent Immigration to Portugal.' Paper presented to the conference on 'Non-military aspects of security in Southern Europe: migration, employment and the labour market', held in Santorini, Greece, Sept. 1997.

Fonseca, M.L. and Cavaco, C. (1997): 'Portugal in the 1980s and 1990s: Economic Restructuring and Population Mobility', in Blotevogel, H. and Fielding, A.J. (eds.) *People, Jobs and Mobility in the New Europe*, Chichester: Wiley.

Guibentif, P. (1996): 'Le Portugal face à l'immigration', *Revue Européenne de Migrations Internationales*, 12/ 1, pp.121–39.

Instituto Nacional de Estatística (1990): *Estatistícas Demográficas 1989*, Lisbon: INE.

Instituto Nacional de Estatística (1996): *Estatísticas Demográficas 1995*, Lisbon: INE.

King, R. (1996) 'Migration and Development in the Mediterranean Region', *Geography*,. 81/1, pp.3–14.

King, R. (1998): 'New Geographies of International Migration', in T. Unwin (ed.) *A European Geography*, Longman, Harlow, pp.281–304.

Kobayashi, M. (1998): 'Narrative Construction of Reality: Portugueseness and Semiperipheral Space', unpublished MA thesis, University of Warwick.

Lewis, J. and Williams, A. (1985): 'Portugal's *retornados*: Reintegration or Rejection?, *Iberian Studies*, xiv/1–2, pp.11–23.

Lewis, J. and Williams, A.M. (1994): 'Regional autonomy and the European Communities: the view from Portugal's Atlantic islands', *Regional Politics and Policy*, 4/2, pp.67–85.

Machado, F.L. (1994): 'Luso-africanos em Portugal: nas margens da etnicidade', *Sociologia: Problemas e Práticas*, 16, pp.111–34.

Machado, F.L. (1997): 'Contornos e especifidades da imigração em Portugal', *Sociologia: Problemas e Práticas*, 24, pp.9–44.

Malheiros, J.M. (1996): 'Communautés Indiennes à Lisbonne', *Revue Européenne des Migrations Internationales*, 12/1, pp.141–58.

Malheiros, J.M. (1998): 'Foreign workers in the Portuguese Labour Market: Facing Illegality and Vulnerability', mimeo.

Martins, D. 'Only 3,000 expatriates expected to vote', *Anglo-Portuguese News*, 11 Dec. 1997.

Miguelez-Lobo, F. (1990): 'Irregular Work in Portugal'. Commission of the European Communities, *Underground Economy and Irregular Forms of Employment (Travail au Noir)*, Luxembourg: CEC.

Mingione, E. (1995): 'Labour Market Segmentation and Informal Work in Southern Europe', *European Urban and Social Studies*, 2/2, pp.121–43.

Newbery, B. 'Slums hide behind boom city', *The European*, 11–17 Nov. 1994

Peixoto, J. (1996): 'Recent Trends in Regional Migration and Urban Dynamics in Portugal'. In Rees, P. et al. ed. *Population Migration in the European Union*, Wiley, Chichester.

Pinto, M.J. (1997): 'EU citizens 25% of total of foreigners', *Anglo-Portuguese News*, no 1939.

Port, L. 'Apathy-or shyness? Few expected to vote', *Anglo-Portuguese News*, 4 December 1997.

Pumares, P. (1998): 'Moroccan Immigration to Spain', in Unwin, T. (ed.) *A European Geography*, Harlow: Longman, pp.250–53.

Rocha-Trindade, M.B. (coord.) *Sociologia da Migrações*, Universidade Aberta, Lisbon.

Serrão, J. (1977): *A Emigração Portuguesa*, Lisbon: Livros Horizonte.

Williams, A.M. (1992) 'The Portuguese Economy in Transition', *ACIS Journal*, 5/1, pp.30–39.

Williams, A.M., King, R. and Warnes, T. (1997): 'A Place in the Sun: International Retirement Migration from Northern to Southern Europe', *European Urban and Regional Studies*, 4/2, pp.115–34.

Williams, C.C. and Windebank, J. (1995): 'Black Market Work in the European Community: Peripheral Work for Peripheral Localities', *International Journal of Urban and Regional Research*, 19/1, pp.23–29.

Immigration, Clandestine Work and Labour Market Strategies: The Construction Sector in the Metropolitan Region of Lisbon

JORGE MACAÍSTA MALHEIROS

IMMIGRANT WORKERS AND THE RECENT EVOLUTION OF THE PORTUGUESE LABOUR MARKET

Although the presence of African workers in the Portuguese labour market goes back to the late 1960s, when colonial war and emigration caused shortages of unskilled workers in sectors like the naval industry, construction and public works, the visibility of foreign communities began to be significant only after the mid-1970s (see Figure 1). The decolonization process, which occurred during the events surrounding the Revolution of 1974, caused a 'boom' in the number of Africans arriving from the PALOPs.[1] Coming along with the *retornados* (people of Portuguese origin living in the Portuguese ex-colonies in Africa), these Africans were the germ of the large African communities established in subsequent years. Therefore, between 1974 and the late 1970s,[2] foreign immigration to Portugal resulted less from the internal pressures of the sectoral Portuguese labour markets, than from a push process generated by the sudden and disorganized transfer of administration in the colonies. The armed conflicts that started in Angola and Mozambique in the independence process were also motives that fed the flow of immigrants who arrived in Portugal in the following years.

Between the early 1980s and the early 1990s, it is possible to consider a second phase in the immigration cycle of Portugal. The number of foreigners kept rising at a reasonable rate but the relative growth of

This paper was developed within the framework of the project 'Internacionalização, Reestruturação Económica e Geração de Novas Marginalidades na Região de Lisboa' of the Department of Geography of Faculdade de Letras (University of Lisbon).

FIGURE 1

EVOLUTION OF THE NUMBER OF FOREIGNERS WITH RESIDENCE PERMITS 1960–1994

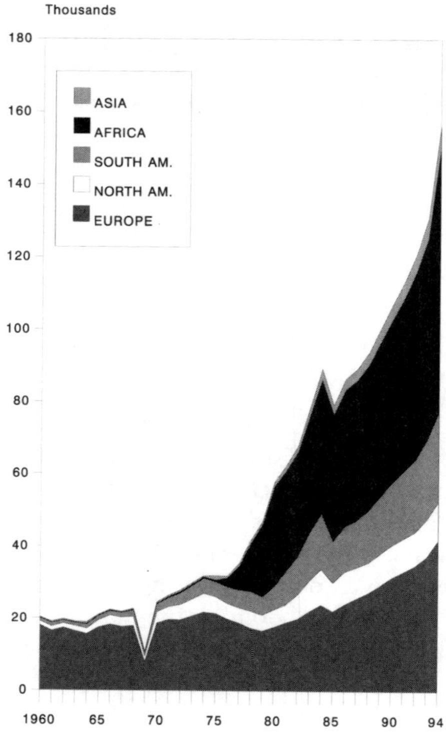

Source: INE, Estatisticas Demograficás Serviço de Estrangeiros e Fronteiras

TABLE 1

RATES OF VARIATION OF DOCUMENTED FOREIGNERS BY GEOGRAPHICAL ORIGIN

	1960/65	1965/70	1970/75	1975/80	1980/85	1985/90	1990/95
EUROPE	-3.08	6.70	14.46	-17.32	24.59	42.38	42.84
NORTH AM.	76.88	57.34	51.07	2.38	65.67	12.60	20.68
SOUTH AM.	34.65	85.15	90.63	56.67	80.65	50.22	48.87
AFRICA	75.00	31.55	127.60	5416.50	26.06	29.38	75.08
ASIA	11.54	68.10	205.38	-3.19	122.38	62.01	62.01
OCEANIA	510.00	-1.64	106.67	20.16	83.22	30.77	33.61
DOUBLE NAT. / STATELESS	-26.56	-34.04	-27.42	146.67	48.65	34.55	22.07
TOTAL	**3.49**	**16.36**	**29.83**	**81.12**	**37.02**	**35.40**	**50.75**

Source: Foreign and Borders Office (SEF).

Asians (mainly Indians, Pakistanis and Chinese) and South Americans (especially Brazilians) became more relevant (see Table 1).

Within this logic, the number of nationalities identified by the Foreign and Borders Office (SEF) increased from 102 in 1981 to 129 in 1991. This diversification of the origins of immigrants points to a change in the position of Portugal in the context of international migration and to a more relevant role of the Portuguese labour market needs in the process of recruitment of foreign workers. By the end of this phase, the polarized pattern of immigration of workers to Portugal was very clear: on the one hand, highly skilled nationals coming mainly from European countries; on the other, unskilled workers arriving from the former Portuguese ex-colonies in Africa but also from other countries like Zaire, Brazil, Pakistan and more recently Morocco and Bangladesh (Malheiros 1996: 96-98; Pena Pires 1993: 185). This polarized pattern of foreign immigrants can also be found in other southern European countries like Spain (Gozálvez Pérez 1996) and fits with global theories that explain the trends towards a polarization in wages and employment positions in the developed countries (Sassen 1989).

TABLE 2

EVOLUTION OF THE ACTIVE FOREIGN POPULATION BY OCCUPATIONAL CATEGORY

OCCUPATIONS	Number of persons 1983	Number of persons 1990	Number of persons 1996	Variation rate 83-90 (%)	Variation rate 90-96 (%)	Variation rate 83-96 (%)
(0/1) Professionals and technicians	4082	12743	20571	212.2	61.4	403.9
(2) Directors and managers	1483	3465	4991	133.7	44.0	236.5
(3) Clerical employees	1508	2592	3429	71.9	32.2	127.4
(4) Employees in commerce, shopkeepers and vendors	2743	4100	7088	49.5	72.9	158.4
(5) Personnel and domestic services	1363	1824	7210	33.8	295.3	428.9
Farmers and agriculture workers	895	910	1093	1.7	20.1	22.1
(6/7/8) Construction and industrial workers	10916	23552	42428	115.8	80.1	288.7
TOTAL ACTIVE	22990	49186	86810	114.0	76.5	277.6

Source: Foreigner and Borders Office (SEF)

An observation of the data in Table 2 shows throughout the 1980s a higher growth rate of skilled professionals in relation to the growth rate of unskilled labourers in industry and especially construction. This situation is related to the first stage of the process of internationalization of the Portuguese economy that enabled an increase in capital flows and a higher penetration of foreign enterprises.[3] Also the modernization process of the Portuguese entrepreneurial structure, partially supported by the inflow of EU funds,[4] has reinforced the needs of experts in areas with a low level of development in Portugal (design, marketing and others). In 1991, the occupation groups that incorporate the qualified professionals (0/1 and 2) had a concentration of around 30 per cent of the active foreign population, a proportion three times higher than the global national average (Peixoto 1994; 1998).

Apparently, the first half of the 1990s seems to correspond to a third stage in the contemporary Portuguese immigration cycle. On the one hand, the relative growth in the number of legal foreigners increased. On the other hand, African communities and unskilled workers reassumed the leading position in this process. Simultaneously, the growth trends of skilled professionals experienced a decrease (see Table 2). In fact, after the early stage of openness of the Portuguese economy, the rhythm of settlement of foreign enterprises decreased and the internal training programmes started to incorporate the occupational areas in deficit. On the contrary, the dynamics of construction and public works during the past six years have contributed support for the growth of unskilled workers of foreign origin, not only in the formal labour market but also in the informal one.[5]

However, the personnel and domestic services sectors have shown the highest employment dynamics amongst the foreign active population, especially in the present decade. This process is highly related to the presence of African women in domestic and industrial cleaning sectors and it reflects important regulatory and economic changes. On the one hand, the regularization processes and the diffusion of the advantages of having contracts and social security have brought to light domestic employees who were previously working on a completely informal basis. On the other hand, several private firms as well as public services decided to contract out services like cleaning, enabling expansion of the firms developing these activities.

THE DEVELOPMENT AND CONSOLIDATION OF AN INFORMAL LABOUR MARKET

Although the development of informal strategies in the labour market affects all immigrants, this situation is more relevant for unskilled workers. Therefore, the discussion of an informal labour market should be placed within the analytical framework of the secondary labour market. According to the dual labour market theory (Mallet 1980; Gambier and Verniéres 1982), the concept of the secondary labour market corresponds to the segment of employment which is characterized by its vulnerability in terms of salary, contractual terms and possibilities of career. Within this market, the offer of potential workers should be differentiated and kept at a high level with the purpose of introducing differentials in wages as a function of non-labour factors like age, sex or ethnic origin (Jackson 1991:27).

Actually, unskilled foreigners have several disadvantages when competing with nationals in the labour market. First, there is the question of formal restrictions (visa requirements, work permits, etc.). Then, they bring their own disadvantages (lack of ability in the language, lack of familiarity with labour market circuits) and have to face the prejudice or even the hostility of some groups in the local population. To overcome these limitations, migrant workers frequently rely on informal strategies, especially if formal institutions (the state, local authorities, trade unions) show an incapacity to help the labour market integration of unskilled foreigners. Among the above-mentioned strategies, there are two inter-related ones that play privileged roles: *the mobilization of family and kinship networks* and *the development of clandestine activities*.

Acting as a fundamental channel of contacts between immigrants and employers, migrant networks provide essential information to those who are looking for a job or need some other kind of support (temporary housing, social support, etc.). As Pohjola (1991:440) says, these networks assume a main role in the 'reorganisation of migrants' lives after the move'. The development of clandestine activities is often a response to legal restrictions that result either from an actual illegal situation or from a wrong interpretation of the benefits and limitations associated with a legal job. Frequently oriented through the circuits of clandestine work, recently-arrived unskilled migrants often accept the rules of the informal labour market not only because they are undocumented but also because their fast accumulation strategies are apparently more easily satisfied if they follow this path. However, if in the short run the profits may appear high (e.g. there are no fiscal taxes, welfare payments, etc.), the consciousness of vulnerability increases with time and the problems become real (under-payment, absence of paid holidays, no social benefits in case of dismissal and, frequently, of accident). Besides, there are important long-term costs related with the practice of clandestine work developed by undocumented immigrants. For instance, in a situation of global or sectoral crisis, unemployment rises and the potential for social tension and conflict increases. On the other hand, a long period of clandestine work without welfare payments is bound to affect negatively both the society and the worker after his working life, especially in the present crises in the national social security systems of many EU countries.

The implementation of an informal labour market for unskilled foreigners is a short/medium run strategy incorporating long term risks. However, it contributes both to a consolidation of the above-mentioned secondary labour market and to supporting the contemporary needs of the flexible production model. Actually, clandestine immigrant workers are a group with a profile adjusted to the new features of the labour market, offering flexibility and short-term adaptational capacity. They are mobile, both geographically and professionally, they are institutionally vulnerable and their ties to the country of destination and to the employers are relatively weak – a situation that increases the possibilities of simplified replacement strategies.

UNDOCUMENTED IMMIGRATION AND LABOUR MARKET VULNERABILITY OF FOREIGN WORKERS IN PORTUGAL – SOME GLOBAL FEATURES

The Second Extraordinary Regularization Process of the Foreign Population held in 1996 enabled the identification of approximately 40,000 undocumented migrants in Portugal,[6] of which 35,000 were recognized like valid claimants (see Table 3).

Despite the over-representation of Africans coming from the PALOPs, their number is lower when compared to the numbers of the 1992/93 Regularization Process. This situation and the diversification in the origins of the immigrants shown in Table 3 points to the maintenance of the trends already detected in the 1980s. Because we are now dealing with undocumented immigrants, it seems correct to view the 1990s as a period of increasing activity of the international networks of clandestine work in Portugal. Information about the extraordinary regularization

TABLE 3
NUMBER OF INDIVIDUAL PROCESSES PRESENTED AND ACCEPTED BY SEF (FOREIGNERS AND BORDERS OFFICE) IN THE 1992/93 AND 1996 EXTRAORDINARY REGULARIZATION PROCESSES

COUNTRIES	**1992/93**	**1996**
Angola	12525 (32.0%)	9.255 (26.4%)
C.Verde	6778 (17.3%)	6.872 (19.6%)
G.Bissau	6877 (17.6%)	5.308 (15.1%)
Mozambique	757 (1.9%)	416 (1.2%)
S.T.Príncipe	1408 (3.6%)	1.549 (4.4%)
Total PALOPs	**28345 (72.4%)**	**23.400 (66.7%)**
Senegal	1397 (3.6%)	672 (1.9%)
Morocco	98 (0.3%)	520 (1.5%)
Brazil	5346 (13.7%)	2.330 (6.6%)
China	1352 (3.5%)	1.608 (4.6%)
Pakistan	286 (0.7%)	1.754 (5.0%)
India	261 (0.7%)	915 (2.6%)
Bangladesh	139 (0.4%)	752 (2.1%)
Other countries	1942 (5.0%)	4.739 (13.5%)
GRAND TOTAL	**39,166**	**35,082**

Source: Foreigners and Borders Office (SEF)

processes as well as job opportunities in sectors like construction and public works are circulated among the potential immigrants. Furthermore, Portugal shares an image of a country with looser border controls than most of the northern and central countries of the EU.

Some interviews with newcomers from China and Pakistan cite ‘entrance facilities’ as a fundamental reason for their presence in Portugal. In this case, old contact systems have assumed a new prominence and become more active, once again with the help of networks connected to the former organization of the Portuguese Colonial Empire (via Mozambique, Goa and Diu in India or Macao in South China). Furthermore, the increase in the number of undocumented migrants coming from China and South Asia reveals the relevant role of the international circuits involving such foreign workers active in Portugal in the 1990s. Recently, SEF officials declared that networks of illegal migration based in South Asia are responsible for a significant number of irregular foreigners trying to enter the country after the 1996 Regularization Scheme.

Despite this last regularization process, there is still an important and indeterminate number of undocumented migrants in Portugal, not only through recent arrivals but also because of those unable to present their documents in 1996. Moreover, the number of clandestine workers is obviously higher because there are some regular immigrants who work without valid contracts. To this situation, it is important to add questions related to some specific groups who are legally forbidden to work, such as asylum seekers. These are somehow compelled to develop illegal activities for their livelihood while Portuguese authorities decide about their definite status.

The over-representation of Africans, especially from the former Portuguese ex-colonies, gives indirect information about the concentration of these undocumented migrants in unskilled occupations (namely construction in the case of males and industrial and domestic cleaning in the case of women, who are fewer). These are, in fact, two activity branches that reveal a high capacity to generate clandestine work. Recent research (Baganha 1997) confirms the high level of labour market vulnerability experienced by the PALOP workers in Portugal because of their smaller proportion of permanent contracts and lower rate of social security enrolment.

This set of different paths towards irregular situations among immigrants contributes to the development of work that fulfils a very important role in the support of the segmented secondary labour market of the above-mentioned sectors of the Portuguese economy (Esteves *et al.* 1991:49). If the incorporation in the networks of informal labour brings apparent immediate advantages for all agents (employers, workers and indirectly the state institutions), the exposure of foreign workers to some situations reveals serious vulnerability. According to some research (for instance, França *et al.* 1992, for Cape Verdeans; Malheiros 1995, for a group of Angolans) as well as the opinion of responsible people in NGOs like the Guinea-Bissau Association or the Portuguese Council for Refugees, the following are the most usual vulnerable situations faced by clandestine foreign workers in Portugal:

- employment without any kind of contract,
- under-payment both in relation to nationals and to their own professional category,
- absence of paid holidays or thirteenth month salary, procedures enshrined in the rules of labour contracts in Portugal,
- frequent refusal of payment after the completion of work (a formal legal working contract does not exist),
- absence of social assistance and insurance for work accidents, and

- aggravated possibility of dismissal due to the lack of documents and the absence of a working contract.

The combination of these situations depicts the unfavourable conditions experienced by clandestine foreign workers in Portugal. However, the example of construction, probably the sector where an informal labour market system is better developed in Portugal, can perhaps throw some light on the relations, advantages and economic consequences that arise from such an arrangement.

INFORMAL RELATIONS AND THE DEVELOPMENT OF A PARALLEL LABOUR MARKET FOR IMMIGRANTS: THE EXAMPLE OF THE CONSTRUCTION SECTOR

As far as Portugal is concerned, the branch of construction and public works represents the best example of an economic sector where clandestine and temporary work, largely provided by African male immigrants, supports not only the recent expansion of the sector, but especially the accumulation strategies of the different types of construction companies and entrepreneurs. In this branch, formal and informal economic strategies show high levels of interaction corresponding to a complex network of interests involving promoters, banks, construction firms and even workers.

Since the beginning of the 1990s, and particularly since 1992 in the Metropolitan Area of Lisbon (MAL), the construction sector has experienced an remarkable dynamic with an annual business increase close to 10 per cent (AECOPS – Portuguese Association of the Enterprises of Construction and Public Works). This process is the result of the simultaneous investment of private (banks, urban estate promoters, major Portuguese companies developing business in the trading area) and public agents; it includes several mega-construction projects (e.g. the new Tagus Bridge and the EXPO 98 precinct).

To face this growth in construction sector demand, enterprises have reinforced their subcontracting strategies, and the total number of enterprises settled in the MAL increased from 2,704 in 1986 to 4,867 in 1993, with an increased proportion of small units (between one and nine workers) from 66.5 per cent to 72.8 per cent, in the same period.[7] In the case of construction and public works, the practice of subcontracting is particularly adjusted, contributing to reduced risks and costs shared by promoters and construction firms. One the one hand, strong demand fluctuations lead construction companies to reduce their permanent workers and to reinforce the subcontracting strategies. On the other hand, the use of subcontractors is associated with a minimal responsibility chain for ensuring control over the working teams (Pinto and Queiroz 1996). It is important to stress that subcontractors are not always small firms responsible for the full execution of certain tasks in the construction or public works projects. Actually, several of the above-mentioned small units are ephemeral, sometimes constituted with the purpose of developing a single specific project and in other cases corresponding to individual entrepreneurs, frequently of African origin, acting exclusively as suppliers of labour (Salgueiro *et al.* 1997).

This process of fragmentation of the construction firms' fabric is associated with a natural increase in the number of workers involved in the branch. In fact, construction experienced one of the highest sectoral employment growth rates of MAL between 1986 and 1994 (23 per cent), surpassed only by wholesale trade and some branches of services to enterprises (Salgueiro *et al.* 1997).

More firms, more workers and increasing precariousness. First, it is important to say that construction is the activity branch with the highest number of short-term contracts and also of workers without contracts (Pinto and Queiroz 1996). According to the National Federation of the Trade Unions of Construction, Wood and Marble Stone of GCPW (General Confederation of Portuguese Workers), the problem of clandestine and precarious workers increased in the late 1980s due to the implementation of strategies aiming to reduce the costs and social responsibilities of construction firms and subcontractors. For instance, it is possible to identify in Table 4 the progressive growth in the number of workers with short term contracts. Also the workers in the situation of holding 'Green Receipts'[8] (false independents) show a continuous increase in the first half of the present decade.

Because the construction sector demands a very flexible labour force, not only because of the mobility of yards but especially due to the strong variations in the demand for new buildings and infrastructure, companies find several advantages in the implementation of the above-mentioned strategies.

If construction and public works correspond to an activity branch particularly adapted to subcontracting strategies and informal work, unskilled and low-skilled immigrants from developing countries frequently present a profile that facilitates their insertion in the clandestine labour market, as was stated above. Therefore, it is not

TABLE 4
EVOLUTION OF WORKERS IN THE CONSTRUCTION SECTOR IN PORTUGAL
1991–1994

	1991 Abs.	%	1992 Abs.	%	1994 Abs.	%
Legal workers	186,376	54.2	192,954	58.9	179,973	53.2
.with a short term contract	*127,194*	*68.2*	*137,815*	*71.4*	*130,173*	*72.3*
. with a permanent contract	*59,182*	*31.8*	*55,022*	*28.6*	*49,800*	*27.7*
Clandestine workers	81,824	23.8	57,146	17.4	62,527	19.4
Total of workers	268,200	78.0	250,100	76.3	245,500	72.6
Total of "Green receipt" workers ("independents")	75,615	22.0	77,663	23.7	92,600	27.4
GRAND TOTAL	343,815	100.0	327,763	100.0	338,100	100.0
ratio of clandestine/ legal workers	0.44	–	0.30	–	0.35	–

Sources: Annual Report of the Bank of Portugal; Employees tables of the Ministry of Employment; National Federation of the Trade Unions of Construction, Wood and Marble Stone

surprising that immigrant workers, especially from the PALOP, are a significant proportion of the labour force in construction in the Metropolitan Area of Lisbon.[9] An abundant labour supply as well as the lack of documents and limited knowledge of the Portuguese labour market pushes foreign workers into accepting more precarious and vulnerable working conditions. This problem, referred to one trade union official, had already been noted on previous occasions, e.g. a paper about the working conditions of immigrants in 1985 (França *et al.* 1992:80).

Despite the reduction in clandestine work in the early 1990s,[10] the number of workers in this situation is still relevant (its ratio to declared workers was one to three in 1994 – see Table 4). Certainly, the number of foreigners among clandestines is more relevant than the global percentage of foreign workers in the construction sector in Portugal. In the research conducted by Pires and Queiroz (1996), the estimate of the total percentage of undeclared workers in the sector in 1991 is placed at 45–50 per cent. Recent studies on active immigrants in the MAL point to a percentage of clandestine workers in the construction and public works branch of close to 60 per cent. In fact, one of the most common contractual procedures between African workers and subcontractors is the so-called 'oral agreement', which means that the worker is available to work for a certain boss, in certain places, while specific construction tasks are required. Once the task is finished, the worker must wait for a new contract from the subcontractor in order to be placed in a new construction yard. Within this logic, salary depends strictly on the number of hours worked (normally eight per day, not taking into consideration eventual extraordinary hours) and non-working periods (e.g. in between the participation in two different construction projects) are also non-payment periods.

In order to have a more comprehensive perspective of these questions, it is interesting to discuss briefly the role of the different agents involved in the network that supports clandestine work in construction. With the intention of reducing costs, the construction companies have progressively developed a system of contracts with subcontractors, who remain responsible both for finding the workers and for the direct working agreements with them. Because the rhythm of construction might be irregular, the labour needs experience short-term fluctuations and the subcontractors must be prepared to hire new workers within one or two weeks (sometimes, even in one or two days). Therefore, subcontractors, frequently of Cape Verdean or Guinean origin, establish direct or indirect (through *engajadores*) recruitment networks. Besides direct contacts with Africa, *engajadores* develop recruitment systems in the peripheral quarters where African population clusters as well as in some specific meeting points (located in the central areas of Lisbon) that act as 'work-exchange' centres.

This cascade-like recruitment system (construction companies – subcontractors – *engajadores* – workers) contributes to increasing the contract vulnerability of foreign labourers. On the one hand, the responsibilities become less clear in this web of agents. On the other, each of the agents tries to accumulate as much capital as possible and the illegal procedures multiply (absence of payment of social assistance, escape of fiscal obligations, development of forms of work without contract). Sometimes, the price accorded between construction companies and subcontractors for the working hour is not respected. There are examples of wages almost 60 per cent under the established agreement – a situation that means a clean profit of 40 per cent to the subcontractor (*Grande Reportagem*, January 1996:40).

Clandestine work in construction benefits in the first place enterprises and subcontractors. However, clandestine immigrant workers can also take some apparent advantage of this situation. First, if they are undocumented the signing of legal work contracts is not possible. Secondly, if they regard themselves as temporary migrants or want to accumulate money quickly, the absence of taxes or social security contributions enables a higher direct gain. Obviously, some lack of knowledge about the advantages of legal contracts brings about this attitude: benefits include the thirteenth month salary, holiday payment, limitations on salary abuse and dismissal and social security contributions (payment in case of accident and unemployment benefits). Finally, there is a mismatch between the working rules (e.g. to keep schedules, to maintain a regular production routine) in western society and the work perception of some Africans. According to the experts of some NGOs (e.g. Guinean Association or the Portuguese Council for Refugees), sub-contractors often complain about the absenteeism of the clandestine workers, this being one of the excuses for some cases of payment refusal.

Besides these agents who are directly involved in the recruitment process, state institutions and trade unions also play important indirect roles (Figure 2). The balance of gains/losses of the state institutions arising from clandestine work is probably positive in the short/medium term. The presence of foreign work reduces potential tension in a sector with some internal labour shortage and contributes to keeping labour costs low. Therefore, government can spare some money in the several public works that have been executed in last years. However, Finance and especially Social Security may face important negative long run effects

FIGURE 2
WEB OF RELATIONS INVOLVED IN THE INFORMAL CONSTRUCTION LABOUR MARKET IN PORTUGAL

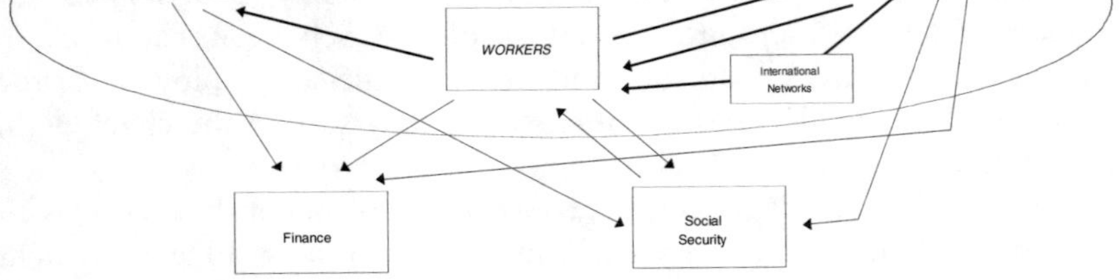

arising from the generalized practice of clandestine work. In situations of unemployment increase or at the time of paying retirement pensions to former workers the balance between state gains (during the working life of the workers) and state expenditures will be negatively affected by the years of clandestine work, when the workers were not inside the formal social security system.

Trade unions try to develop initiatives with the goal of improving contractual relations and working conditions of the unskilled foreign workers in construction. Nevertheless, their activity faces some constraints. On the one hand, the solution to the question of subcontractors seems to be a bit controversial for trade unions. On the other hand, if they complain to the work inspectorate about the use of clandestine workers in some yards, these people can be confronted with serious problems, especially if they are undocumented foreigners. Finally, unions in this sector have been trying to develop a set of positive initiatives (co-operation in the extraordinary regularization process, direct contact with firms in cases of payment refusal or abuse of workers, preparation and spreading of documents concerning the rights of foreigners) which try to contribute to the development of an advantageous process of labour market integration of the unskilled African workers.

SOME BRIEF CONCLUSIONS

Like other intermediate countries, Portugal presents a polarized pattern of a foreign active population dominated by highly skilled European professionals and unskilled African workers – the latter mainly from the former Portuguese ex-colonies in Africa. The upkeep of a secondary labour market with a continuous supply of unskilled labour depends on the presence of foreign workers, mainly in the less prestigious sectors which require flexible labour, such as construction or industrial and domestic cleaning. The development of situations of clandestine work involving undocumented migrants is an extra contribution to segment and weaken the position of workers in the vulnerable secondary labour market. Thus, and despite the effort of the Schengen countries in strengthening border controls and fighting illegal employment, the pressure of labour demand in some sectors may sustain the channels of clandestine imported workers from non-EU countries.

As far as Portugal is concerned, construction is one of the sectors with highest levels of clandestine work and precariousness in employment relations. Supported by strong demand, construction firms have developed a complex subcontracting network which includes several layers before reaching the workers. High labour needs justify the recruitment of African workers for the fulfilment of unskilled tasks, not only because construction is a socially devalued sector where unskilled functions are over-represented (Salgueiro 1997), but also because of internal labour shortages in this branch as a result of internationalization. In fact, whereas the national construction market recruits African workers, Portuguese firms place Portuguese construction workers in several German yards, but also in France, Spain or Saudi Arabia. The relationship between immigration and emigration schemes in the construction sector certainly deserves more research.

However, besides construction, male clandestine foreigners can also be found in restaurants, shops, street markets (pedlars) and women especially in industrial and domestic cleaning. The development of the service economy will certainly lead to a development of clandestine (or semi-legal) activities in the tertiary sector. Moreover, the probable end of the golden age of the construction and public sectors in Portugal will lead to an increase in employment problems for the African communities. New public works projects (e.g. the construction of a new international airport) and alternatives in commerce may mitigate the expected problems, but are solutions with a limited scope.

Finally, it is important to stress that the development of better labour market integration of the foreign unskilled workers is a hard and complex task. Despite the positive initiatives[11] of the Socialist Government elected at the end of 1995, the effects are still small. For instance, to fight the vulnerability generated by clandestine occupation in construction it is essential to improve the control systems over both large and small construction firms. Therefore, a stronger role for the labour inspectorate and the enactment of penalties for subcontractors who exploit foreign workers is clearly necessary.

Other initiatives include the development of institutional support for labour market incorporation, including language teaching (even for those who came from the former Portuguese colonies) and training courses as well as the development of initiatives aiming to inform immigrants of their rights. The success of these processes depends, amongst other things, on the development of outreach practices not only by NGOs, but also by government and local authorities. Changing people's practices requires a pro-active institutional attitude, that, in the present case, means contacting the immigrants in their places of work and residence.

The relative success of the 1996 Extraordinary Regularization Process, where outreach methods were implemented, shows the importance of this argument.

NOTES

1. PALOP stands for African Country of Portuguese Official Language.
2. This period corresponds to the first phase of the contemporary Portuguese immigratory cycle. The period of the late 1960s and early 1970s should be assumed like a pre-cycle moment, cut by the 1974/75 events.
3. As shown by Ferrão and Fonseca (1989: 256) and Duarte (1994), the growth rate of foreign investment in this period reached very high levels.
4. These funds have become very significant after formal entry into the EEC in 1986.
5. Despite this evidence, the complete understanding of this third stage still needs confirmation. In fact, the growth in the number of foreigners registered after 1994 is largely caused by the inclusion of the results of the 1992 Regularization Process in the SEF data. Therefore, the acceleration in the growth rhythm of the foreigners in 1994 and 1995 is not only related to new arrivals but also with the inclusion of the former undocumented immigrants. This situation is more relevant among the African nationals, and particularly among those coming from the PALOP, because these were the groups who presented more regularization demands.
6. This regularization process took place between June and December 1996 and was directed at all non-EU foreigners irregularly settled in Portugal who arrived in the country before June 1995, in the case of people coming from non-lusophone countries, and before December 1995, for those who were nationals of Portuguese-speaking nations.
7. Data of the Personnel Tables of the Ministry of Labour and Social Solidarity.
8. This situation corresponds to the workers who are classified as independents, although they and the dependent workers share the same labour rules (working hours, subordination to direct and permanent instructions of a master, etc.).
9. According to the trade union cited, the number of African workers in the construction sector, especially from the former Portuguese colonies, is close to 50 per cent in the Lisbon Metropolitan Area. As a curiosity, it is interesting to remark that five of the 20 members of the board of directors of the Lisbon section of this trade union are Africans; also important is the number of Cape Verdean activists in several companies and construction yards.
10. Both campaigns of Trade Unions and the replacement of clandestine situations by other kinds of semi-legal procedures like the 'green receipts' have contributed to this situation. However, the rush to finish several projects in the course of 1997 and 1998 has probably led to a new increase in the number of illegal situations. Unfortunately, these data are not yet available.
11. The Second Extraordinary Regularization, the creation of a special Government body to deal with the minorities problems and the pedagogical work agreements with the construction firms of EXPO correspond to a few examples of this'new attitude'.

REFERENCES

Baganha, M.I. (1997): 'Immigrant Insertion in the Informal Economy – The Portuguese Case'. CES-University of Coimbra (project report, unpublished).

Duarte, G. (1994): 'Investimento Estrangeiro Imobiliário no Área Metropolitana de

Lisboa'. MA thesis, Dept.Geography, Faculdade de Letras da Universidade de Lisboa (unpublished).

Esteves, M.C. (org.) *et al.* (1991): *Portugal, País de Imigração,* Lisbon: Instituto de Estudos para o Desenvolvimento (I.E.D.).

Fonseca, L.; Ferrão, J. (1989): 'Investimento estrangeiro e desenvolvimento regional: o caso do investimento espanhol em Portugal', *Finisterra,* 24(48), Centro de Estudos Geográficos, pp.251–78.

França, L. (coord.) *et al.* (1992): *A Comunidade Cabo Verdiana em Portugal*. I.E.D., Lisbon: Cadernos 23.

Gambier, D.; Verniéres, M.(1982): *Le Marché du Travail*, Paris: Economica, Paris.

Grande Reportagem, 58, January 1996, Lisbon.

Gozálvez Pérez, V. (1996): 'L´immigration étrangère en Espagne (1985–1994)'. *Revue Européenne des Migrations Internationales*, 12 /1, Université de Poitiers – Migrinter – C.N.R.S., pp.11–38.

Jackson, J.A.(1991): *Migrações*, London: Escher.

Mallet, L. (1980): *Le Marché Local du Travail*, Paris: Editions du C.N.R.S.

Malheiros, J.M. (1996): *Imigrantes na Região de Lisboa: os anos da mudança. Imigração e processo de integração das comunidades de origem Indiana,* Lisbon: Colibri.

Malheiros, J.M. (1995): 'Refugees in Portugal and Spain: a Preliminary Approach on Reception Policies and Integration prospects', in DONNE, M., *Avenues to Integration – Refugees in Contemporary Europe*, Ipermedium/Univ. of Rome, pp.145–77.

Peixoto, J. (1994): 'As migrações de profissionais altamente qualificados no espaço europeu: do "brain drain" ao "skill exchange"', *SOCIUS Working Papers*, 1/94, Lisbon: ISEG.

Peixoto, J. (1998): *'As Migrações dos Quadros Altamente Qualificados: Mobilidade e Transferências Intra-Empresariais em Portugal e no Espaço Internacional*'. Dissertação de Doutoramento apresentada no Instituto Superior de Economia e Gestão da Universidade Técnica de Lisboa (unpublished).

Pires, R.P. (1993): 'Immigration in Portugal. A Typology Essay' in TRINDADE, M.B.Rocha *Recent Migration Trends in Europe*, Lisbon: Universidade Aberta/I.E.D, pp.179–95.

Pinto, J.M.; Queiroz, M.C. (1996): 'Mobilidade da Mão-de-Obra na Construção Civil', *Sociologia, Problemas e Práticas*, 19, Lisbon: ISCTE.

Pohjola, A. (1991): 'Social Networks: Help or Hindrance to the Migrant?', *International Migration*, 34/3, pp.435–44.

Salgueiro *et al.* (1997): 'Internacionalização, Reestruturação Económica e Geração de Novas Marginalidades na Região de Lisboa'. Departamento de Geografia, Universidade de Lisboa (project report, unpublished).

Sassen, S. (1991): *The Global City: New York, London, Tokyo*. Princeton, N.J.: Princeton University Press.

Greece: The Contours of a Fragmented Policy Response

MARTIN BALDWIN-EDWARDS and
ROSSETOS FAKIOLAS

In this article, we outline the main trends of immigration into Greece, the policy responses taken in various relevant areas, and give a preliminary analysis of data from the 1998 regularization programme. These data are the first in Greece to give some real indication of the characteristics of the massive number of illegal immigrants. Finally, we propose an analytic framework which attempts to make some sense of the inchoate policies and policy outcomes in this area.

TRENDS IN IMMIGRATION

Despite problems with the quality or even existence of migration data in Greece, some clear trends can be discerned. Return migration of Greeks was prevalent in the post-junta years (the late 1970s) and subsequently declined; by the 1990s, return migration and emigration of Greeks equalized equal at around 3–5,000 per annum (Salt *et al.* 1994:193). Yet another category of 'ethnic Greeks' emerged in the late 1980s as significant: Pontian Greeks from the USSR began to arrive in large numbers in 1989, peaking at 14,000 in 1990–91.

Throughout the post-war period there had been typically 24–34,000 foreign nationals (including ethnic Greeks and EC nationals) registered in Greece, representing some 0.7 per cent of the labour force. By 1990 this had increased to around 170,000 immigrants (Fakiolas and King 1996:176); yet by 1996 there were merely 80,000 legally present foreigners in Greece, with about 30,000 work permits recorded (OECD 1997). To some extent, this decline in numbers can be explained by statistical confusion or even obfuscation; however, as we shall see, another explanation lies in the impact of immigration legislation passed in 1991.

The figures for the 1991 Census – the last one held – reveal a total foreign population of 167,000 of which 32,000 were EU nationals. Table 1 gives a crude breakdown of the data. Of course, the Census is unlikely to yield information about illegal aliens, and may well understate the size of the registered foreign population. The data show a significant number of recorded Albanians, Former USSR nationals and Turks; it has been suggested that the vast majority of these are ethnic Greeks, who have failed to change their nationality (Fakiolas 1995). In essence, the Census captures a picture of legally secure immigrants, whose numbers are dominated by ethnic Greeks, EU nationals, North Americans and Australians.

TABLE 1

FOREIGNERS IN GREECE, 1991 CENSUS (000S)

Nationals of:			
	UK	11.0	
	Germany	8.5	
	Italy	4.2	
	France	3.4	
	EC total		**32.6**
	Cyprus	14.7	
	Yugoslavia	1.3	
	Austria	1.1	
	Sweden	1.1	
	Other Europe		**20.0**
	Albania	20.6	
	USSR	12.9	
	Poland	9.6	
	Former Socialist bloc		**48.5**
	Turkey	11.1	
	Philippines	3.6	
	Iraq	2.1	
	Syria	2.1	
	Pakistan	1.9	
	Lebanon	1.9	
	India	1.7	
	Asia		**28.8**
	USA	13.9	
	Canada	4.7	
	S. America	2.1	
	America		**20.9**
	Egypt	4.0	
	Nigeria	0.5	
	Morocco	0.3	
	Zaire	0.2	
	Africa		**8.7**
	Australia	6.5	
	TOTAL		**167.3**

The decline in legal immigration is mirrored by the trend in illegal immigration over the 1990s. In 1980, the estimates of illegal migrants ranged from 15,000 (Ministry of Public Order) to 40,000 (ILO, cited in Petrinioti 1992:15). By 1988, the range was 70,000 to 105,000 (cited in Baldwin-Edwards 1991:201) and for 1991, Petrinioti suggests 180,000 (Petrinioti 1993:18). The limits of credulity were apparently reached in 1992 with an estimate of 400,000 (CEC 1993:16), yet by 1994 the government estimates were as high as 500-600,000. The magnitude of the stock of illegal immigrants appeared to stabilize at around that level, which nevertheless represents some 12 per cent of the labour force (OECD 1998:115).

Although by the late 1980s Greece had received a large number of Polish refugees and illegal immigrants (Romaniszyn 1996), the main cause of mass illegal immigration seems to have arisen from the collapse of communism in Eastern Europe. In particular, Albania has seen a massive exodus of its population to Greece. Despite many Albanians having claim to Greek ethnicity, and therefore the right to enter, the Greek government has discouraged such movement (Salt *et al.* 1994:193). The major nationalities illegally present in Greece are primarily Albanian, followed by Poles, East Europeans and Filipinos (Papantoniou *et al.* 1996). Recent data from the legalization programme partially confirm this, although with some reservations.

POLICY RESPONSES

The response of the Greek state to the new immigratory pressures has been complex and contradictory. The official line has been – although it is unclear that it remains so – that 'Greece is not a country of immigration' (Glytsos 1995:168).

One set of policy initiatives lies in the immigration law passed by the Greek Parliament in October 1991. Law 1975/1991 replaced Law 4310/1929 which had been in effect for more than 60 years. Subsequently it has been claimed by the Minister for the Interior in 1992 that the Law has serious shortcomings and was adopted in a 'panic situation' in response to the 'Albanian crisis' (CEC 1993:40). The passage of the bill was difficult and opposition parties condemned it for xenophobia and a policing philosophy, as well as taking no account of immigrants already present in the country.

The new Law replaced the aliens law of 1929 and sets out much more detailed requirements. It does not apply to Greek nationals, stateless persons and those under the jurisdiction of EU legislation. (Article 17 allows for a ministerial decision to construct a special status for ethnic Greeks, but this has not been done.) The police are empowered to check those entering or leaving the country for appropriate travel documents; strict entry requirements are laid down; illegal aliens can be expelled without trial; and a special police force is set up.

The second section of the Law deals with legal stay of aliens, family reunification and work permits. Residence permits are granted for employment with pre-entry authorization; they are employer specific and valid for one year, renewable up to five years. After five years, a two-year permit can be given by joint decision of the Ministries of Public Order and of Labour. After 15 years' residence (excluding years of study) and ten years' social insurance contributions, a permit of indefinite duration can be granted. Family reunification is covered for the first time in Greek law. Aliens holding a two-year residence permit can request similar residence permits for their immediate family (defined as spouse, parents and unmarried children aged under 18).

The arrangements for work permits continue a practice that had been adopted previously: this required employers to obtain permission from the local manpower office before the foreigner had entered Greece. It would not be given if the vacancy could be filled by the local labour force, and moreover was specific for employer, employee and a limited period of time. Not only does the new Law continue this arrangement (other than to include EU nationals, ethnic Greeks and refugees), but it imposes a quota for salaried employment – the figure to be determined by three ministries.

Other provisions in the Law relate to public policy limitations, 'administrative deportations' on the grounds of public policy, and obligations of individuals. These include aliens' obligations to report a change of address or status, and Greeks' obligations to report arrival and departure dates of aliens. Fines and prison terms are available as penalties for those who provide false documents, transport, employment or in any way facilitate the entry and stay of illegal aliens. Article 11 provides for a list of undesirable aliens, to be excluded from Greek territory. An Interministerial Decree of 1992 elaborates the mechanisms by which this can happen: by a court ruling of expulsion, and by administrative expulsion determined by the Ministry of Public Order – the latter on the grounds of national security, public order or health. There is a clear provision for such information to be communicated to other EU states, in accordance with the Dublin and Schengen Treaties.

The Law also regulates, in Articles 24 and 25, the legal status of refugees. A presidential decree was issued in 1993, with detailed procedures for the determination of refugee status (Sitaropoulos 1994). The decree implements refugee determination procedures identical in form to those in the rest of Europe – rejection on the grounds of passing through a safe third country, of manifestly unfounded applications, and of not filing the application immediately on arrival in Greece. In 1996 a new law was passed to extend health care and temporary employment rights to asylum seekers and recognized refugees. It also contained measures for family reunion of recognized refugees, fast-track asylum application procedures and temporary protection status (OECD 1998:116). Another presidential decree, which has been under preparation for some time, is expected to be issued in 1999.

Work and Residence Permit Arrangements

Both residence and work permits are required for legal work in Greece, although residence is permitted without the right to work. Residence permits are issued to foreign passport holders by the Ministry of Public Order, regulated by the 1991 Law. Their duration ranges from a few days to five years or more (see the explanation above).

Table 2 shows the trend in granting residence permits – essentially increasingly restrictive from the mid-1980s, most particularly in the granting of new permits. More detailed analysis (not shown here) reveals that even within the restrictive trend there is a small increase in the number of Russians – presumably ethnic Greeks from Pontos – from 8,700 in 1989 to twice that figure for 1991–95. Similarly an increase in permits for Albanians is noted – presumably also ethnic Greeks. The most dramatic decline is in the number of permits for Poles, from 11,700 in 1989 to 1,400 in 1993. However, these figures are potentially highly misleading as they are statistics relating to the permits themselves rather than to individuals. Their highly variable duration prevents us from drawing any solid conclusions.

Work permits are generally employer and job specific, of a year's duration, and must be obtained before arrival in Greece. If the employment ceases, the alien must leave the country. The legal demands on an employer of non-EU labour are onerous, and include a sizeable deposit, proof of a minimum annual income of about $17,000, proof of social insurance contributions for renewal of contracts, and employment of five Greeks for engagement of a foreigner and of another ten for each additional alien.

TABLE 2

RESIDENCE PERMITS ISSUED, RENEWED AND TOTAL VALID (000S)

YEAR	Issued	Renewed	Total Valid
1988	n.d.	n.d.	110.4
1989	n.d.	n.d.	100.3
1990	25.5	31.6	87.9
1991	22.5	31.6	86.3
1992	18.9	30.7	89.3
1993	16.5	29.8	90.6
1994	17.8	27.6	75.1
1995	n.d.	n.d.	78.9
1996	n.d	n.d.	79.2

Sources: cols. 1 and 2: Papantoniou *et al.* (1996); col. 3: OECD (1997)

Looking at the granting of work permits over the period 1980–96, a pattern of consistent restriction emerges. Despite massive illegal immigration, and illegal employment for such immigrants, there has been little change in the number of work permits issued – around 26,000 to 30,000 a year, with seasonal variations (OECD 1997, 1998). Table 3 gives summary data for recent years; the decline in EU numbers is presumably through the granting of 5-year permits, as required by EU law. Thus there has been a small increase in the number granted to non-EU nationals in recent years.

TABLE 3

FOREIGNERS EMPLOYED WITH WORK PERMITS 1991–1997 (000S)

Year	Total	Males	Females	EU countries	Ethnic Greeks
1990	27.0	17.4	9.6	10.3	4.8
1991	28.4	16.6	11.8	14.4	3.2
1992	33.9	18.6	15.4	20.0	3.9
1993	30.0	16.1	13.8	19.6	3.0
1994	28.7	17.0	11.7	13.6	3.2
1995	27.4	16.8	10.1	11.5	3.5
1996	25.0	15.2	9.8	9.4	3.7

Source: Ministry of Labour and Social Security

Note: The data above do not include about 5,000 recognized refugees and foreigners employed in the Greek merchant fleet (about 13,000).

The 1998 Regularization

After protracted consideration in drafting two Presidential decrees on the legalization of illegal immigrants, which had been criticized for lack of dialogue with immigrant associations in Greece, the process took a turn for the worse when the July 1997 cabinet meeting to approve the decrees decided at the very last minute to exclude nationals of Albania and other countries bordering Greece. This decision was subsequently rescinded by the Prime Minister after uproar from the General Confederation of Greek Workers – Greece's largest trade union – and other influential pressure groups.

The two Presidential decrees of 29 November 1997 establish a two-stage process: a 'white card' or permit of temporary stay, which itself is a prerequisite for applying for the 'green card', or permit of limited duration of stay. For the white card, although many bureaucratic requirements were made (see Baldwin-Edwards 1998), employment status was confined to evidence of application for a social security contributions (IKA) booklet. However, the card was intended to last only 6 months, expiring on 31 May 1998. The Green Card can be given in two forms: Type A, lasting 1–3 years; and Type B, lasting 5 years. The basic requirement is proof of employment for 40 days over the period 1 January to 31 July 1998, with consideration given to duration of employment, length of residence in Greece and profession *inter alia*. Type B requires proof of five years' residence in Greece and an annual income in excess of 800,000 drachmas ($2,500).

Both White and Green Cards give equal rights to nationals in wages, working conditions and appeal to authorities; the Green Card gives the right to leave and re-enter for a period of two months, the Type B Green Card grants the right to family reunion of dependants.

The procedures surrounding the application process have been severely hindered by bureaucratic problems – primarily inefficiency and lack of communication between government agencies. Thus the deadline for applying for the Green Card has been moved forward four times already (July, October, December 1998, and April 1999). 373,000 applications for the White Card had been received by June 1998 and by November, just over 100,000 applications for the Green Card (*Athens News*, 22 Nov. 1998). By December 1998, only 38,000 White Cards had been awarded, and 2,700 Green Cards (OAED data).

The award of Green Cards is determined by a committee consisting of a magistrate, representatives from OAED, the Ministry of Labour, the Police Aliens Bureau, and the General Confederation of Greek Workers.

At the last report, the rate of examination of applications was only 250 per month by five committees in Athens (*Athens News*, 22 Nov. 1998). Examination of applications requires a Ministry of Justice criminal record certification, which the ministry takes 18 months to provide. Many immigrants cannot have their application considered before 2000, as a consequence. Another serious problem is the refusal of IKA, the social security agency, to issue booklets to immigrants for the payment of their social security contributions.

Analysis of Data from White Card Applications

In the seven months after the end of the registration period in May 1998 and up to the end of that year, OAED concluded four analyses of the relevant data, with progressively larger samples of 10,000, 26,396, 40,820 and 50,961 applicants. The data presented below come from the largest sample of the last analysis concluded on 2 October 1998. Apparently, only marginal differences appear from one analysis to another.

Country of origin. Table 4 gives a breakdown by nationality and the gender distribution for each nationality. As expected, the great majority of applicants are Albanian. The biggest surprise is the very low number of Poles: previous estimates of illegal immigrant stocks (see Papantoniou *et al.* 1996) had put them as the second largest national grouping, with a level about one-third that of the Albanians. Thus they are vastly under-represented in the regularization programme, and presumably will remain in Greece illegally – even if only for short periods. The precise reasons for the low application rate are a matter for conjecture at this time. The other main nationalities are Egyptian, Bulgarian and Pakistani. The number of Filipinos applying is also low: residence permit data show their official numbers to have declined from just under 5,000 in 1991 to under 2,000 in 1996. There has been no research suggesting actual decline in numbers, therefore presumably they too will remain illegally.

Two explanations may suffice for the very high application rate of Albanians versus the very low rate for Poles and Filipinos. First, the Albanians have been linked with criminal activity (in public perception at least) and have many difficulties with the police. Neither the Polish nor the Filipinos, nationalities which have been long resident in Greece without drawing undue attention to themselves, have such problems. Secondly, it may be that their employment has illegality as its defining condition: that is, as *legal* immigrants they are too expensive. There is

TABLE 4

STRUCTURE OF APPLICANTS FOR REGULARIZATION BY COUNTRY OF ORIGIN AND GENDER (PERCENTAGES)

Country of origin	M + F	% male
Albania	52.5	74.4
Egypt	6.2	95.5
Bulgaria	5.9	39.1
Pakistan	5.9	99.6
Rumania	4.3	68.4
Poland	3.1	60.5
Bangladesh	2.7	99.3
India	2.4	98.1
Ukraine	2.3	20.7
Syria	2.3	95.7
Philippines	2.1	18.5
Nigeria	1.2	79.0
Others	9.1	51.4

Source: OAED, National Employment Observatory. Report of 2/9/1998

Notes: a) 139 applications did not have country of origin
b) The total number of applications for regularization amounted to 373,000
c) 'Others' consist of applicants from about 90 different countries with under 1% of the total each.

limited evidence to suggest that employers are refusing to pay social security contributions – one of the chief requirements for the Green Card (*Athens News*, 22 Nov. 1998). Although the White Card did not require this, Poles and Filipina may have ascertained such reluctance at the start of the regularization. For Albanians, the immediate benefits of legality may have outweighed the potential costs.

Gender. Two nationalities stand out as having very high female proportions – Philippine (81.5 per cent) and Ukrainian (79.3 per cent). 60 per cent of Bulgarian applicants are female, also. From empirical research, we know that Filipinos and Bulgarians are extensively involved in housekeeping; the Ukrainians, quite large in number (around 8,000) are recent arrivals. Their employment may be in the services sector (which is virtually unresearched) and also in prostitution – which appears to exploit East Europeans extensively. Certain nationalities are almost exclusively male – Egyptian, Pakistani, Bangladeshi, Indian and Syrian. Polish and Bulgarian show the most balanced gender distribution – perhaps because of their proximity and the ease of family migration.

Regional analysis by gender shows a M/F ration of 2.3:1 for the greater Athens area; in the rest of Attica, the agricultural areas, the ratio is about 4.5:1. This confirms the view of little work in agriculture for women, whereas urban areas have high demand for female housekeeping and other service sector jobs. The most extreme contrast is between Kavala, northern Greece with a ratio of 5:1, and the Dodecanese islands with a ratio of 1.5:1, the latter reflecting the ample employment available in catering and housekeeping for affluent Greek families.

Age structure. The data show that the overwhelming majority of applicants are young: 88 per cent are between 15 and 44 years old. Nearly 100 per cent of applicants are of working age. In the older age cohort of 45–64, women predominate with a M/F ration of 1:2. 14 per cent of female applicants are in this age bracket, presumably reflecting the lesser physical demands of cleaning and housekeeping jobs, compared with male employment in construction and agriculture.

Marital status. Table 5 shows applicants by marital status and gender. A surprisingly large proportion are married, although the data do not show whether this is caused by the large Albanian majority or not. 45 per cent of married applicants declare two or more dependent family members, which is large than usual in contemporary Europe.

TABLE 5

APPLICANTS FOR REGULARIZATION BY MARITAL STATUS AND GENDER

Marital Status	%	% of males	% of females
Married	54	51	60
Single	40	45	28
Divorced	3	1	8
Not declared	2	3	2
Widows (ers)	1	0	3

Source: OAED; National Employment Observatory

Formal education and professional qualifications. Data are not available for education level by nationality. Table 6 gives a crude picture. Overall, 68 per cent have secondary or tertiary education, and a high rate of women with tertiary education (17 per cent). The illiteracy rate is quite low, given the large number of Albanians – although accuracy of data in this respect may not be high.

TABLE 6

STRUCTURE OF APPLICANTS BY LEVEL OF EDUCATION (PERCENTAGES)

Educational Level	Total	Male	Female
Illiterate	4.0	3.4	1.9
Primary educn.	26.3	28.4	20.8
Secondary	55.5	54.7	57.7
Tertiary	12.3	10.6	16.7
Did not declare	3.0	3.0	3.0

Source: OAED; National Employment Observatory

As far as professional qualifications are concerned, 38 per cent did not answer. This is a problematically large omission. 23 per cent declared they were unskilled manual workers, 19 per cent qualified technicians, 7 per cent street hawkers, 3 per cent 'scientific' or fine arts, and 2.8 per cent agriculture and animal husbandry.

Policies to Combat Illegal Migration

The most notable responses to illegal migration have been increased policing of border areas and deportations. In February 1992, it was determined that controls along the borders with Albania, Yugoslavia and Turkey should be strengthened with the aid of seven mobile patrols (CEC 1993: 39). In February 1994 the Minister of Public Order announced a special unit of 400, with helicopter support, to patrol difficult border areas – particularly with Albania (*Kathemerini* 22/2/94 p 5).

Deportations in the period 1987-1991 amounted to 12,291 with the greatest number being Poles, Yugoslavs, Egyptians, Pakistanis and Syrians, in order of magnitude (Petrinioti 1992:16). Deportations, i.e. removal from Greek territory after due legal process, have increased slightly in the 1990s. However, it is 'expulsions', first authorized in the 1991 Law which have been extensively utilized – most notably for Albanians but also for some other nationalities such as Iraqi. Table 7 shows the data for significant nationalities. The figures have remained fairly constant over this period, but whether this reflects a steady stream of migrating Albanians or a limited capacity to intercept is largely a matter for conjecture.

Trafficking of Migrants and Prostitution

Over the past three years, Greece has been a major hub for trafficking in migrants. In 1996 there were more than 2,500 arrests of traffickers in

TABLE 7

EXPULSIONS FROM GREECE 1991–95, SIGNIFICANT NATIONALITIES (000S)

Nationals of:	1991	1992	1993	1994	1995
Albania	84.3	277.0	221.0	216.5	241.2
Bulgaria	0.0	0.4	1.0	0.8	1.4
Iraq	0.2	0.3	11.5	1.8	3.9
Pakistan	0.0	0.3	1.5	1.6	1.8
Romania	0.5	2.2	2.2	2.0	0.4
Turkey	0.0	0.1	0.4	0.6	2.3
Bangladesh	0.0	0.0	0.0	0.4	0.5
GRAND TOTAL	86.0	282.0	239.0	225.0	250.4

Source: Baldwin-Edwards (1998)

Greece, which may be only a small proportion of the trafficking networks (*Athens News*, 4 Feb. 1997). The IOM considers Greece to be an important transit country for trafficking of women from the CIS, Asia, Caribbean and Dominican Republic. Greece is also seen as a gateway for drug smuggling into Europe, with particular problems of remote coastlines, numerous islands and police corruption, according to a US State Department Report (*Athens News*, 1 Mar. 1998).

Despite a measure of success in arresting and clamping down on migrant and drug traffickers, it has emerged in the last six months that the Greek police and others have been actively involved in the rackets. In August 1998, three police officers were arrested in Thessaloniki for protecting prostitution rings (*Athens News*, 23 Oct. 1998); nine policemen were arraigned in October in Pyrgos for involvement in the procurement of Romanian prostitutes, three of whom were minors. After 'nearly daily reports of police corruption, from protection of prostitution rackets to drug trafficking' (*Athens News*, 31 Oct. 1998), the Minister of Public Order was dismissed on 29 October 1998. On 3 November, 11 police officers were charged on counts ranging from extortion to breach of duty: among them were former Athens police chief Vassilopoulos, his deputy Papadakis, superintendent Yiannes and Florendis, a senior advisor to the sacked Minister (*Athens News*, 5 Nov. 1998). In one officer's bank account $2.7m was discovered, it was reported.

According to one source, the principal reason for the unravelling of police corruption is that of political rivalries. The key informant in the revelations had fallen out with the ministry leadership and their political patrons (*Athens News*, 8 Nov. 1998). One day after a 'complete purge' of the vice squad, two prostitution rings (specializing in women from former Soviet republics) were broken with 33 arrests in 13 Athens brothels (*Athens News*, 14 Nov. 1998). On 20 November, charges were issued for procuring and forcing into prostitution against a police constable, who had imprisoned two prostitutes in his flat, and a retired police officer. The two men were allegedly involved in a 'particularly unsavoury' prostitution ring run by a popular singer: despite neighbours' repeated requests to the police, no action had ever been taken. Also on 20 November a retired police brigadier-general was arrested for running a racket selling forged documents to illegal migrants for acquiring residence permits. The Athens public prosecutor has apparently found, in the Ministry of Public Order's records, substantial evidence of fake residence and work permits obtained through police complicity with Greek and Albanian gangs engaged in organizing forced prostitution rackets (*Athens News*, 21 Nov. 1998).

Asylum-seekers

There has been a consistent problem with the Greek state and asylum seekers (see Black 1992; Stavropoulou 1994). Until the 1990s, the state simply tolerated applicant refugees, leaving much of the process to the UNHCR. Thus, most ended up as illegal immigrants, who have been obliged to apply under the regularization procedure in order to remain legally. A refugee camp at Lavrion houses 300 people, but has never been sufficient. In Koumoundourou Square in Athens squat some 1,000 Kurds, mainly from Iraq. They live in tents, have no sanitary facilities, and are dependent on charity for food and clothing. According to the UNHCR, procedures are not being followed by the Greek state: applicants have been given interview dates in the next century and despair. They have been refused temporary residence permits, and the right to work (*Athens News*, 23 Oct. 1998). At another unofficial 'camp' – Palia Pendeli – 250 Kurds are housed by *Médecins sans Frontières*. The housing consists of tents, although there are washing and cooking facilities. The camp is allowed to submit just one asylum application per week (*Athens News*, 22 Nov. 1998). When applications are allowed to be processed, the official recognition rate for Kurds is 0.5 per cent, compared with a general rate of 4 per cent (*Athens News*, 23 Oct. 1998).

Greece has now been condemned by Amnesty International, Helsinki Watch and the Greek Minority Rights Group for its treatment of refugees. Amnesty International is demanding the publication of the long-awaited presidential decree, the cessation of deportations without due process and proper training of the police in asylum matters. Three violations of the human rights of Kurdish refugees are cited: the refusal on 22 September 1998, by police on Crete, to accept 167 applications for asylum assisted by Amnesty International and UNHCR; a similar incident with 275 Kurds in another part of Crete in October 1998; and the deportation of Kurds without due process from Kavala to Turkey as 'illegal immigrants' (*Athens News*, 4 Nov. 1998). The attempted deportation of a Syrian refugee, convicted and imprisoned in Greece for drug trafficking, back to a death sentence in Syria has led to denial that he was a refugee. Dokuz arrived in Greece in 1989 and was assessed by the UNHCR as a refugee, but never accepted by the Greek state as such. Another case of 58 Iraqi Kurds on the island of Kos is cited, where they were initially given asylum cards which were then withdrawn and the holders jailed (*Athens News*, 14 Nov., 10 Dec. 1998).

TOWARDS AN ANALYTIC FRAMEWORK

At first glance, the Greek pattern of policy response looks incoherent. We suggest here that, in the political and policy arena, three broad patterns of behaviour can be identified. These we label 'institutional/bureaucratic', 'external relations', and 'modernizing/technocratic'. These different orientations can be in opposition or in synchrony; individual actors or groups of actors can span more than one pattern of behaviour. Nevertheless, we maintain that the analytic framework has considerable utility.

Institutional/Bureaucratic

Essentially, the argument here is that traditional structures and patterns of behaviour shape, if not determine, policy and outcomes. Civil servants in Greece receive little pre-service or in-service training, lack expertise in modern methods of management and do not keep up with technological developments (Sotiropoulos 1995). The Greek police represent an even more extreme version of this characterization. The weak self-regulation of the Ministry of Public Order, along with apparently none at all in the police forces, has permitted the institutionalization of a new form of corruption – trafficking in migrants and drugs, and related prostitution. Whereas many of the traditional forms of clientelism and corruption were relatively benign, the new phenomenon of mass immigration has presented new opportunities for corruption. The low salaries of the police, poor training and low public esteem have aided that transition.

Generally, the bias of legal training of civil servants presents problems of policy management. Rather than focusing on outcomes, policy-makers pay undue attention to legalistic formulations. In the case of the Regularization programme, for instance, it was thought quite sufficient to translate the legal texts of earlier Spanish, Portuguese and Italian programmes in order to learn from those countries' experiences. The programme shows quite clearly the results of such a strategy.

Asylum-seekers have felt the full brunt of the ineffectual Greek state. Inadequate training and communication between state agencies essentially denies the right to apply for asylum. Indeed, most police appear to be unaware of anything other than illegal immigration – into which category asylum seekers are placed.

In all three of these areas, state capacity reveals itself to be inadequate to the demands of a changing world environment: institutionalized patterns of behaviour have not encouraged rational solutions to new problems.

External Relations

This orientation has two modes: relations with lesser (primarily Balkan) powers, and EU relations. In the first case, we can note the consistent pattern of mass expulsion of Albanians from Greek territory not through their illegal presence *per se*, but as reprisal against Albanian policy. In the summer of 1993, some 20,000 Albanians were expelled following the expulsion of a Greek priest from southern Albania; in 1994, the furore over the trial of five Greek minority activists in Tirana resulted in the expulsion of more than 100,000 Albanians from Greece. In 1996, more than 7,000 Albanians were expelled from Greece: this time the motivation was less clear. One commentator even suggests intra-state intrigue to undermine the Foreign Minister's impending visit to Albania, the 'normalization' of Greek-Albanian relations and the proposed Regularization Bill (Dimitras 1998).

In the second case, we note the determination of Greece to enter Schengen, to have Greece's borders accepted as the external frontier of the EU, and European recognition of Greece's role in fighting drug trafficking etc.

In the preparation of the Regularization Bill, submissions from ministries were invited. The Ministry of Foreign Affairs had reservations about legalization on the grounds that it would give rights to immigrants; along with the Ministry of Defence, it also feared the creation of national or religious groups (Fakiolas 1998). Thus we can conclude that this foreign policy orientation views immigrants and immigration purely as objects of manipulation for policy objectives: the role of immigrants in Greek society and economy is disregarded, along with fundamental human rights obligations.

Modernizing/Technocratic

The whole regularization process – which has occurred in Greece at a much later stage than in the other southern European countries – is an example of this tendency. It has been pioneered by the Ministry of Labour (unfortunately with the bureaucratic problems already noted), but its intentions seem clear. This orientation accepts the reality of immigration into Greece, and also accepts that at least some of them will remain. Thus access to Greek citizenship needs to be reconsidered, and such a stance has been adopted by the Labour Minister.

When the regularization bill was nearly derailed (by excluding Albanians), it was trades unions and immigrant assocations who lobbied for a retraction of that change. The Prime Minister revealed himself as being in the modernizing camp by overruling the last-minute reckless derailment.

In other related matters, we might note the role of the Ministry of Education in granting education rights to all (including illegal) migrant children, along with setting up a special task force to look at the problems for minority and immigrant children. In the area of health, there has been a willingness to treat in the state hospitals large numbers of illegal migrants – many of whom have travelled from Albania for the sole purpose of treatment.

SOME CONCLUSIONS

Two outstanding features of Greek policy emerge: first, that there is really no actual policy or policy objectives on immigration; secondly, that there is so little information on all aspects surrounding immigration that policy is extremely difficult to formulate anyway.

Taking the first point, it is still unclear how the Greek state wishes to deal with immigration. Does it want to move to a *Gastarbeiter* policy, or does it accept permanent immigration as a reality? What should be the criteria for admitting legal immigrants, and what actually are the criteria for granting green cards and work/residence permits? Access to Greek nationality is another difficult issue, made more restrictive in the early 1990s. We have advanced the tripartite analytic framework to illustrate the incoherence of state policies, and it is these competing interests and perspectives which have formed policy. The supposed common denominator – the 1991 Law – is simply exclusionary, whereas its implementation is variable.

The second point concerns statistical and other data, relating to the labour market, the role of *legal* immigrants in the economy, and any sort of even crude data about the massive munber of illegal immigrants. Without accurate data and real research on these issues, no policy of directing immigrant employment toward unfilled jobs is feasible. The large informal economy makes even good statistics fairly meaningless, therefore empirical research is necessary. As recorded unemployment rises in Greece, and economic restructuring proceeds, these information gaps will become much more serious.

State capacity to respond has been severely defective. The time taken to act has been excessive; even now, with the regularization programme, the speed with which state agencies provide documentation and OAED processes the applications is absurdly slow at the end of the twentieth century. These defects have not been remedied and no plans appear to be in hand to do so. The result of these inefficiencies is that all illegal immigrants with a white card application – the actual card should have expired in July 1998 – were privileged to stay and work in Greece. Thus 373,000 illegal immigrants suddenly became legal, although mostly working in the informal economy.

Asylum-seekers have not been so privileged. Greece has shifted from its former position of toleration, although without providing adequate assistance, to a policy of intolerance and refusing to allow asylum-seekers even to apply. The outcome is, perhaps, not so very different from the exclusionary measures passed by other European countries, but hardly defensible, nevertheless.

A preliminary assessment of the regularization programme suggests that it has achieved little. Probably it has benefited the Albanian community, who have been protected from deportation; perhaps it has shifted the agenda a little more towards modernizing and accepting the reality of immigration. It has certainly benefited serious criminals involved in drug trafficking and forced prostitution, through the 'softly-softly' approach in policing immigrants over the regularization period. Yet large sectors of the illegal immigrant community – most notably Poles and Filipinos – appear to have had minimal involvement with the programme. New illegal immigrants have arrived, and many who were here failed to apply anyway. The outcome has been a curious mixture of semi-legal immigrants with regularization applications, the few legal immigrants, and a large unknown number of illegal immigrants. Given that most of the white card applicants will not get a green card, the situation pertaining prior to the programme will be reproduced around the year 2000 or 2001. Some of the formerly illegal immigrants will have temporary work permits, so this will represent a small advance. As in other southern European countries, this could have been achieved more easily and cheaply by granting work and residence permits in larger numbers. Improved access to such permits will be essential to avoid future problems, but seems unlikely to occur.

Since this article was written, many things have changed. The most important, of course, is the NATO-Serbia conflict and the mass migration of Albanians in the Balkan region. Greece's relations with her neighbours are now more important than ever, and a heightened awareness of illegal migration is inevitable. The Greek regularization programme, which benefited predominantly Albanians, appears to have more or less foundered with the issue of only 40,000 or so Green Cards. The principal reason is bureaucratic failure, although legalization probably priced most immigrants out of the labour market anyway. A specific problem has emerged with the drafting of the procedures, namely that they excluded immigrants legally resident but illegally working: this was particularly relevant for the Polish community, and explains their very low application rate.

A new asylum decree law, delivering a formal procedure for asylum applications, has been hailed by the UNHCR as 'the most progressive in Europe', although we wait to see its results. The Kurds of Koumoundourou Square in Athens were urgently moved on in the wake of the Ocalan crisis, emphasizing the difficult foreign policy aspects of immigration into Greece. The issue of trafficking in migrants and forced prostitution appear to have receded into the background, although 'modernization' of the police services is promised as a major policy objective. Finally, we should note that a draft immigration bill – intended to address the considerable defects of the 1991 Law – is in progress. It can only be hoped that it will solve the major problem of a 'non-policy' and facilitate legal, rather than clandestine, immigration. It will be no easy task, requiring both institutional and labour market reform; it remains an imperative, however, for both the indigenous and alien populations of Greece.

REFERENCES

Baldwin-Edwards, M. (1991): 'Immigration after 1992', *Policy and Politics* 19/3, pp.199–211.

Baldwin-Edwards, M. (1998): 'The Greek Regularization: a Comparative Analysis with the Spanish, Portuguese and Italian Experiences', University of Reading, Centre for Euro-Mediterranean Studies Working Paper, April 1998 [on Web at http://www.rdg.ac.uk/EIS/GSEIS/emc].

Black, R (1992): 'Livelihood and Vulnerability of Foreign Refugees in Greece', London: Department of Geography, King's College, Occasional Paper 33.

CEC (1993): 'Immigration – the situation in the EC member states in 1992', Brussels: DG V General Report by RIMET [Working Document V/6714/93-EN].

Dimitras, P. (1998): 'Greece: Albanian Immigrants for Hire or Expulsion', Greek Helsinki Monitor, mimeo.

Fakiolas, R (1995): 'Preventing Racism at the Workplace in Greece', mimeo., paper presented to European Foundation for the Improvement of Living and Working Conditions, Dublin

Fakiolas, R. (1998): 'Μετανάστευση' [Immigration], in X. Petrinioti and G. Koukoules (eds): *Επετηρίδα Εργασίας 1997* [Greek Labour Yearbook 1997], Athens: Panteion University Press, pp.19–34

Fakiolas, R. and R. King (1996): 'Emigration, Return, Immigration: A Review and Evaluation of Greece's Postwar Experience of International Migration', *International Journal of Population Geography* 2, pp.171–90

Glytsos, N. (1995): 'Problems and Policies Regarding the Socio-Economic Integration of Returnees and Foreign Workers in Greece', *International Migration* XXXIII/2, pp.155–76.

OECD (1997): '1996 SOPEMI Report on Greece', prepared by Nikos Petropoulos, mimeo.

OECD (1998): *Trends in International Migration: SOPEMI Annual Report*, Paris: OECD.

Papantoniou, A., M. Frangouli and A. Kalavanou (1996): 'Migrants' Insertion in the Informal Economy: Deviant Behaviour and the Impact on Receiving Societies', Athens, mimeo

Petrinioti, X (1992): 'Immigration into Greece by Persons Originating from Third Countries', (unpublished study commissioned by EEC DG V), Athens, April 1992.

Petrinioti, X. (1993): *Η Μετανάστευση προς την Ελλάδα*, [Immigration into Greece] Αθήνα: Οδυσσέας.

Romaniszyn, K. (1996): 'The Invisible Community: Undocumented Polish workers in Athens', *New Community* 22/2, pp.321-33.

Salt, J, Singleton, A and Hogarth, J (1994): *Europe's International Migrants: Data Sources, Patterns and Trends*, London: HMSO.

Sitaropoulos, N (1994): 'Greek Immigration and Refugee Law – an Update', *Immigration & Nationality Law & Practice*, 8/2, pp.57–61.

Sotiropoulos, D. (1995): 'The Remains of Authoritarianism: Bureaucracy and Civil Society in Post-authoritarian Greece', Centro de Estudios Avanzados en Ciencas Sociales, Instituto Juan March, Madrid, Working Paper 1995/66.

Stavropoulou, M (1994): 'Refugee Law in Greece', *International Journal of Refugee Law*, 6/1, pp.53–62.

Socio-Spatial Dynamics and Exclusion of Three Immigrant Groups in the Athens Conurbation

THEODOROS IOSIFIDES and RUSSELL KING

INTRODUCTION

The general aim of this article is to investigate the role that work, space and housing conditions play in the social marginalization and exclusion of foreign workers in Athens. The main empirical base of the article is 135 interviews with three groups of immigrant workers – Albanians, Egyptians and Filipinos – each from a different part of the world and each with different gender and labour market characteristics. These interviews were supplemented by participant observation in districts of Athens characterized by high concentrations of immigrants.

In addition to its empirical contribution, this paper is part of a wider theoretical project aimed at 'inserting' migrants into new models of southern European economy and society. In two other papers (Iosifides and King 1996; King and Konjhodzic 1996), an attempt has been made to place immigrants within the specific southern European model of the capitalist economy developed by Mingione (1995), amongst others (e.g. Garofoli 1992; Hadjimichalis 1994). Here we concentrate on placing immigrants within southern European urban societies. In a book and in a series of stimulating papers, Leontidou (1990; 1993; 1995; 1996; 1997) has drawn attention to both the specificity and variety of southern European cities. What is lacking in her accounts is an indication of where the 'new immigrants' fit in. This paper cannot answer this research question for all of southern Europe, nor even for all the principal cities of Greece. What we do offer is some evidence relating to the life experiences of recently-arrived immigrants in Athens.

This material is presented under three headings. First, we summarize

We should like to thank the journal's two referees for their helpful comments.

the employment characteristics and labour market positions of the three immigrant groups. A fuller account of this aspect of the migrants' lives is provided elsewhere (Iosifides 1997a), but a recapitulation is necessary here, however, as essential background to the second and third sections. In the second section we discuss space, place and the distribution of the three groups. Third, we analyze their housing characteristics and living arrangements, including residential mobility and satisfaction levels. In the conclusion we return to the theoretical frame and attempt to establish the evolving structural role of immigrant workers in the Athenian economy and society.

Before we come to the substantive empirical results and associated discussion, three short background contexts need to be set out: the recent migration situation in Greece; the urban context of Athens; and a note on the methodology of the field research.

THE MIGRATION CONTEXT

In common with the other southern EU countries, Greece has recently been transformed from a traditional emigration country to one of immigration (King and Rybaczuk 1993). For most of the twentieth century Greece has been a country of mass emigration. Between 1900 and 1974 an estimated 1.8 million left; initially the majority destination was the United States, but after the 1950s most emigrating Greeks went to West Germany (Fakiolas and King 1996). After 1970, however, emigration started to decline and return migration became increasingly dominant in the balance of migration flows. Return took place for a variety of reasons, amongst which the stagnation of demand for migrant labour in Germany, the improvement of employment prospects in the Greek economy and the natural wish of many migrants to return home through nostalgia were probably the most important.

In the 1980s, foreign immigration replaced the return migration of Greeks as the key element in the positive migratory balance. Geography played a key role: the position of Greece at the south-east corner of Europe facing the south and eastern Mediterranean shores, its long mountainous frontier to the north, its islands extending close to the Turkish mainland, and its heavy reliance on tourism and shipping made it relatively accessible and easy to enter for potential migrants. The imposition of strict immigration controls by the northern EU countries and the improvement of the Greek economy and standard of living were other factors diverting migrants to Greece. Also extremely relevant were the intense economic and demographic push pressures in countries just the other side of the Mediterranean (King 1996). Yet another important push factor, of almost explosive proportions, was the freedom of movement granted to citizens of the former socialist states of Eastern Europe after 1989. The massive influx of Albanians into Greece in the early 1990s can be largely attributed to this geopolitical factor.

In this article, however, we wish to stress the importance of labour demand emanating from the specific socio-economic characteristics of Greece. Four inter-related features of the Greek economy explain this demand. These are the persistence of a large informal economy; the fragmentation of the economy into a myriad of small mainly family-run enterprises; the seasonality and labour intensity of many sectors of the economy such as agriculture, fishing, tourism, construction and shipping; and finally the rejection of low-paid, low-status jobs by natives due to higher educational levels, higher socio-economic aspirations and the delayed labour market entry of the young. These are defining parameters of the southern European economic system (Mingione 1995), but they tend to present their sharpest expression in Greece (Iosifides and King 1996).

There are various categories of immigrants in Greece including ethnic Greeks from Albania and the former USSR, legally resident foreigners from other EU countries, refugees etc., but the most numerous category of recent arrivals is made up of immigrants from several East European, African and Asian countries. Since the vast majority of immigrants are undocumented, either arriving clandestinely or on tourist visas which have since expired, only very approximate estimates exist of their numbers. The four largest groups are non-ethnic-Greek Albanians, Poles, Egyptians and Filipinos. There are smaller but nevertheless significant immigrant communities from Iraq, Pakistan, former Yugoslavia, Bulgaria, Romania and several African countries. Aggregate estimates put the overall number of immigrants who are potentially economically active at between 350,000 and 500,000; that is between 8 and 11 per cent of the total Greek labour force of 4.4 million (Fakiolas 1997). Hence Greece, in proportion to its population, has more immigrants than the other southern EU countries (King and Konjhodzic 1996).

THE URBAN CONTEXT: ATHENS

The Athens conurbation dominates Greece in terms of its share of both population and economic activity. Athens contains 30 per cent of the Greek population, although recently the conurbation has begun to lose population to the outer metropolitan periphery and to other regions of the country (Leontidou 1995). Similar trends can be observed with regard to economic activities: during the 1960s and early 1970s almost half of national industrial employment was concentrated in Athens, but by 1990 this proportion had fallen to one-third. The recent tendency towards the decentralization of population and industrial activity from the capital can be explained in the context of Greek capitalist development. Improvements in rural conditions and incomes, financial transfers to less developed areas, large allocations of public funds to agriculture and the proliferation of negative externalities in Athens have all led to the relative improvement of the economic position of provincial Greece in recent years (Hadjimichalis and Vaiou 1990). Due to the combination of legislative prohibitions and special incentives, larger establishments have shown a faster rate of decentralization, whilst involutionary industrialization in Athens proceeds by a multiplication of small units. The persistence of a large informal sector in Greece is highly correlated with the fragmentation of the economy into small units and is largely an urban phenomenon.

Greek urban development displays some unique characteristics which differentiate it from the experiences of more advanced West European countries and which therefore provide a different setting for the incorporation of recent immigrants in urban space. As Leontidou (1990) has shown, the development and expansion of Athens was historically based mainly on popular control of land on the urban fringe, early informalization of the housing sector and spontaneous unplanned urban growth. More recent changes and developments have led to an urban system characterized by middle-class speculation and suburbanization, economic tertiarization and informalization, and an increasing homogenization of urban space except for specific enclaves of wealth and poverty (Leontidou 1993).

Within this urban context, what is more relevant for the purposes of this study is to examine the emergence of new enclaves of poverty and marginalization in the city where the presence of recent illegal immigrants is bound up with processes of degradation and 'de-gentrification'. Extensive observation and field research in the conurbation revealed that immigrants were to be found both in the poorest districts (Piraeus and Egaleo to the west, Vathis and Omonia in the centre) and in some of the wealthiest areas such as the north-eastern and southern suburbs (Figure 1). This latter finding, surprising at first sight, can be explained by two factors, to be explored in more detail later on: the first concerns the nature of immigrants' employment and applies mainly to female migrant domestic workers, and the second is related to the fact that even the wealthiest parts of Athens contain small pockets of low-income residents and of poverty (Balourdos *et al.* 1990). Figure 1 shows that central Athens incorporates several districts with a relatively high degree of concentration of immigrants; these areas are also increasingly characterized by prostitution, drug trafficking, criminality, degraded accommodation and poor-quality infrastructure. There has been a significant drop in land and dwelling prices in recent years and a growing degree of abandonment and de-gentrification in these districts. A recent survey comparing the residential location of the Athenian population in 1980 and in 1995 found that 71.5 per cent of the inner-city population had moved from the central area, transferring mainly to the northern and southern suburbs (reported in the newspaper *Kathimerini*, 10 January 1996). The buildings of the central areas thus vacated have been increasingly taken over by immigrants, corresponding to the rapid growth in their numbers over the past ten years.

FIGURE 1

MAIN AREAS OF IMMIGRANT SETTLEMENT IN ATHENS WHERE FIELD RESEARCH WAS CARRIED OUT.

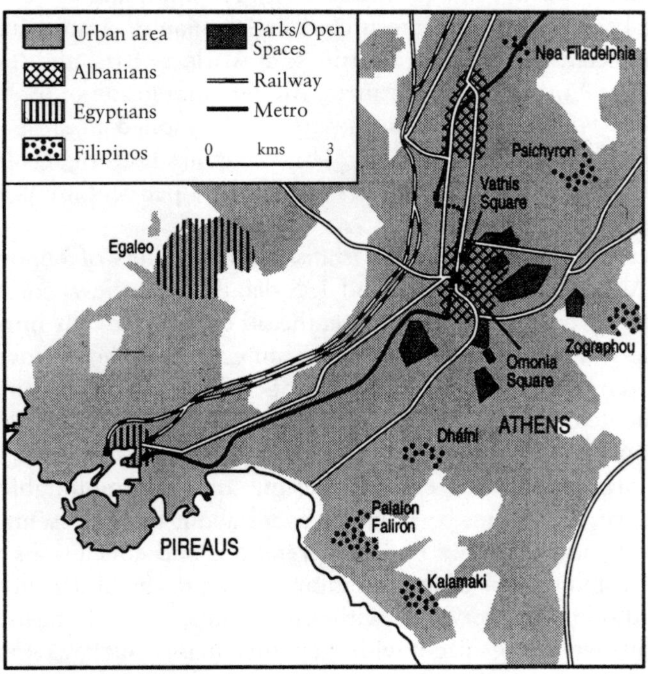

METHODS

Field research in Athens was conducted using a combination of methods.[1] Snowball sampling was used to obtain 135 interviews with immigrants living and working (or seeking work) in the conurbation: 46 with Albanians, 48 with Egyptians and 41 with Filipinos.[2] The limitations of snowballing are well-known and were counteracted by two strategies: dispersing the initial contacts amongst different areas of Athens and types of migrants; and a request to a selection of the interviewees to direct the interviewer to different types of migrant for follow-on interviews. This type of non-probability sampling was justified because of lack of knowledge about the immigrant population in the city and hence the impossibility of constructing a reliable sampling frame. Most immigrants in Athens are 'illegal' in the eyes of the Greek authorities and, apart from the Filipinas, are characterized by residential instability. Despite their precarious situation, relatively few immigrants refused to be interviewed. This was because great care was taken to explain the purposes of the survey and to ensure confidentiality, and because good use was made of key intermediaries to reassure interviewees. Most interviews were conducted in Greek, some in English (with Filipinas) and some (with the help of a key informant as interpreter) in Albanian or Arabic. Interviews were conducted in a variety of settings: at work, in flats, and (especially with Filipinas) in community centres. An initial intention of interviewing a quota of Polish immigrants had to be abandoned because of their dispersal and invisibility in the city. This group has no formal community structure and one estimate suggests that only 15 per cent are year-round residents (Romaniszyn 1996).

We have to acknowledge the statistical limitations of our interview sample. Although on the one hand 135 detailed interviews constitutes a reasonable corpus of information, on the other hand we only interviewed something like one per thousand of the immigrants in the Greater Athens area. Given the obvious problems of collecting information from undocumented immigrants and of the lack of knowledge of the target population (making it impossible to set up a rigorous sampling frame), these shortcomings in research design are insurmountable. As a consequence, we cannot be fully confident about the representativeness of our data, and therefore our interpretations and conclusions must be regarded as indications of the situation existing in the mid-1990s.

In addition to interviews with immigrants, several meetings and discussions were organized with key informants such as immigrant representatives and community leaders, employers, Greek policy-makers and officials. Finally, information was gathered in the form of observation, field notes and informal discussions with groups of immigrants in their habitual meeting places.

IMMIGRANTS IN THE ATHENS LABOUR MARKET

As economic migrants, the chief objective of Albanian, Egyptian and Filipino immigrants is to find remunerative work. The combination of their undocumented status, poor educational background (except Filipinos), lack of knowledge of Greek (except for some ethnic-Greek Albanians), and the changing social structure of Greece itself, tends to relegate immigrant workers to the lowest levels of the labour market. Hence they are required to perform jobs which are dirty, dangerous, boring, servile and often characterized by high rates of insecurity and seasonality. Much employment takes place in the informal sector, which means that the immigrant workers have no protection and are paid well below statutory minimum wages. The immigrants' illegal status allows them to be exploited in this way and prevents them from taking action. For them, even scraps of work in the lowest echelons of the Athenian labour market are preferable to a life of poverty and unemployment in their home countries.

Despite these common features of immigrants' work, significant differences were found with respect to the types and sectors of work performed (Table 1). The most distinctive group are the Filipinas whose gender orients them overwhelmingly to the domestic help, childcare and nursing sectors. Only three male Filipinos were interviewed: one each employed in the construction, cleaning and small-firm sectors. The Albanians and Egyptians in Athens are male-dominated groups; only three female Albanians and six female Egyptians were interviewed in the survey. The employment profile of Albanians and Egyptians is similar but not identical. They have two sectors in common – construction and small firms – but, in addition, Albanians work in the cleaning and decorating sector, which Egyptians do not, whilst Egyptians are the only group to have developed a specialism in street-vending.

A few words are necessary to explain the definitions of these employment types, since some of them encompass a number of different situations, partly reflecting how interviewees' responses were categorized and partly reflecting the nature of the informal labour market in Athens. Construction opportunities for immigrants involve two subsectors:

TABLE 1

TYPE OF EMPLOYMENT OF IMMIGRANTS IN ATHENS

	Albanians	Egyptians	Filipinas	Total
Construction	22	18	1	41
Cleaning, decorating	10	1	1	12
Small firms, catering	13	15	1	29
Street-vending	0	13	0	13
Domestic help	0	0	28	28
Nursing, baby-sitting	0	0	8	8
Other	1	1	2	4
Total	46	48	41	135

Source: Iosifides (1997b)

house-building and associated repair work, where immigrants are taken on as helpers; and large, mainly public, civil engineering projects such as road-building, where immigrants are hired by subcontractors to cut labour costs. In recent years, opportunities in the latter of these two types have grown substantially due to the start-up of several major projects in the Athens region, amongst which the most notable are the new airport and the new underground railway system. Cleaning also involves two subsectors: work in the household domain (house-cleaning, painting and decorating etc.), and similar work done in larger public or private buildings (offices, banks etc.). The 'small firm' sector in Table 1 is the most diverse and includes small manufacturing firms and workshops (e.g. in clothing and paper), removal firms and work in restaurants, hotels and takeaways. Street-vending involves the sale of lottery tickets, clothes, leather goods, cheap jewellery etc., either from fixed stalls or by hawkers who simply walk around the city with their wares. Most of the domestic helps work as live-in maids, but some Filipinas do this work on a live-out contract basis. This sector overlaps to some extent with the final major category in Table 1 where 'domestic' work involves child-minding and the care of elderly people.

Another way of analyzing the work performed by immigrants in the informal economy of Athens is to examine the level of occupational precariousness. Table 2 shows both instability between types of job done (based on the employment categories used in Table 1), and the insecurity of each period of employment, based on the length of time the current job had been held at the time of interview. A clear continuum between the three nationalities is revealed. The Albanians have the greatest mobility between employment types, and also the highest degree of employment insecurity as measured by the shortness of the 'contract' of the current job (in practice, of course, such contracts hardly exist, except at a purely verbal level). The Filipinas, by contrast, are overwhelmingly linked to a single type of employment, and their employment arrangements are fairly long-term, although still informal in the majority of cases. The Egyptians occupy an intermediate position.

TABLE 2

INSTABILITY OF EMPLOYMENT OF IMMIGRANTS IN ATHENS

	Albanians	Egyptians	Filipinas	Total
No. of employment types				
1	24	38	38	100
2	15	8	3	26
3 or more	7	2	0	9
Length of current job				
0–3 months	20	11	2	33
3–6 months	8	4	2	14
6–12 months	9	11	2	22
1–2 years	5	12	15	32
over 2 years	0	10	18	28
temporarily unemployed	4	0	2	6
Total	46	48	41	135

Source: Iosifides (1997b)

The above data indicate both an overall relegation of immigrant workers to the most marginal, poorly-rewarded and insecure jobs, and also a certain ethnic segmentation within the immigrant labour market. Albanians have the greatest degree of job precariousness as they are concentrated in construction, cleaning and tourism-related small firms. Egyptians are in the middle, since they are mainly employed as workers in small firms or self-employed as street-traders, although a significant minority were engaged in construction work. The most 'secure' group are the Filipinas where the vast majority have held the same job for at least a year.

This hierarchy is repeated across other aspects of the migrants' background and experience, according to interview data. For instance, Albanians possessed the poorest educational background: 29 had only primary education or less, compared to 26 Egyptians and 13 Filipinas, whereas 14 Filipinas were graduates but only one Egyptian and one Albanian. Albanians were the youngest (average age 24.1 years, compared to 25.3 for Egyptians and 29.1 for Filipinos) and most recently arrived of the three groups (all Albanians had arrived since 1990, whereas four Egyptians and 16 Filipinas had arrived prior to 1990). Finally, interview data showed that Albanians received the lowest wages for their work – an average monthly income of £220 compared to £255 received by the Egyptians and £227 by the Filipinos (but most members of this last group also had accommodation and food costs included so that their disposable income net of living costs was higher than both the other two groups).[3] Albanians earn less both because of the fact that they pick up the lowest-paid and most precarious jobs and also because they are paid lower wages than other immigrants even for the same job. Lazaridis (1996) found that the presumed association of Albanians with criminal activities meant that employers were less willing to hire them and so offered them lower wages.

The quantitative data discussed above implies the robustness of a 'full' sample survey which we cannot of course claim, as was noted earlier. In particular, the situation of the Albanians in Greece is far more complex than we have indicated in the simple comparisons above. Low educational attainment and lack of knowledge of the Greek language are not necessarily the main factors accounting for Albanians' marginal position in the labour market; nor indeed are these factors completely true in themselves. For instance it is known from other surveys (Barjaba 1997; Fakiolas 1997; Lazaridis 1996) that many Albanians working in Athens have high levels of education. They may have backgrounds as teachers, scientists or musicians, but they earn many times more than their Albanian salaries by working in the informal economy in Greece: a form of 'brain waste' that has been described by Rhode (1993) in the context of other East European migrant nationalities working in the 'West'. Regarding language, it must be remembered that many Albanians coming from the south of their country (where emigration to Greece has been highest) know the rudiments of the Greek language, which is widely spoken in that region. Moreover, Albanians generally show an impressive ability to learn Greek once they are in the country, so language becomes less of an objective handicap to their integration. In retrospect, it may be that our Albanian sub-sample was biased towards recent arrivals and those in precarious employment. Even this, however, is speculation.

What our findings do show are, first, that there appears to be an entrenched demand within Greek society for low-wage foreign labour.

This enables, secondly, overall labour costs of enterprises to be reduced and encourages Greek families and households to employ cheap immigrant workers to carry out home-based tasks. Immigrant workers are a mechanism to bring much-needed flexibility to the overall Greek labour force. This is especially true in rural areas where seasonality of labour demand in agriculture is marked (Lianos *et al.* 1996). Bilateral agreements concluded in 1995–96 with Bulgaria and Albania for the recruitment of seasonal workers were a recognition of this need. Thirdly, there is a substantial degree of polarization and segmentation within the Greek labour market, especially within the informal sector which is itself characterized by heterogeneity and ethnic stratification. The remainder of this paper will examine to what extent these findings are paralleled by other facets of immigrants' lives in the city.

SPACE AND PLACE FOR IMMIGRANTS IN ATHENS

The role that space plays in the marginalization of immigrants in Athens is multifaceted. For example, in the first stages of Albanian immigration into the country, most immigrants sheltered in certain squares, in underground and railway stations, and in abandoned or semi-derelict properties dotted around the city. Several Albanian interviewees referred to the extreme hardship and insecurity they faced on their first arrival in the city. In all cases, except the Filipinas, immigrants occupy cheap and low-quality accommodation, either in areas which are generally poor and deprived, or in small sub-areas within middle-class districts.

The nature of places which contain concentrations of immigrants has changed over the years, partly because of their very presence. Apart from their physical presence, there are other characteristics which make such places 'different'. For example, foreign newspapers and magazines – Arab, Albanian, and so on – are dominant in shops in these areas. Several cafes, bars, clubs and gambling-houses are largely occupied by immigrants, and signs written in the native languages of the immigrants can be found everywhere. The signs usually give or ask for information relating to employment and accommodation. The whole environment in these areas strikes native Greeks as dominated by the foreign presence and makes them appear even more alien, deprived and rejectable.

Yet these areas cannot be defined as ghettos. The notion of the ghetto, derived from the experience of the Jews in Europe or of black urban America, means a compact, homogenous concentration with clear boundaries. Strictly speaking, immigrant areas in Athens cannot even be defined as enclaves. The term 'enclave' implies that internal cohesion forces are dominant. Although social networks and solidarity do play a role in the spatial concentrations of immigrants in Athens, external forces, such as housing discrimination and the housing market, explain better their residential characteristics, as we shall see later on. Hence immigrant concentration in Athens is mostly involuntary, and this is an additional indication of immigrants' marginalization and social exclusion. However, because these areas are mixed, comprising both immigrants and accommodation for local people who have weak purchasing power or a desire for cheap, temporary flats (e.g. single old people, students), they are perhaps better termed as immigrant clusters (cf. Knox 1995).

In an environment of social exclusion, the social significance of place amongst different immigrant groups is very important. Apart from accommodation, certain places in Athens act as meeting and recreational areas, functioning also as market places and points of information exchange about almost all aspects of life and work in the city. Especially during the evenings, a number of squares (for example the Agios Spyridonas square in Egaleo or Vathis square in central Athens) are transformed into meeting places of different national groups (Egyptians, Iraqis and other Arabs in the former, Albanians in the latter), and into places of sharing of useful information and experiences about new employment or accommodation opportunities. Surrounding these squares are eating places and clubs which are mainly patronized by the immigrant groups. During the early mornings these same squares function as market places for the hiring of labour; potential employers arrive and take on the short-term labour they need for a particular job.

Finally there is the role of Athens itself as a place on the mental map of immigrants arriving in Greece. Although the provincial Greek economy offers opportunities and demands for immigrant labour – notably in seasonal work in agriculture in the irrigated plains and in tourism in the islands – most immigrants aim for Athens (see King *et al.* 1998). The capital presents a wider range of employment opportunities because of its large informal sector and its multiplicity of small firms, providing a broad availability of low-paid jobs in several sectors, as we have seen. Even though most of the work available is temporary and insecure, unemployment is avoided by moving quickly from one job to another, or by holding two or more part-time jobs simultaneously. Another advantage of Athens as perceived by immigrants is its availability of cheap accommodation in run-down areas of the city abandoned by the outward migration of local people. Housing needs can be more easily met in Athens because of the size of the housing market, especially the informal rented sector. The existence of more-or-less established immigrant groups in the city is an attraction for new arrivals who find co-nationals, even relatives and people from their own home town or village, ready to help (but also sometimes to exploit) them. Finally, the chances of avoiding arrest and deportation are higher in Athens than elsewhere in Greece, because of the anonymity of life in a big city and the greater degree of absorption in the labour market of the parallel economy (Romaniszyn 1996).

HOUSING

The instability and marginalization in the labour market described earlier are mirrored in the immigrants' quest for accommodation (Table 3). The overall situation is that over 60 per cent have experienced at least one change of address since their arrival in Athens, and a third have lived at five or more addresses. Moreover there are significant differences between the immigrant groups. Albanians have the highest degree of residential instability; this is related, above all, to their main type of accommodation in squalid 'hotels'. The most stable group are the Filipinas, over half of whom have been at the same address since they arrived. This contrast between Albanians and Filipinas is all the more marked because, on average, the Filipinas have been living in Athens for much longer than the Albanians. On the other hand, Filipinas' residential stability is easily explained by their work as live-in domestics. The Egyptians hold an intermediate position in Table 3, polarized between stability and mobility.

TABLE 3
RESIDENTIAL CHANGES DURING IMMIGRANTS' TIME IN ATHENS

	Albanians	Egyptians	Filipinas	Total
None	9	18	22	49
Once	5	9	10	24
Two or three	6	4	7	17
Four or more	26	17	2	45
Total	46	48	41	135

Significance: chi-square 19.9, d.f.2, $p<0.001$ (rows 1-2, and 3-4, collapsed)

Source: Iosifides (1997b)

The two most commonly cited reasons for residential change are dissatisfaction and expulsion. Dissatisfaction with housing conditions or rent levels plays an active role only when opportunities for real improvement appear. In most cases an extremely poor accommodation environment is tolerated simply because better conditions are impossible to find. The most important reason for a move is expulsion. Rental arrangements for the immigrants and the relationship between them and the landlord are nearly always totally informal, lacking any written contract or other legal safeguards. Because of this, expulsions of immigrants are frequent, depending on the whim of the owner. Finally, a few immigrants reported that they had changed residence because they wanted to be nearer the city centre or their workplace.

The living arrangements of immigrants in Athens reveal the important role of their social networks of friends and relatives in the city. Only a tiny minority of immigrants interviewed (four Egyptians) lived alone. The great majority live with relatives and with friends of the same nationality, except Filipinas, most of whom (28 out of 41 interviewed) live with their employers. Very few immigrants can afford to live alone and to pay on their own the whole amount of the rent and other bills such as water and electricity. Costs are reduced as the number of people sharing increases. Amongst Albanians, cases were found of ten and even twenty persons sharing a single, albeit large, 'hotel' room. Sharing costs and accommodation in this way also provides short-term protection for those who are temporarily unemployed.

Sharing accommodation has important social dimensions; social networks are built and reinforced which are crucial for the individual's survival as an illegal immigrant. Living in areas of high criminality and in a broader environment of hardship and vulnerability, residential groupings of immigrants offer security and respond more successfully in cases of emergency. Strong collective bonds, especially between room-mates, and solidarity and mutual assistance in almost all matters were evident from interviews, discussions and participant observation. Amongst specific areas of mutual support are personal security, employment, economic and health problems, recreation and contacts with the home country. These residentially-based support networks are especially strong and important amongst Albanians who (unlike the Filipinas, for example) lack a formal community structure, and who, interestingly, exhibit a high level of mistrust towards other Albanians, let alone Greeks.

Moving on to accommodation types, Table 4 shows that there are clear contrasts between the three immigrant groups: Filipinas live mainly with their employers, Egyptians are almost all in rented flats and houses, whereas Albanians are the main occupants of inner-city 'hotels'. These so-called hotels have had a chequered history. In the 1950s and 1960s they functioned as military barracks, and in the 1970s they were used as temporary shelters for refugees from Cyprus, Kurdistan and elsewhere. During the 1980s they were closed down because of maintenance problems and declining quality, but were opened up again when the influx of Albanians came after 1990 (Psimmenos 1995). Given this history, it is not surprising that living conditions and facilities in these 'hotels' are extremely bad; many now operate as brothels as well. One reason for the virtual entrapment of large numbers of Albanians in these hotels is the higher degree of housing discrimination towards this group due to the development of the stereotype of the Albanian illegal immigrant as 'cunning, primitive, untrustworthy' (Lazaridis 1996: 344).

TABLE 4

TYPE OF ACCOMMODATION OF IMMIGRANTS IN ATHENS

	Albanians	Egyptians	Filipinas	Total
Hotel	24	3	0	27
Rented flat/house	21	45	13	79
With employer	1	0	28	29
Total	46	48	41	135

Source: Iosifides (1997b)

Levels of satisfaction from housing conditions display significant differences between the three immigrant groups (Table 5). Albanians are the most dissatisfied – unsurprising given the squalid conditions of the 'hotels'. Egyptian interviewees were the most satisfied, with the Filipinas occupying an intermediate position. Dissatisfaction of the latter mainly derives from the fact that they live with their employers in an atmosphere often characterized by tension, personal isolation, authoritarianism and, not infrequently, sexual harassment.

TABLE 5

LEVELS OF SATISFACTION OF HOUSING IN ATHENS

	Albanians	Egyptians	Filipinas	Total
Satisfied	6	26	22	54
Neutral	25	16	12	53
Unsatisfied	15	6	7	26
Total	46	48	41	135

Significance: chi-square 21.5, d.f.4, $p<0.001$

Source: Iosifides (1997b)

One important characteristic of the immigrants' opinion about housing is the relativity of their expression of satisfaction. Normally, housing satisfaction amongst the general (i.e. non-immigrant) population is related to high quality, amenities, large size and good location (Kouveli 1993). All these housing characteristics are absent for immigrants, except some of the Filipinas. Immigrant housing satisfaction is instead related more to the existence of a good relationship with the landlord and the likelihood of a long-term and secure period of accommodation; indeed, several respondents expressed satisfaction simply because they had a roof over their heads.

Nevertheless, satisfaction levels do vary by type of accommodation, being lowest for 'hotels'. Taking all the responses together, the main causes for complaint were the expense of rents given the poor quality and dirty state of accommodation provided; the lack of basic amenities such as hot water and a reliable supply of electricity; the high number of people with whom kitchens, bathrooms and toilets had to be shared; the dilapidated and even dangerous nature of the building structures which lacked proper security; and frequent overt discrimination in access to housing. Visiting immigrants' flats and multi-occupied rooms, the main impression is one of extreme overcrowding and lack of privacy. Many such rooms and flats are in highly disadvantageous positions: often in basements, lacking windows and access to fresh air, cold and damp in winter, hot and stuffy in summer. Interviewees complained of constant monitoring by landlords and hotel-owners and of frequent intrusions and abuse by people who had no right to enter their accommodation. Lack of privacy and invasion of poorly-defined personal space and free time were also chronicled by Filipinas living with their employers.

Many interviewees, especially the Albanians, reported that Greek society gives them a bad name because they can only afford to live in marginal and degraded areas which are also characterized by prostitution and open drug abuse. These interviewees repeatedly affirmed that they are not part of this criminal subculture but simply poor workers who are denied access to alternative housing because of price, discrimination and their undocumented status. Living in run-down inner-city areas leads to the internalization of their marginal and excluded position within Greek society and thus lowers self-esteem and aspirations for improvement.

Information gathered from several interviews revealed the ways in which the discrimination experienced in the labour market, discussed earlier, is repeated in the housing market. Most landlords refuse to lease to immigrants; those who do, impose terms and conditions which would not apply for Greek tenants – two or three months' rent in advance (the norm is one month), regular but unannounced inspections, and no formal contract. Many immigrants reported that the only way to lease a space was to obtain a warranty from a native Greek, usually their employer. From an economic point of view, the housing of immigrants can be interpreted as reflecting the risk premium demanded in any commercial dealing which involves high levels of uncertainty. Housing restriction therefore plays an extremely important role in the concentration of immigrants in badly-maintained, low-quality accommodation whose demand by natives is very limited.

DISCUSSION

Since the late 1980s and early 1990s immigration has introduced new elements in Southern Europe's regional and urban labour markets: 'Third World' and ex-socialist countries have willingly supplied workers to do the jobs which native workers have declared themselves unwilling to do because of low wages, poor working conditions, and the low prestige of certain types of work. Hence Greece, along with other southern European countries, has provided a continuing vindication of Piore's (1979) thesis that immigrant workers are functional to the ongoing development of capitalism in its various forms, generating and responding to the demands of a progressively dualistic labour market. Whilst this article has explored some features of the work experiences of three groups of immigrants in Athens, its main purpose has been to uncover other aspects of their lives, especially those related to housing and socio-spatial marginalization. In this concluding discussion we return to the more conceptual questions posed at the beginning of the article and attempt to place our empirical material within the theoretical context of the changing nature of the urban economy and society of Athens, and of western cities in general.

The first point to stress is the obvious parallelism between migrants' experiences in the labour market and in society at large. In both cases they suffer what Sivanandan (1988) has called 'super-exploitation'. This willingness to tolerate low wages, tough working conditions and almost sub-human living arrangements derives from three interconnected factors. The first is the desperate situation in migrants' home countries where, had they stayed, they most probably would have been worse off, at least in terms of income-earning capacity. Hence, despite the risks involved and the difficulties of finding jobs in Athens, the majority of immigrants earn five or even ten times more than they could in their own countries. Some save in a couple of weeks more than they could in many months or even years in their respective places of origin. Secondly, their illegal status – a product of Greece's 'non-policy' on migration of allowing a large number of migrants to enter clandestinely yet (until the very recent regularization) refusing to grant them any kind of legal or citizenship rights – creates a status for them as 'non-persons', the ultimate in social exclusion (Fakiolas and King 1996). This situation, whereby immigrants have no place in Greek society but only function as disposable workers, is reinforced by widespread stereotypes of immigrants (especially Albanians) as criminals and trouble-makers (Lazaridis 1996). Thirdly, contemporary immigration to Greece (and other parts of southern Europe) has taken place within the evolving global map of migration in which 'Fortress Europe', the removal of the Iron Curtain and other aspects of the New World Order have provided new forces shaping international migration flows in the 1990s. Within Greece, immigrants have been 'used' to minimize wage costs and hence maintain the competitiveness of Greek enterprises.

This last point bears further scrutiny as it highlights the role of immigrants in the changing economic and social geography of Athens (and, more widely, of Greece and southern Europe) in the last 10–20 years. Following Dell' Aringa and Neri's analysis of the Italian case (but which applies with equal force to Greece), immigrants are central to the overall strategy of holding down wages, at least in certain segments of manual employment; and they offer to employers a positive incentive to shift productive resources from the legal economy to the informal sector (Dell' Aringa and Neri 1989). Various estimates indicate that Greece has the largest 'black market' sector of any EU economy, accounting for approximately 30 per cent (some would say up to 35 per cent) of GDP in the early 1990s (Williams and Winderbank 1995). Although immigrants are prominent as a seasonal (and black market) labour force in agriculture and tourism in Greece, their main participation is in the urban service economy of Athens where they perform a variety of tasks such as house-cleaning, child-minding, house repairs, building work and street-hawking, as we have seen. In virtually all respects (street-vendors are a partial exception), these jobs involve an almost servile relationship with the hirer of the migrant's labour. Whilst on the one hand this situation recalls the hierarchical social composition of the nineteenth century European city with its housemaids, cooks and servants, in other respects the Athens case shares many features of the social and economic restructuring of late-twentieth century global cities described by Sassen (1991; 1994).

Whilst Athens is far from being a global city in the Sassen sense, it does possess a number of features which align it with the trends described by Sassen for cities like New York and London. Indeed we believe that, in some respects, Athens can be considered as a prototype for the trends towards informalization of work and the increased social inequality and restructuring of consumption into high-income and very low-income strata which are a central part of Sassen's analysis. In making this suggestion we are endorsing, but with different evidence, Leontidou's (1993) belief that Mediterranean cities have long contained powerful 'postmodern' characteristics which prefigured the post-Fordist restructuring of large industrial cities in the Anglo-American realm.

Let us explore this line of analysis in a little more detail. The marked tertiarization of urban economies involves not only types of output and services associated with high-level technical knowledge and the professions but also a wide range of low-wage, unskilled jobs, which are both directly linked to the new expanding service economy (office cleaners, hotel and restaurant workers, construction site labourers etc.) and pamper the personal needs of the new service class, who cluster and reproduce themselves in big cities (house-cleaners, baby-sitters, gardeners, decorators etc.). Many of these low-grade jobs now operate within the informal economy; they are part of a restructuring of the urban labour market which, in addition to the well-known parameters of flexibilization and casualization, also involves a shift of labour market functions to the household or community (Sassen 1995). This shift can be observed in two senses: first in the way that individual householders, members of the new service class, act as employers and managers of casualized, often immigrant labour for household-related drudge tasks; and, second, in the way that immigrant groups, once they have established a specialism in a given area of employment in a given city, tend to bring in other members from their country of origin, fulfilling also a training and socializing role of settling them into the workplace and the neighbourhood (Sassen, 1996).

The question now arises as to the relationship between immigration on the one hand and the trend towards greater flexibility and informalization of the urban economy and the labour market on the other. We shall confront this question both in general terms and by returning to the Athenian case. It is often assumed that Third World (and in the case of Athens, East European) migration has 'caused' informalization. It is true that immigrants have seized opportunities created by the restructuring of urban societies but they are not necessarily the creators of these opportunities (Pugliese 1993; Sassen 1996). The new immigrant employment niches, such as those we have observed in Athens, are a structured outcome of current trends, which are partly general to advanced economies and partly rather specific to the Athenian milieu where inherited social structures and practices have accentuated many of the processes of informalization and the consequent incorporation of immigrant labour.

The next stage is to clarify what these Athenian specificities are. To a large extent these are characteristic of most south European cities, but Athens presents them in perhaps their clearest form. Some of them have been mentioned already: a long-established and heterogeneous informal sector which interconnects with the formal sector in a number of ways and which is based on a phenomenally high rate of self-employment – for Greece as a whole 50 per cent, much higher than any other EU country (Mingione 1995). This atomization of production and services is based on one-person or small family enterprises such as shops, market stalls, restaurants, workshops, building trade activities, removal firms etc., which are firmly embedded in the socio-economic fabric of the city and have long experience of dodging the depredations of the regulated economy. Immigrants have fitted easily into these concerns as assistants, occasional helpers and unskilled manual employees. Moreover the free-wheeling, fragmented Athenian economy has allowed some immigrants to become self-employed as street-vendors, market stall traders, window-cleaners etc.

But the economic structure and organization of the city is only one aspect of Athens' specificity. Social and demographic processes have added another important set of contexts for the explosive growth in the number of immigrants in Athens since the 1980s. Greece has also experienced the dramatic fertility collapse seen in Italy and Spain since the 1970s so that, with very low and sub-replacement fertility levels for the past two decades, the number of new labour market entrants is being greatly reduced.[4] Moreover, high levels of participation in higher education have a further dual effect on young people's passage to their working lives: first, the entry to employment is delayed by the prolonged years spent at college and university; second, aspirations are directed away from manual and low-status employment to the fields of business, the professions and the civil service. These processes are particularly marked in Greece where parents place enormous value on the education of their children (often to the extent of sending them abroad to obtain a more prestigious degree), and go to extreme lengths to support them into their mid- or even late-20s in order that they are not compelled to take a socially-demeaning manual job. This social value put on education and the prestige attached to different forms of work reinforce the dual labour market mechanism by which immigrants are increasingly needed to do jobs rejected by Greeks. Unemployment is no barrier to the functioning of the dual labour market: indeed its rather high rate (10 per cent in 1997, with youth unemployment at least twice as high) is a testimony to the sacrifices that families are willing to make to support adult children at home rather than have them take on jobs which would lower family status and marriage prospects.

Two further social processes are at work in Athens to reinforce the needs and opportunities for immigrant workers. The first is the way that the rejection of manual work also extends to the home domain so that household tasks – painting and decorating, cleaning, repair work, gardening – are increasingly passed over to low-wage immigrant labour in order to create more leisure (or work) time for household members. The southern European bourgeoisie, both old and new, are certainly less keen on 'do-it-yourself' than their northern European counterparts! The second process, amply documented in King and Konjhodzic (1996), is the increasing participation rates of women in the labour market: young, educated Greek women in particular are unwilling to accept the traditional Greek mother/homemaker roles of the previous generation. Given the lack of state support for nurseries and the equal lack of commitment on the part of most Greek men to share cooking, house-cleaning and child-rearing responsibilities, there has thus arisen a powerful demand for immigrant workers – typically Filipinas – to take on these household tasks. Moreover the acquisition of a foreign maid has itself become a status-symbol for middle class and even some lower middle class Athenian families.

CONCLUSION

Hence we conclude that, in addition to a specific model of south European economy and urban life, we can add a specific type of immigration which nests within the urban socio-economic form dominated by tertiarization (bearing in mind that most southern European cities, missing the Fordist period of industrialization, have always been based on services and small enterprises) and by informalization. The southern European form of immigration involves, of course, heavy participation in the informal sector and in the atomized service economy, as well as high levels of illegality (higher in Greece than elsewhere in southern Europe). Other key features are the existence of ethnic and gender links to specific job niches (so that some migration streams are almost exclusively female), and very high levels of socio-spatial exclusion – either within the individual household for live-in domestics or in rejected pockets of urban space for other migrants. In Athens we have seen that Albanians, Egyptians and Filipinos, for the most part undocumented, unprotected and unrecognized, tend to accept any kind of working situation and any kind of residual accommodation. Despite the general homogenization of the city recorded by Leontidou (1990), immigrant clusters and colonies are the new emerging *loci* of extreme poverty and deprivation. The concept of the 'dual city' starts to apply in the Athens case. There are, on the one hand, 'native spaces' with little or no immigrant presence; and on the other hand, 'different' or 'mixed' spaces with a strong immigrant imprint. These latter areas have undergone a transformation into 'alien' spaces according to the immigrants' needs and socio-spatial concentration/exclusion, and the clear rejection of these areas by the indigenous population.

Psimmenos (1995) suggests that the 'dual city' of Athens is taking on an almost South African mentality as the majority become ever more willing to exploit the immigrants as a slave-like labour force to create more free time and leisure for themselves. He also documents in a more psychoanalytical way how the creation of a peripheralized labour force in the centre of Athens has been reflected in the rise of illicit economic activities and in the rapid devaluation of social standards and life chances of the immigrants, who are pushed into a way of life of social exclusion, loss of power and even denial of identity. Saddest of all are the Albanian children who are coerced into prostitution. Athens exemplifies the duplicitous view that Albanians and other immigrants can be exploited for their labour and paid the lowest wages possible, yet since they are illegal immigrants and 'so should not be in Athens anyway', their concentration in rejected spaces in sub-human living conditions is somehow justified. Time will tell whether the dual city of Athens will be a permanent or ephemeral phenomenon. A first step would be for the Greek authorities to grant basic human rights to those whose labour Greek society so willingly and profitably exploits.

The recent regularization generated ambiguous results. During the regularization the police were under instructions to ignore illegal immigrants. This led to an even greater official tolerance of immigrant mafia organizations, dominated by those from Albania and Russia. The wave of social unrest in Albania prompted by the collapse of the pyramid investment schemes in 1997 also appears to have spurred an increase in Albanian criminality in Greece. Hence a criminal minority's exploitation of an unregulated situation has damaged the entire immigrant community's standing. Meanwhile, racism is becoming endemic and directed against virtually all non-Greeks. This has been exacerbated by several street killings — some by machine-gunning motorcyclists — which have upset the traditional social peace and stability of Athens. The result is a public discourse of opposition to *all* foreigners, who are said to be 'destroying Greece'.

NOTES

1. The field research in Athens was carried out over eight months during 1995–96 by Iosifides; for further methodological details see Iosifides (1997b).
2. Since the vast majority of immigrants from the Philippines in Athens are females, we henceforth denote them as Filipinas.
3. Of course, asking undocumented migrants about their earnings is not unproblematic, and some respondents declined to give precise answers. However, we believe the figures quoted here to be broadly reliable, not least because they were cross-checked with employers and other key informants.
4. Assuming unchanged (i.e. continuing low) fertility behaviour, the impact on choking off new (young) labour market entrants will become more marked in the future. Meanwhile the labour market continues to expand through increasing female participation and immigration. Official data record a growth in the labour force from 3.96 million in 1987 to 4.38 million in 1997.

REFERENCES

Balourdos, D., Kappi, H., Kostaki, A. and Papatheodorou, H. (1990): 'Household Income Distribution in Greater Athens', *TOPOS, Review of Urban and Regional Studies* 1/90, pp.109–35 (in Greek).

Barjaba, K. (1997): *Between Social Integration and Exclusion: Albanian Immigrants in Greece*, Gorizia: Istituto di Sociologia Internazionale di Gorizia (mimeo).

Dell' Aringa, C. and Neri, F. (1989): 'Illegal Immigrants and the Informal Economy in Italy', in: I. Gordon and A. Thirlwall (eds.) *European Factor Mobility: Trends and Consequences*, Basingstoke: Macmillan, pp.133–47.

Fakiolas, R. (1997): 'The Impact of Migration on the Greek Labour Market'. Paper presented to the Conference on 'Non-military aspects of Security in Southern Europe: Migration, Employment and Labour Market', Santorini, 19-21 September.

Fakiolas, R. and King, R. (1996): 'Emigration, Return, Immigration: a Review and Evaluation of Greece's Postwar Experience of International Migration', *International Journal of Population Geography,* 2, pp.171–90.

Garofoli, G. (1992): *Endogenous Development in Southern Europe*, Aldershot: Avebury.

Hadjimichalis, C. (1994): 'The Fringes of Europe and EU Integration: a View from the South', *European Urban and Regional Studies,* 1, pp.19–29.

Hadjimichalis, C. and Vaiou, D. (1990): 'Flexible Labour Markets and Regional Development in Northern Greece', *International Journal of Urban and Regional Research* 14, pp.1–24.

Iosifides, T. (1997a): 'Immigrants in the Athens Labour Market: A Comparative Study of Albanians, Egyptians and Filipinos', in R. King and R. Black (eds.) *Southern Europe and the New Immigrations*, Brighton: Sussex Academic Press, pp.26–50.

Iosifides, T. (1997b): 'Foreign Immigration and the Labour Market in Athens', University of Sussex, unpublished DPhil thesis.

Iosifides, T. and King, R. (1996): 'Immigration to Southern Europe: the Socio-Economic and Labour Market Contexts', *Journal of Area Studies,* 9, pp.70–94.

King, R. (1996): 'Migration and Development in the Mediterranean Region', *Geography* 81, pp.3–14.

King, R., Iosifides, T. and Myrivili, L. (1998): 'A Migrant's Story: from Albania to Athens', *Journal of Ethnic and Migration Studies,* 24, pp.159–75.

King, R. and Konjhodzic, I. (1996): 'Labour, Employment and Migration in Southern Europe', in: J. van Oudenaren (ed.) *Employment, Economic Development and Migration in Southern Europe and the Maghreb*, Santa Monica: RAND, pp.7–106.

King, R. and Rybaczuk, K. (1993): 'Southern Europe and the International Division of Labour: from Emigration to Immigration', in: R. King (ed.) *The New Geography of European Migrations*, London: Belhaven, pp.175–206.

Knox, P. (1995): *Urban Social Geography: an Introduction*, Harlow: Longman.

Kouveli, A. (1993): *Research on Housing and Construction Companies in Greece*, Athens: EKKE (in Greek).

Lazaridis, G. (1996): 'Immigration to Greece: A Critical Evaluation of Greek Policy', *New Community,* 22, pp.335–48.

Leontidou, L. (1990): *The Mediterranean City in Transition: Social Change and Urban Development*, Cambridge: Cambridge University Press.

Leontidou, L. (1993): 'Postmodernism and the city: Mediterranean versions', *Urban Studies* 30, pp.949–65.

Leontidou, L. (1995): 'The re-polarization of the Mediterranean: Spanish and Greek Cities in Neoliberal Europe', *European Planning Studies,* 3, pp.155–72.

Leontidou, L. (1996): 'Alternatives to Modernism in (Southern) Urban Theory: Exploring In-between Spaces', *International Journal of Urban and Regional Research,* 20, pp.178–95.

Leontidou, L. (1997): 'Five Narratives for the Mediterranean City', in R. King, L. Proudfoot and B. Smith (eds.) *The Mediterranean: Environment and Society*, London: Arnold, pp.181–93.

Lianos, T., Sarris, A.H. and Katseli, L.T. (1996): 'Illegal Imigration and Local Labour Markets: the Case of Northern Greece', *International Migration* 34, pp.449–84.

Mingione, E. (1995): 'Labour Market Segmentation and Informal Work in Southern Europe', *European Urban and Regional Studies,* 2, pp.121–43.

Piore, M.J. (1979): *Birds of Passage: Migrant Labour and Industrialized Societies*, Cambridge: Cambridge University Press.

Psimmenos, I. (1995) *Migration from the Balkans: Social Exclusion in Athens*, Athens: Glory-Book Papazisis (in Greek).

Pugliese, E. (1993): 'Restructuring of the Labour Market and the Role of Third World Migrations in Europe', *Society and Space,* 11, pp.513–22.

Rhode, B. (1993) 'Brain Drain, Brain Gain, Brain Waste: Reflections on the Emigration of Highly Educated and Scientific Personnel from Eastern Europe', in R. King (ed.) *The New Geography of European Migrations*, London: Belhaven, pp.228–45.

Romaniszyn, K. (1996): 'The Invisible Community: Undocumented Polish Workers in Athens', *New Community,* 22, pp.321–33.

Sassen, S. (1991): *The Global City: New York, London, Tokyo*, Princeton: Princeton University Press.

Sassen, S. (1994): *Cities in a World Economy*, Thousand Oaks CA: Sage Press.

Sassen, S. (1995): 'Immigration and Local Labor Markets', in A. Portes (ed.) *The Economic Sociology of Immigration*, New York: The Russell Sage Foundation, pp.87–127.

Sassen, S. (1996): *Transnational Economies and National Migration Policies*, Amsterdam: Institute for Migration and Ethnic Studies.

Sivanandan, A. (1988): 'The New Racism', *New Statesman and Society* 1/22, pp.8–9.

Williams, C.C. and Winderbank, J. (1995): 'Black Market Work in the European Community: Peripheral Work for Peripheral Localities?' *International Journal of Urban and Regional Research* 19, pp.23–38.

Trafficking for Sexual Exploitation and the Sex Business in the New Context of International Migration: the Case of Italy

GIOVANNA CAMPANI

In the sphere of the Daphne project, I participated in a study on the trafficking of immigrant women for sexual exploitation. The outline created by the research is represented, on the one hand, by the transformation of the international migratory context, where the trafficking of human beings is worsening every day – migration as a 'business' (Salt 1997); and on the other hand, by the debate raised by the issue of prostitution, oriented towards the modification of the regulations in effect, and how it is approached in various European countries.

Hinging between trafficking and prostitution lies the worldwide development of the sex industry, which already, in the 1980s, Lin Lean Lim (1989, 1991), an acute scholar of migratory phenomena, had pinpointed as one of the 'occupational' sectors employing a large number of immigrant women. At the time, Lim was referring especially to Asiatic countries – mainly Japan, Malaysia and Thailand. Some ten years later, a relatively high number[1] of foreign prostitutes was noted in Europe, along with 'entreneuses', dancers, mail-order brides, etc. This presence suggests a connection between female immigration and prostitution.

The connection between female migration and prostitution is principally attributed today to the growth of the sex industry as a transnational enterprise. But this reality, which is fairly simple, is not always pointed out by the media, who instead focus on prostitutes and sometimes on clients and pimps. Emphasis is placed on the link between prostitution and immigration, reaching the collective imagination and producing stereotypes and partial representations that falsify the variegated reality of female immigration, and make it difficult to pinpoint the specifics of the existing migratory phase.

The link between female-prostitute immigration was certainly present in older migratory phases (for example, the colonization of the Americas[2]) or more recent ones (rural-urban migration in Europe in the last century), while it was almost non-existent in other migratory phases (in post-war migration, for example, in which they pushed their way up from southern Europe or from the Mediterranean basin towards northern Europe). The connection between female migration and prostitution must therefore be put into context with regard to the migratory phase and must be redefined concerning the contexts and fluxes. Even today the practice of prostitution pertains more specifically to certain groups of immigrant women and certain countries. Only from certain countries, as in the case of Nigeria, are the female migrants destined for the sex industry.[3] Similarly, aside from the global dimensions of the phenomenon, there is no doubt that the traffic is directed more towards certain countries than others, and that the sex industry is growing more in certain countries than in others.

Therefore, what is the specificity of the connection that exists today between migration, traffic and women who have migrated for prostitution? The study conducted certainly cannot respond in an exhaustive manner, but it indicates, at least for Italy, the principal dynamics of the phenomenon. In this article, beyond presenting the study conducted, we attempt to provide a general outline of the trafficking of immigrant women for sexual exploitation.

TRAFFICKING OF MIGRANTS IN GLOBAL NEOLIBERALISM

In Italy, as the PARSEC study points out, the presence of foreign girls who practice prostitution became visible in the early 1990s and continued, in different phases, in successive years. In the early 1990s in Europe, the theme of the trading of women for sexual exploitation emerged and rapidly became one of the worries of the politicians of the European Community, later the EU. The first series of recommendations to the member states was, in fact, approved by the Justice and Home Affairs council of the European Union in November 1993.

It was consistently in the 1990s that transnational trafficking of human beings, 'hardly a global issue in the 1980s' (Kyle 1998), became a form of trafficking worth many millions of dollars according to the U.S. immigration and naturalization services. Confronted with it, the United States was apparently powerless, finding it impossible to prevent in its place of origin. The United Nations estimates the value of the trafficking business to be seven billion dollars per year (Caldwell 1997); the

International Organization for Migration estimates it to be higher – 12.5 billion (Menschenschmuggel 1998). According to the United Nations, four million people are trafficked every year in the world, but again, according to the IOM, the number of people being trafficked is much higher, given that the Organization estimates that 500,000 women alone are trafficked in Eastern Europe (as estimated by Marco Gramegna). All of these data are, however, uncertain and indicative only of the very frequent occurrence of the phenomenon.

In the case of transnational trafficking of human beings in general, and of women in particular for sexual exploitation, the emergency dates back less than ten years. Following growing social visibility and interest on the part of international bodies and governments, the concern and search for strategies and measures of containment began.

It is precisely because the emergency and social visibility of the phenomenon, as well as its study and intervention, are all so recent, that data are lacking. Such data would allow us to understand both the 'social organization' at its point of origin (and it is precisely this aspect which remains obscure, according to the few scholars in this area) and the stages of the journey. Certainly hypotheses are made; and we know some of the mechanisms. The Russian mafia, for example, is extremely active in the trade of human beings. We know that certain Russian cartels work in strict collaboration with other criminal organizations – Italian, in particular (Ziegler 1998). The trafficking journeys are extremely complex, with different points of grouping and passage.

In order to comprehend the complexity of the trafficking, various factors must be kept in mind. On the one hand, trafficking adheres to the classic business model with costs/risks/benefits, and is comprised of enterprises of various dimensions. These can utilize, with optimal or minimal force, relations of power in the countries involved; let us remember the scandal of the visas given to Nigerian women in Italy, which were obtained thanks to the complicity of the officials in Italy and Lagos. The biggest enterprises can even turn to partners who are often high-level political and economic actors who also closely influence the decision-making poles in the countries (Tamzali 1997). On the other hand, on a 'lower' and not 'higher' level, a great number of people not necessarily tied to crime take advantage of the activities connected to the exportation of migrants and have no interest in stopping it. In fact, while the big crime organizations run their trafficking operations on a transnational level, a local level, in both the countries of departure and arrival, supplies foundations of sustenance through petty crime and private citizens. The fight against traffic clashes here with the existence of a vast network of interests which are only comprehensible if we keep in mind the general mechanisms of migration and the specificity of the current migratory context.

> Traditionally, many potential migrants have sought help from networks of family or friends who have emigrated before them. The networks and members of the ethnic community facilitated migration. They provided initial information, helped obtain the legal documents required, and found work. More recently, these traditional networks have been substituted or incorporated in trafficking operations. Traffickers of humans now operate internationally or in multiple markets and cultures. (Kyle 1998)

Though Kyle's statement may seem one-sided and the substitution of networks with solidarity by trafficking may be excessive, it helps us get to the heart of the matter. In the current context of international migration, characterized by the blocking of labour immigration in developed countries, the networks are no longer able to fulfil their role of attraction and sustenance for the new immigrants without turning frequently to illegal practices. But illegal practices are often more effective, just as they are practices of professionals of crime, who have, in fact, discovered this business. The latter have heavily entered into the new 'business' of the century (Salt 1997) – the trafficking of migrants.

The combination of legal and illegal practices in the phase of entry into the new country was present, for the most part, in the history of migration, but it was of limited importance when regularization was a simple practice for migrants.[4] Illegality assumes another dimension today, given that in the face of the closure of the frontiers for those coming from the southern hemisphere, the presence of 'professional' organized crime appears to be necessary.

On the other hand, the migratory pressure from different countries and continents towards developed countries is greater today than it was in the past, while the fall of communism in the USSR and in Eastern Europe, an epochal phenomenon which has not earned enough attention, has opened a new geographic space for migration. Already in the early 1980s, to describe the new context of international migration, the OSCE talked about globalization and acceleration of migratory fluxes. Steven Castles and Mark Miller talk about migration in our time as a global phenomenon, characteristic of the end of this century and of the millennium: 'the Age of Migration'.

Migratory pressure sits on a growing line of North-South polarization, along which the demographic, economic and social statistics (quality of life indicators, for example) are increasingly easier to differentiate.

The increase in migratory pressure due to the deterioration of living conditions in the southern part of the world clashes with the closure of developed countries: in some cases, the reaction to the closure may manifest itself in the form of a collective explosion in the countries of departure (let us think of the case of Albania). Nevertheless, more often than not, those who want to emigrate find individual solutions and revert to the trafficking networks. The trafficking channels the pressure, even offering (terrible as this statement may seem) the prospect of an individual way out, to be paid for at a very high price. Nevertheless, it is a prospect. Emigration at all costs, even through traffickers who ask a very high price, represents, in the words of Ruggiero (1997) 'an individual resistance by way of physical relocation'. But this individual resistance represents, in fact, setbacks in collective projects in the countries of origin (development, socialism, etc...).

The increase in migratory pressure is one of the consequences of the economic, social, political and cultural transformations that have occurred in the past 20 years in the countries of departure as in the countries of arrival. These transformations are being introduced in the economic globalization process, making the market the only regularizing force and forcing the break-down of any protectionist barrier preventing the circulation of the merchandise. At the same time, economic globalization is closely tied to the increase in the level of communication and information on a global level. The same characteristics intrinsic to economic globalization facilitate the traffic.

Economic globalization represented, in fact, the end of 'national development' for many countries which were in a phase of development: the populations no longer believe in the future of their countries and consider emigration to a rich country to be a much more interesting prospect for their personal futures. The same is true for economies in transition, such as in Eastern Europe. Although the end of communism has opened up prospects of individual promotion, competition, it seems that the harshness of the rules of the game, and the presence of crime in the economy, offer prospects of an individualistic nature and do not encourage collective trust for the country's future. Thus the presentation of developed countries' model of existence and the circulation of information about them make it seem that anyone can imagine the possibility of emigrating.[5]

The cultural globalization (global American culture, in fact the 'Mac

World' culture) and neoliberalism, constituting today's dominant ideology, applied more by many right-wing than by left-wing governments,[6] represent ulterior support for trafficking. This is true both for the legitimization for any activity that produces wealth (thus even the sex industry, as is already the case in the Asiatic countries, for example in Thailand or in Eastern Europe), and also for the influence they can have on the mentality of those being trafficked (they are willing to pay, *often individually*, large sums of money just to ensure their departure). We will come back to the importance of cultural globalization in the development of the sex industry later in the article.

It is precisely in the contradiction between economy and global information, and a 'national' work force which provides an opening for trafficking, according to David Kyle, one of the few researchers who is currently working on these themes. At the root of the present situation of trafficking which has become a 'global' problem, there is the

> true moment of global capitalism and of triumphant neoliberalism (Post-Keynesian Liberalism), the configuration of capital 'without frontiers' and global markets of consumerism and services, on one hand, and a work force which is still closed within the borders of the other. (Kyle 1998)

There is this contradiction: a workforce for which frontiers exist in an economy which no longer has them, created by the necessary and sufficient conditions for global clandestine trafficking. 'The integrated global economy has at least one principal contradiction. While free trade allows for the growing mobility of capital and goods, this liberalization is not extended to human beings.' (Seabrook 1996)

The contradiction is much more disruptive, in that within the developed countries' economies, there is an ever-present 'grey area' of black-market jobs, for which subservient and flexible labourers, like the clandestine labourers, are needed. In this grey area, there are varied spheres of activity, ranging from productive semi-legal activity to that which is openly criminal.

> These quasi-legal productive sectors border on openly criminal economies, which draw profits from illegal labour and the trafficking of human beings. In some cases, the groups of organized crime straddle the semi-legal economy and the true criminal economy, and offer a variety of work opportunities to the individuals being trafficked in Europe. (Ruggiero 1997)

In some cases the illegal, trafficked immigrant can find work within the same enterprises rooted in Western Europe by organized crime (restaurants, casinos, trafficking, housing complexes, brothels) (Ziegler 1998).

Within the 'grey area,' between legal and illegal, are numerous activities linked with services, among these are services extended to private parties which are on the rise. The increase in female migration in the past twenty years has mainly been caused by an increase in services (in southern Europe, for example, immigrant women initially came in order to work as domestics).

Other than the growth of domestic labour, after a period of decline during the 1960s (Campani 1997) and in the care-giving professions (nurses, carers for the elderly), the increase in services also relates to consumer habits on the part of the populations of the developed world – in recent years, the activities linked to tourism and the entertainment industry. The development of the sex business must also be understood with regard to the increase in this type of activity.

In conclusion, since contraband and trafficking have a long history (as we will see in the analysis of the trafficking of women), the new development today is the dimension that trafficking is taking on, in the context of a capitalistic global economy, *whose intrinsic characteristics promote trafficking*.

In the specific case of the trafficking of women for sexual exploitation, its current development can be included in the growth of an activity hovering between legal and illegal (where the scales tip towards illegal) sex business. The sex industry is promoted in the context of globalization, by the growth of the consumer market and the new neoliberal ideology that clashes with family traditions and roles which had typically remained steadfast for centuries, proposing money and consumerism as the values to be pursued, and promoting the practices and experiences of individualism.

It is absolutely not our intention to pass moral judgement, nor is it moralistic, on this type of ideology: some observers denounce its devastating effects in the majority of developing countries (for example, the practice of selling one's daughters to the sex business in some areas of Nepal, girls sacrificed not only for survival, but also because of the families' desire to participate in consumerism; or the spread of AIDS in Thailand). Other scholars, however, even though they are fewer in number, sometimes highlight the role of 'modernization' which is expressed, for example, in forms of convenient provision for the prostitutes and the various sex industry structures in a phase of economic growth in Thailand. Yet, we can establish in general that Asiatic documentation and that which is generally non-European is much more critical towards neoliberalism than European documentation: a neoliberalism which justifies everything, including sex tourism for the sake of profit.

THE TRAFFICKING OF WOMEN FOR SEXUAL EXPLOITATION

The trafficking of women for sexual exploitation is a component of global trafficking of human beings, constantly on the rise in the above-described context of global economic liberalism. Organized crime, the managers of global trafficking, can very easily bring in those people being trafficked as destined for their activity (as is often the case of women in prostitution). In fact, in the expanding sex industry, organized crime (often in collaboration with petty crime) has a strong presence.[7] As with trafficking in general, the trafficking of women takes on new dimensions and characteristics today, even though it is certainly not a new phenomenon.

The first international accord for the repression of 'white slavery' (it was called thus at the time of trafficking) dated 18 May 1904, was followed by the International Convention of 4 May 1910 (again for the repression of white slavery) and by the International Convention of 30 September 1921 for the trading of women and children. In 1922, the Society of Nations Conference established an advisory committee for the trading of women and children, and in 1933, the first International Convention for the Trading of Women and Children was adopted. After the Second World War, the United Nations took up this theme again and in the seventeenth session in 1948, the Economic and Social Council invited the General Secretary of the United Nations to draw up the plans for a new Convention of a general scope covering the repression of the trading of women and children and the prevention of prostitution. The new development in the Convention of 1949 was that compared to the former documents, there was a connection established between trade and prostitution, while until then the two problems had been kept separate. In the debate on prostitution today we will see that the current tendency is to question this connection between exploitation of prostitution within countries and trafficking, as had been established by the Convention of 1949.

Today, the trafficking of women is directed from south to north, or south-south or east-west. The women who are trafficked are ones who come from poor countries and are brought to rich countries or countries in which, generally, beyond the local clientele, there is sex tourism.[8] Extremely lucrative in the era of globalization (a symbol of globalization itself), sexual tourism is a new phenomenon, and one which has important implications for the development of the sex industry.

Compared to the era in which the first conventions were signed, the directions of the trading or trafficking fluxes changed: white slavery assumed north-south or north-north fluxes. The studies conducted in the 1930s showed that the traffic went from Europe (mainly France, Italy, Spain, Germany, Austria, Hungary, Greece, Poland, Rumania and Turkey) towards Central and South America (Mexico, Panama, Argentina,[9] Brazil, Uruguay) and towards North America. The city of Alexandria, Egypt, was one of the principal ports through which the girls passed. Since Europe was the principal place of origin (white slavery, white slaves), in Asia, Chinese women were often trafficked to fulfill the needs of the brothels.

Compared to the past, the trafficking of women for sexual exploitation has greatly increased. The European Commission's report on the trafficking of women for sexual exploitation sounds like this:

> There is no doubt that the trafficking of women by organized crime is on the rise. Although there are no exact figures, (...), the IOM (International Organization for Migration) estimates that in 1995, about 500,000 women were being trafficked, the majority of them illegal, towards countries of the European Union, and studies of the NGO International Campaign Against Child Prostitution in Tourism in Asia has recently noted the trend of the trafficking of a high number of women and girls in Russia, the Ukraine and Belorussia towards the West. The figures declared by the National NGO also suggest an increase in the number of women coming from Central and Eastern Europe. (Commission of the European Communities 1996)

Ziegler cites Interpol's figures of the trafficking of women for 1997, which are even higher than IOM's: one million. The criminal organizations have Kiev, St. Petersburg, Alma-Ata, Tachkent and elsewhere in which modelling agencies or employment agencies for young dancers, run advertisements in the local papers.

If Eastern Europe has become one of the principal places of origin of the women who are trafficked into the European Union, trafficking equally involves the following:

- some African countries (in the case of Nigeria, for example, where the women are trafficked into Italy, and Ghana, where the women are trafficked into Germany) (Ruggiero 1997),
- various countries of Latin America (as is the case of the Dominicans trafficked into Spain and of the Dominicans and Brazilians to Switzerland),
- various Asian countries (Thai and Philippine women trafficked into Germany).[10]

The trafficking of women for sexual exploitation is not limited to the European Union: it is common in Asia, in the countries where there are thriving sex industries. Many Asian countries, such as Thailand, the Philippines or Sri Lanka, have followed, in the past twenty years, a policy which exports labourers. In the beginning it was male labourers, principally directed towards the Gulf countries; but the need for male labourers has decreased, while the need for female workers, domestics, nurses and baby-sitters has increased. Domestic labour, overall, especially in the Gulf countries where many Asian women are sent, is often very hard and does not spare women from domestic violence (being raped by one's employer is common, judging from the accounts given). Other than domestic labour, there are no exceptional employment opportunities. In the face of these meagre prospects, an increasing percentage of women leave, in most cases choose to leave officially and unofficially, to work as entertainers or sexworkers. Migration for prostitution is illegal, but the girls can obtain an entertainers contract, as is the case of many Philippine and Thai girls who go to Japan. The entertainers contract represents legal immigration for the activities connected with the thriving sex industry. There are agencies, often above every suspicion, which offer legal entertainers or dancers contracts to Philippine and Thai girls. But not even a legal contract is a guarantee of acceptable living conditions. The example of Japan, though an industrialized and democratic country, is significant.

Japan legally hires Philippine and Thai women for its entertainment industry. According to Japanese sources, there are about 50,000 women who enter with official contracts every year. Of course, even in these cases, living and working conditions can be much worse than promised. But the worst conditions are met in the cases of women who are illegally hired, to whom 'respectable' jobs are promised and who instead find themselves involved in the prostitution racket. Philippine sources estimate that 40,000 Philippine women work legally in the Japanese sex market and that the numbers of those who work illegally are just as high. Thai sources estimate that 70,000 (*Bangkok Post*, 19 March 1993) Thai women work as prostitutes in Japan (but these estimates seem, to some authors such as Boonchalanski and Guest, excessive).

In October 1985, a trafficking case was discovered in Bangkok: a Japanese and a Thai were accused of illegally exporting Thai women to Japan using fake identification. The women were destined for prostitution and had to pay large amounts of money in order to depart.

The abuses suffered by the Philippine and Thai women who illegally enter Japan fill the pages of the Asian papers. The tales of the constraint mechanisms of which the trafficked women are victims are sadly similar to those of which the women immigrants in Europe are victims: they are sold, their passports are seized and they must repay a debt.

While Thai women emigrate (in the hopes of higher earnings), or are trafficked into Japan or to Western Europe, especially to Germany, Holland and Scandinavia,[11] Thailand has become the place of arrival for many economic immigrants from Burma (about 330,000, many of which are women, a good number of them trafficked, in the sex industry and many men who run it), from India and Bangladesh (about 100,000), from China (about 100,000, of which many are women trafficked from the Hunan province), and about 20,000 from Cambodia and Laos.

Among these immigrants exists a number of trafficked women. Asia Rights Watch, scrutinizing rights in Asia, published a report on the trafficking of Burmese women to Thailand in December of 1993.

> Thirty girls and women were interviewed in depth, and it was revealed that about 20,000 Burmese women were hired and sent to the sex industry in Thailand. The women are generally tricked by agencies which promised legal work in Thailand. They are brought to the border, often by unsuspecting relatives, who receive money – up to 800 dollars – which then becomes the prisoner's 'debt'. Any young woman who tries to leave the brothels risks arrest- the police are often brothels' main clients – or it places the family at risk – which will be persecuted because the debt was not paid. Women work between 10 and 18 hours a day, 25 days a month and receive between 5 to 15 clients per day. (Seabrook 1996: 136)

Burmese women are the principal victims of trafficking and forced prostitution. Hnin Hnin Pyne, in her thesis, 'AIDS and Prostitution in Thailand, a Study of Burmese Prostitution Cases in Ranong', subdivides the induction into prostitution into three channels: *voluntary*, where the woman herself goes into the sex industry structure (brothel or massage parlour); *forced*, when parents or other relatives push the girl to prostitute herself for money; and *involuntary*, when there is coercion and trickery. According to this thesis, the majority of Burmese women entered the sex industry by way of coercion and trickery.

From Cambodia and Laos there are also trafficked women destined to work in the brothels in Bangkok. There are also cases of kidnapping from these two countries. The development of trafficking towards Thailand is in response to the constant rise and new demands for women on the part of the sex industry.

TRAFFICKING AND THE SEX INDUSTRY

We have said that the trafficking of women for sexual exploitation takes on new characteristics today in relation to increased internationalization and the involvement of criminal organizations in this industry. Prostitution today therefore seems to be a business which has been placed in a sector, which, apart from the prostitute and client, requires a complex structure and investment of large amounts of money.

Having made it clearer as to what we mean by way of the sex industry, that is, a structure or sector within which prostitution occurs, namely, the prostitute-client relationship.

> Here are some categories with which to begin. There are those which can be called services: prostitution, striptease and phone sex. And there are the products: pornography and erotic aids. In the two sides of the industry, a handful of creative and well-run businesses are making a turnover more than ever – for example, through 'hostess' agencies or high-class escorts, or through Internet, or by intelligently exploiting pieces of the market. The traditional businesses, especially small or artisan-type ones, are under the threat of extinction. What is happening? The principal change, as for many other industries, is globalization.

Thus writes *The Economist* in an article published in February 1998, entitled 'The Sex Industry,' adding 'To Buyers and Sellers, the Sex Trade is Just Another Business' as the subtitle.

Globalization, as *The Economist* further explains, has made it such that thanks to international tourism and business trips, prostitution has become extremely well-paid in most poor countries: the girls of Riga and even Budapest who prostitute themselves in hotels earn twenty times what a university professor or a head physician of a hospital earns each month! In the West, the girls of Riga and Budapest force the market prices to fall: on a lower level, whether it is the most banal pornography or street prostitution, only suppliers with good prices survive. Globalization has also made it such that erotic aids are made in China, and Western pornographic film producers have moved their studios to Budapest, which has become the principal centre of such productions in Europe, rather than Amsterdam or Copenhagen. The actors' rates have plummeted dramatically. Even acts that suggest injury or humiliation only cost the producer two or three hundred dollars, about one-third of the rates paid ten years ago.

In the current context there is increasingly less independent prostitution. This does not mean that voluntary prostitution does not exist as a choice, but it is not an 'artisan' practice, except in rare cases. The situation of 'artisan' prostitution, or rather what is left of it, varies, however, from one country to another, forming a group of factors which is extremely complex to evaluate.[12]

Within a globalized capitalist economy, survival of a small 'artisan' and 'interstitial' economy can find great difficulties and occupy limited niches of the market. Today, prostitution tends to be a capitalist business like any another, made up of a group of directors and wage earners, whose every move is kept under watch, and the ties with crime, traffickers, with the consumers (the clients) and with the police, are perfectly structured. *Because these are the conditions which allow it to obtain that which every self-respecting industry seeks: profit*. And, as we have pointed out numerous times, this capitalist enterprise is expanding thanks to the conditions offered by globalization.

In the documentation consulted on Asian countries, especially Thailand[13] and the Philippines, we found very few, if any, references to 'artisan'[14] prostitution. It would seem a little different, for now, the case of Latin America, where prostitution tied to internal migration exists, destined for a prevalently local clientele (see note 12 in the present article referring to the shanty towns of Brazil and Bacelar's study, *Familia Prostituta*).

Europe's situation is different, and at least for the autochthons, is better compared to the current one in Asia, due to the social and political structure, to the legal system and also of the relations of this sort, changed through years of feminist fighting. But the situation is rapidly changing due to the arrival of immigrants, as *The Economist* rightly points out; also the break-up (in terms of social structure and values) of many countries of Eastern Europe, which represents a favourable trend for the recruitment of women for prostitution and pornography, allowing costs to be lowered and profits to be increased. Currently, the involvement of crime in trafficking and the increase of the supply of prostitutes, is a stage in the construction of the sex industry, structured according to the above-described manner (that is, with directors, wage-earners, precise ties with crime, the goods-women suppliers, the clients, the police).

The expansion of the trafficking of women for sexual exploitation and the expansion of the sex industry, which becomes a source of high profits for some groups and not for the women or men who practice prostitution, need other conditions. One of the conditions often raised in the readings consulted is a situation in which there is poverty, misery, and a lack of opportunity, combined with the transformation of traditional values into a consumeristic model. We will cite a consultant for UNICEF for Nepal whose comments might possibly be valid for Eastern Europe too.

There is an enormous sex market in Southern Asia, particularly in the south-east. One of the most lucrative businesses is the trafficking of girls to nearby countries. The Nepalese government estimates the number of girls of Nepal in India alone to be 200,000, of which 20 per cent are children. A great number of girls and young women are forced or sold by their parents, husbands, relatives, or by family friends: people in whom the girls had put their trust. The potential revenue generated by the sex market has few, if any, rivals in the villages. The sex business offers the chance to make a quantitative leap in the earnings that one would normally find only in a context where there is higher education, small industries on a large scale and services where the opportunities for wage-earning jobs are plentiful. Since the majority of these factors are absent in rural Nepal, the sex market wields a great economic attraction (Knuttson 1996:109-110).[15]

We repeat, analogous phenomena occur in Eastern Europe and are at the root of the flux of women trafficked into Europe. In the study of the case of Italy and of the various typologies of women being trafficked, we will get a better idea of the dynamics which we have described on a general level.

THE NORMATIVE ITALIAN OUTLINE

In order to define the normative Italian outline in the matter of international trafficking destined for prostitution and sexual exploitation of women, the norms of immigration and prostitution should be considered. These are both sectors in which legislative action was often markedly late in coming about, or at any rate inadequate, compared to the emerging phenomena.

The first Italian law on immigration No. 943 dates back to 30 December 1986 and consists of 'Norms on the Matter of Employment and Treatment of Non-EEC Workers and Against Illegal Immigration'. Law No. 39 of 28 February 1990, the 'Martelli Law', confronts the problem of illegal immigration in a marginal manner: Article 3, Sub-Section 8 punishes one who promotes the illegal entry of foreigners; aggravating circumstances can be applied (with tripled prison sentences and multiplying the pecuniary penalty by 25), if it is done for profit, or by three or more persons in concurrence with one another.

Subsequently, according to Article 7, Sub-Section 2, among the crimes that bring about the expulsion of foreigners are violation of the 'Provision on the matter of entry and stay, or on the matter of the intermediation of workers, as well as exploitation for prostitution or the crime of rape and of other crimes against one's sexual freedom'.

The decree law No. 489 of 18 November 1995 (that is, the so-called Dini Decree, reiterated twice, the last time on 19 March 1996 with No. 132), has still not been converted into a law, other than revising the norms relative to expulsion (Art. 7) and the repression of activities directed to promote the illicit entry of foreigners (Art. 8).

The norms of Art. 7 prove to be altogether tougher compared to previous legislation, but do not contain explicit references to trafficking oriented towards prostitution.

It is not because of studies like ours that governments have become conscious of the need to provide for specific norms on the trafficking of women for sexual exploitation. The new legislative proposal on immigration presented by the government provides for, at the same time, simpler and more direct measures of expulsion and more severe penalties for those who manage the trafficking as well as support for the women who bring charges against traffickers and their accomplices.

It can be said that this last measure was a suggestion proposed by the study that we piloted. In reality, the people who work in assisting immigrant prostitutes pointed out the importance of giving visas to those who press charges (there is already a right to justice, but it is a very limited one), provide possibilities for employment, and assist them with living arrangements (through shelters). At the end of this process, we would also need to provide, for those who do not want to go back or, for safety reasons, cannot, the possibility of following training courses in order to find work. The other part of legislation in hand concerns norms in the matter of prostitution.

Law No. 75 of 20 February 1958, the 'Abolition of the Regulation of Prostitution and Fight Against Exploitation of Foreign Prostitutes', better known as the 'Merlin Law,' named after the Socialist parliamentarian who proposed its approval, is a law which de-criminalizes the crime of prostitution in cases where it is practised privately, eliminating those operating in brothels, which were, up until that time, inspected by the state, and making it and all other related activity a crime punishable by law.

Art. 1 forbids 'the operation of brothels' in Italy, and Art. 2 orders the brothels to be closed with the so-called 'locales of prostitution' (their closure was to take place within six months from the time the law was passed).

Thus since 1958 the matter has been regulated as provided by Art. 3, which modifies the provisions contained in the Penal Code, Art. 531-535. These articles are in Section IX of the Penal Code, 'Offences Against Public Morality' and in particular, Heading II, 'On Offences of Public Decency and Sexual Propriety.'

Based on these provisions, the following instances are thus punishable:

- ownership, operation or rental of a house in which prostitution is practised,
- any form of participation in the aforementioned activities,
- tolerance of the practice of prostitution in locales open to the public or used by the public (hotels, boarding houses, associations or other forms),
- employment of a person for such ends and the facilitation of the initiation of prostitution,
- initiation of prostitution, whether privately or in public forms, and
- exploitation of prostitution in any form.

Furthermore, and here is where we enter the heart of the matter, the following are also punishable:

- moving to a new locality or a different State from one's own in order to practise prostitution and facilitation of departure, and
- participation in domestic or international organizations to employ

persons intended for prostitution or the exploitation thereof, or support with respect to such organizations.

We will add that the aforementioned crimes are punishable even if committed in a foreign country, and even if it is for induction we wish to make it clear that it is punished 'as long as it is provided for by international law'.

As prostitution itself is not a crime, the suits filed and the trials are often for induction, exploitation and encouragement of prostitution. In 1994, 967 persons were turned in, of which 258 were foreigners. The foreigners are therefore over-represented in this type of crime. Albanians are predominant (75) and Ex-Yugoslavs (65) followed by, but trailing way behind, Nigerians and Tunisians. Among those who were reported, the majority were men, except in the case of the Nigerians, among whom women make up 50 per cent of those reported (9 out of 18).

NUMBER AND TYPOLOGIES

How Many Are There?

During our study, we have sought to establish quantitative estimates, by way of interviews with privileged witnesses and immigrant women.

The estimates proposed, finally, are the result of comparisons made between information received by women who were interviewed, censuses which were informally taken by social workers and associations, opinions of volunteer association workers who were interviewed, and estimates proposed by journals. Beginning with this information, domestic estimates were proposed, with lowest and highest figures: these general data must be considered as the general outline into which any sort of analysis can be placed. They are certainly approximate, since the phenomenon was little-explored despite its great social importance.

The estimates produced – through the afore-mentioned criteria – are summarized in Tables 1 and 2, which demonstrate as a whole a phenomenon shown to be between 18,800 and 25,100 units variably distributed in the domestic territory. The larger numbers seem to be concentrated in the North with numbers between 8,800 and 11,300 units, followed by the central regions with 5,600 to 7,000 units and by the South (including the islands) with 5,100 to 6,800 units.

As it is possible to verify with Table 1, the regions with the highest number of foreign girls who prostitute themselves are Lazio and Lombardy. These have respectively, 4–5,000 and 3,500–4,500 estimated

TABLE 1

ESTIMATES OF NUMBER OF FOREIGN PROSTITUTES IN ITALY

REGIONS	*CITIES*	*minimum*	*maximum*
Veneto		**800**	**1200**
	Venice	500	800
	Vicenza	150	200
Emilio Romagna		**1200**	**1800**
	Bologna	500	800
	Rimini	400	600
	Ravenna	200	400
Lombardy		**3500**	**4500**
	Milan	2000	2500
	Brescia	800	1000
Piedmont		**1200**	**1800**
	Turin	700	900
Latium		**4000**	**5000**
	Rome	3000	3500
	Latina	500	700
Abruzzo		**600**	**800**
	Teramo	200	300
Campania		**1500**	**2000**
	Naples	1000	1200
	Caserta	300	500
Other Regions		**6000**	**8000**
TOTAL		**18800**	**25100**

Source: Elaboration of the research team.

TABLE 2

ESTIMATES OF NUMBER OF FOREIGN PROSTITUTES IN ITALY, BY GEOGRAPHICAL AREA

Geographical Area	*minimum*	*maximum*
North	8100	11300
Centre	5600	7000
South and islands	5100	6800
TOTAL	18800	25100

Source: Elaboration of the research team

in number; they represent major attracting regions of placement since the appearance of the immigratory phenomenon, both because of employment opportunities in small businesses and the service sector and also because of the opportunities of socialization that the big metropolises offer – in particular, Rome and Milan.

These cities seem to be consequently those with larger numbers of prostitutes; as a whole, in fact, they make up about one fourth of the general total, with regard to the lowest estimates (5,000 out of about 18,800 units) and a little more than one-third with regard to the highest estimates (9,500 out of 25,100 units). The other region in which the phenomenon has been estimated to be of great dimension is Campania – with 1,500–2,000 in number, of which a good part resides in the city of Naples and in the immediate surrounding area (for example, the Bay of Domizia along the route of the northern coastline and the surrounding area with Caserta towards the inland areas).

The difficulty in establishing these estimates has not yet been emphasized: it is caused by the great geographic mobility of the prostitutes. These movements can be performed daily (from the place of residence to the place where they practice prostitution); of short duration (one week, ten days) within the same region; of longer duration, of one to two months, for 'a season', which would imply a temporary move of their usual residence. These movements can be done on a spontaneous or individual basis, or more commonly, organized by a pimp and traffickers, who manage various prostitute 'networks'.

In the general outline of these estimates, we also tried to establish the proportions of women 'trafficked', meaning that they had come through trafficking networks and were tricked with regard to their final destination. This has proved to be very difficult, and our sample includes overall, women who had to escape their conditions, turning to organizations providing aid.

Socio-Demographic Characteristics

Beginning with the information collected, it is possible to establish the phases during which prostitution of female immigrants became visible and evolved, and to locate it in Italy's immigration as a whole. The period 1989–1991 certainly represents a turning point; these are the years in which the Eastern countries progressively entered a transition, immigration from these countries increased (surpassing the fluxes of North Africans), and the war in Ex-Yugoslavia broke out. In the wave of immigration from Eastern Europe, it is still difficult to define the groups practising (of their own accord or because they are forced) prostitution: the term, 'Polish,' often indicates any woman from Eastern Europe (Russians, Ukrainians, Romanians, Slovenians, Bosnians, Hungarians). Along with Eastern European prostitutes, other immigrant women practice prostitution: thus we are dealing also with Brazilians (often transvestites) and other Latin Americans. When the second wave began, starting from 1991, the majority of women were Nigerians, often trafficked and brought to Italy through trickery,

Beginning in 1993–94, the majority of immigrants were Albanians, who came in illegally from Albanian cities, often with male relatives, friends, and fiancés, and were pushed into prostitution. The flux of Nigerian women also continued. From 1995–96, the prostitution business increasingly involved more young Albanian girls, often abducted, trafficked, and coming from villages in central parts of the country. The easy-to-come-by visa scandal began, concerning visas granted by certain employees of the Italian Embassy in Lagos, and this has slowed Nigerian immigration a little.

The socio-demographic characteristics vary, evidently depending on the national group and the wave that arrives. We will thus create a general outline – a detailed description will follow – of the two national groups. The most numerous are the Nigerians and the Albanians. The majority of immigrant prostitutes are unmarried women, who are alone, and who have been tricked with the promise of marriage or of artistic and prestigious careers outside of their country.

Among Latin-American women and those of Eastern Europe (with the exception of Albanians) we also find married women, or more often divorced or widowed ones, who have left their children behind in the country. They are generally older women (aged 24–30), whereas Albanian women are younger (some of them minors, aged 14–18), and Nigerians ranging in age from 19–24.

Their social class, on a professional level, and level of education, varies both from one group to another and within the same group. It is very difficult to establish professional typologies from interviews conducted, given the variety of answers received. What can be said is that their origin – i.e. rural or urban – has a determining influence on their professional placement. In an urban setting, it varies greatly: from manual labourers to teachers (among the women of Eastern countries), from waitresses to students (the youngest ones). Cases in which they had previously been practising prostitutes are rare.

We can get a clearer idea of the levels of education. We can establish, beginning with our interviews, that the majority of women had eight years of education; a group of women had slightly more education. The groups can be broken down into those that have little education and those that are highly educated. This varies, overall, as we have already stressed, from one group to another.

Among Nigerians, there is a high number of uneducated women who have never attended school; in particular those who arrived in recent years from the agricultural regions. These can be traced to the South (for example, the regions of Makurdi and Yola), range in age from 15–20, and those from Lagos and Kadan in particular had medium to low levels of education.

With regard to the Albanians, the girls, all of whom are very young, have medium to high levels of education (some, among the oldest ones of urban origin, have even attended a university). The differences depend on their place of origin, whether it is rural or urban. In the last wave, made up of young girls from the countryside, the level of education is lower.

The Latin Americans and women of Eastern Europe are almost all of urban origin and, with the exception of the Peruvians, have a medium to high level of education. It is in this group that the 'free choice' of prostitution is the most common.

Living Conditions in Prostitution. Possible Typologies.

The living conditions of the immigrant prostitutes depend very much on previous life experiences (whether they were already prostitutes or not) and the degree of violence at their place of departure, in that the girls take it for expatriation: it is, in effect, one of the fundamental instruments of control on her (and their families), especially in some groups, for example, the Nigerians.

That said, three typologies can be established according to concrete practices, depending on the ways and places in which prostitution is practised:

- practice of the profession in flats,
- in public places (interviews, dancers, etc...), and
- on the street.

Living conditions, the type of independence possible, and the severity of exploitation vary depending on the typology; the practice of prostitution in flats assumes that there is much more independence than in the other two typologies. It is a typology in which Italian women are in the majority. Among foreigners, there are mainly Russians, Columbians and Argentinians.

'Hidden' or 'masked' prostitution is practised in public and private places, in the form of other businesses, dancers, strippers, pornographic film actresses; it does not differ much from prostitution in flats, and therefore there is still independence in the form of practice of the profession. The difference mostly consists in the role of mediation, controlled by agencies or by managers of the locales where prostitution is practised. It is precisely in the role of agency and manager of the locales that there are trafficking practices with regard to women who hoped to have artistic careers and who find themselves forced to practise prostitution.

The nationality of the women in question is generally Eastern European, Brazilian, Columbian and, in lesser numbers, Philippine. Polish, Rumanian, Hungarian and Ukrainians would seem more widely-introduced in the circuit of actresses and strippers and less so in public and private places; Brazilians and Columbians are, for the most part, placed as dancers and showgirls. Philippines are mostly singers or dancers.

But prostitution is, for the most part, the business of foreigners, and foreigners who, for the most part, are trafficked (up to 75–80 per cent according to our estimates), and in street prostitution. Living and working conditions represent forms of generalized subordination, first of all to the 'pimps', 'macros', and, secondly (especially for some national groups), by networks of criminal organizations, both of the same nationality as the women, and Italian with transnational connections.

Street prostitution is generally ended when the debts contracted with the international agencies who guarantee emigration are reimbursed, both when the women involved are not aware of the business they will have to practise, and when they are not pushed into prostitution in a violent manner or because they are forced to do so.

In effect, the debt with the future 'pimps' is incurred in the period which precedes emigration and must be reimbursed in the first months of stay in Italy. Basically, the debt, instead of becoming lower often becomes higher, as the pimps provide housing at outrageous prices. The girls' passports are often withheld as a guarantee that they will pay, and threats to family members at home weigh heavily upon them.

NATIONAL GROUPS

The national groups which experience to a great extent the 'pimps' (often organized groups of delinquents) are the Albanians and Nigerians, even if their general characteristics – at the root of the respective national groups – obviously pose similarities and differences.

The *similarities* are verified, specifically:

- the young age at first entry of the girls involved – under 18 years of age (even lower for Albanians and slightly higher for Nigerians),
- partial awareness, of certain small proportions of the women in question, of the business in which they will engage in Italy,
- complete unawareness – verifiable in the majority of the cases (including the sub-category of the previous point) – of the violence they will endure and the complete psycho-physical subordination to the pimps and the groups that they represent,
- specific difficulties – verifiable in the course of the practice of the trade – of initiating processes of release from the conditions forced on them by the pimps,
- being caught, even in psychological-existential terms, in dynamics of the re-enforcement of living conditions associated with prostitution.

The *differences* are verified, specifically:

- in the methods of contact, interviewing and of convincing the girls to emigrate,
- in the 'contract' methods, in the cost of emigration and in the forms of payment/restitution of the loan,
- in the characteristics of the ties between the pimps and the country of origin, as well as the various roles the pimps themselves assume,
- in the forms (known) of escape from the above-mentioned vicious circle.

The Albanians

In the case of the Albanians, the contacts that push them to emigration take place in general through friends and acquaintances, sometimes even through amorous relationships. In some cases, less commonly, the girls are victims of veritable abductions. To reach Italy, the girls follow the same routes as the other illegal immigrants (motor boats, rowing boats, etc.) passing through the Channel of Otranto. The cost of the trip varies from 3 to 5 million Italian lire.

The relation between the trafficked girls, subsequently forced to practice prostitution on the streets, and the pimps is often a direct one. The pimps are generally small-time criminals, often young, who blinded by easy money, do not hesitate to throw onto the streets their female schoolmates, their childhood female friends, and even their fiancées.

We are dealing with violent crime of an aggressive nature, but often, of an 'artisan' nature, in the sense that the pimps are often independent or grouped into small groups. For the moment, organized crime does not have complete control over Albanian prostitution even though the ties begin there (certain pimps are also involved in drug trafficking).

The Nigerians

They are recruited in the slums of Lagos or Benin City or in rural villages in Southern and Eastern Nigeria. The contracts, persuasive efforts and, subsequent surveillance of the women are made through a person who is not of the other national groups – a woman of another type, generically called Madam or Mother, meaning 'priestess.' It is she who acts as mediator for the girls and the organization that arranges the departures. In Italy, some time ago, the daughters used to keep the Madam as a reference, and it was to her they sent their money to repay their debt.

Between the girls and the Madam, who stays in the country of origin, the designated tie is consecrated by way of magical practices (voodoo rituals, according to different witnesses); it is therefore very strong and cannot be broken. To this fear of violating a magic norm, the presence of a Madam in Italy is added in order to control the girls; she controls and organizes groups of girls, and is the go-between for the criminal organization behind the trafficking of Nigerian women.

Therefore, the control of the girls operates on three levels: through the Madam in Nigeria, the Madam in Italy and the broad network of organized crime which is in contact with the Italian Madam. The existence of these levels of control therefore make it difficult for the girls to attempt to escape.

The Others

With regard to the other national groups, despite the initial ties we can ascertain that there is greater independence in the practice of prostitution. This applies both to Latin American women and women from other Eastern countries. This is also possibly because these women are, in general, older than the Albanians and the Nigerians.

THE WAYS OUT

Beginning with interviews, it can be said that the ways out of the condition of immigrant prostitutes depend on typology and context. In general, age and experience play an important role (as we have seen, this implies the difference between Albanians and Nigerians, on one hand, and the other nationalities, on the other), but intervention and 'external' action taken on the part of the pimp – departures, family, friends, social workers (government or association), the police or even clients – are often determining forces.

Even when a girl has matured, external support is often necessary in order to make the transition to breaking with the conditions of prostitution. There, often parents' or friends' roles prove to be essential. We will not discuss the clients, whose role is often ambiguous, even if often they are the ones who inform the girls of the existence of the assistance-providing associations. In fact, it is above all, these associations which have an essential role: they make contact with the girls in the street, offering hot drinks and information on HIV. Once rapport is established, the associations invite the girls to come to the association and to take advantage of the services offered. The police forces intervene for administrative checks, but sometimes at the girls' request. Sometimes they intervene because the girls find themselves abandoned. Police forces sometimes collaborate with volunteer associations, at the very least informing them as to the whereabouts of the girls.

CONCLUSION

Is it possible to draw any conclusions either from the analysis of this international outline or from Italian research? Compared to what was said relating to the development of trafficking and the development of the sex business, separating trafficking or the white slave trade from prostitution currently seems much more difficult than it was at the beginning of the century. It is evident that the trafficking has been introduced into the growth of a sector of activity worth billions, that in some countries has acquired legitimacy as an economic propulsor, and which traffickers and organized crime try to establish in other countries too (for example in Eastern Europe). A lucrative business in a globalized world, the sex industry tends, furthermore, to expand, multiplying the supply and creating demand, moving the women through trafficking and the clients through sex tourism.

Yet despite constant legal and illegal interfacing, on which the sex industry operates, despite the effects of the development of the sex industry in more involved countries, on women and their families, from a human rights standpoint, and also one of public health (the development of AIDS), government policies reside in ambiguity. On the one hand, they augur preventative measures and containment of this expansion, and on the other, they hesitate to target an extremely lucrative business, which could in a certain sense become a part of the entertainment industry. In this ambiguity, the measures for prevention or containment, and sanctions too, should not target the weaker element – the prostitutes. Instead, in the case of the trafficked prostitutes, it is necessary to put measures of protection for them alongside the fight against trafficking. But if it is principally the illegal which should be targeted, it is also necessary to halt the apparently legal (houses of ill repute, brothels) which take advantage of the illegal. In fact, there is no guarantee that a legal brothel or massage parlour is not connected with the criminal trafficking networks (as happens in Japan). The topic of legislative intervention seems, in fact, poorly proposed today if the terms of the debate focus on prostitution solely in terms of the client-prostitute relationship, maybe even the pimp, without keeping in mind the global structure of the sex industry.

In south-east Asian and Eastern countries, the development of the sex industry certainly does not produce change in the roles which are usually in some way emancipatory: it comes through the support, if not the accentuation, of female subordination, through the objectification of women who can be bought for men's sexual pleasure. The development of trafficking (and we know of the methods used to subdue women) and of the sex industry, develop through relationships usually socially constructed and based on unresolved female subordination.

In the West too, the development of the sex industry emphasizes the objectification of women (or of men) as the object of sexual pleasure through constant urging to consume (as with the supply of prostitutes or the proposition of sex tourism) and the relationship of power with money. It is on these topics that it is necessary to begin reflecting: certainly the objective of changing mentalities seems unattainable for now, but it is also obstructed by the idea that prostitution is unavoidable, being the oldest trade in the world.

The connection between trafficking and prostitution for the development of the sex business causes the distinction between voluntary and involuntary prostitution to be lost. The grey area of trafficking is never completely involuntary nor is it voluntary: it is an area of social suffering and comprehensive economics. Cases of abduction are fairly rare; more usual are cases of trickery, family complicity and countless seductions. The lack of work opportunities can push women to work voluntarily in the sex business, in contexts which are breaking down social barriers little by little, and ethical and psychological ones too. The breakdown of values, challenging cultural and economic models in the face of the Western consumerism model, do the rest.

Finally, the topic of economic law is posed – the right to live, to have a secure job, not to be dependent on prostitution as the only form of work open to women. Since all civil law and policies in the West set down a fundamental right, the right to life itself, 'without the right to grow up in a peaceful situation, free of being needy or malnutrition, illness and premature death, all of the other rights are cancelled out' (Seabrook 1996:1).

We will again quote, because we believe them to be extremely clear and enlightening, the words of an activist of an association in Bangkok – Empower – which helps prostitutes to put themselves on a level of greater equality with the clients.

> We go to the universities too, with programs in an attempt to change the up-coming generation's behavior. Well-educated youths do not think that it is beneficial to control their desires, and the context we work in only makes this worse. 'Liberalization' is one of the words in fashion; and it spreads into various areas of the economy, where its effects can be disastrous. There is much hypocrisy in this. A consumer society increases desire immensely: but cutting out all repression, strange desires necessarily emerge. To deny this is hypocritical, when many dehumanized, irregular behaviors, are not only condoned, but are considered essential for economic growth. We do not see our distortions because we are accustomed to them. Only in the face of pedophilia and other horrors do we see our worst side in the mirror, and we do not like that which we see.' ('Beth', in Seabrook 1996:85–86)

To follow through on the fight against the trafficking of women for sexual exploitation, it would most definitely have to move on to working on mentalities so that it would not go in the direction of reinforcing a neoliberalism which, without changing these types of relationships on a deeper level, has devalued past models and norms. The fight against trafficking moves on to the re-establishment of a set of values shared by all, societies of departure and arrival, and in opposition to the neoliberal ideology or at least its worst aspects. In the era of globalization, it seems impossible to reach this objective, but it proves necessary before the processes of disintegration, of which the sex industry, trafficking and sex tourism are products. Writes Seabrook:

> It is fiercely ironic that sex tourism must be a symptom of globalization, the integration of the world in a single economy, where both the workers and the clients are products of disintegration – of local communities, the dissolution of roots and belonging, the break-up of old work models and traditional ways of life, and the psychical disintegration of many people who are caught up in great epic changes, of which they have little understanding and over which they have even less control. (Seabrook 1996:170)

NOTES

1. It is always difficult to estimate figures for the number of immigrants present; however, we are dealing with many thousands of women, as the estimates of Italian research conducted by PARSEC indicate.
2. In the novel *Los Pasos Perdidos*, Alejo Carpentier remembers, in speaking about the New World, 'las clasicas rameras, despedidas para la Nouvelle Orleans con marcia de pifano como en una opera de repertorio...' the classic streetwalkers, sent to New Orleans, strolling about to the sound of flutes piping, as in an opera of the repertoire. The opera to which Carpentier is referring is *Manon Lescault* by Giacomo Puccini, in which the unhappy Manon, a fallen angel in Abbé Prevost's novel, must make a terrible voyage with prostitutes. One who is not a fallen angel, but instead a lucid observer of the bourgeois double-standard, is Moll Flanders, whose mother was a prostitute who became an honest land-owner in Virginia. Moll follows a path that leads her from illegality to respectability, choosing thievery and her love for a street bandit over prostitution. Moll has lucidly understood that the trades of thief and banker are not so different. The history of female prostitution in the era of colonization has not yet been written. In Argentina, studies on prostitutes who came in because of the great numbers of single men who were alone are underway. On the other hand, Dolores Juliano, an Argentine anthropologist who works in Barcelona, in an unpublished article on racism and sexism, rightly notes that the 'scarcity' of women in the Latin American context in the era of colonization has certainly changed the type of relations and has also provided a different role for the prostitutes, rendering that reality very far from ours...
3. It is absolutely not our intention to state that all immigrants from certain countries are prostitutes. With this topic, in fact, the risk of stereotyping is very high. It is not, however, possible to ignore the cases of certain nationalities, the presence of prostitutes (Albanians and Nigerians in Italy, for example; the Dominicans in Spain or in Holland, the Ghanese in Holland, or the Eastern Europeans in Holland, France, Luxembourg...) is higher than in others. The causes of this phenomenon reside principally in the organization of the trafficking networks. In the study conducted by PARSEC for the

IOM, the number of foreign prostitutes in Italy was estimated at a minimum of 18,000 (up to 25,000), which is not a very large percentage with respect to the number of female foreign residents, but neither is it an insignificant figure, especially considering the limited number of nationalities involved.

4. We must not forget that, in the time of the occupation during the 1950s and 1960s (the 'trente glorieuses'), in France, Italian immigration, but Portuguese too, was often clandestine (who can forget the old Neo-Realist film, *The Path of Hope*, in which the French border guards allow a clandestine group of Sicilians in the 'Eldorado' of the time?). But since work was easy to find, it was sufficient that a clandestine immigrant present a work contract obtained there, in order to legalize his situation. In this context, the illegal immigrant, at the very most, forced to turn to a 'smuggler' of Ventimiglia, to whom many Italian immigrants in France have said they turned.
5. The phenomenon of anticipatory socialization had already been proposed in the 1960s by Italian sociologists Alberoni and Baglioni.
6. Cornelius Castoriasis, who passed away in 1997, states in his last interview published in August 1998 by *Le Monde Diplomatique* that the predominance of neoliberalism ideology is exemplified by left-wing or centre-left governments of Great Britain, France and Italy. We are dealing with three left-wing or centre-left governments which practice, more or less, the same policies of the liberal right-wing ones in countries in power such as Germany or even Spain... the only basic differences, with respect to welfare and neoliberal ideology, between the 'Right' and the 'Left' remain still in some countries of old and strong social democratic tradition, where moreover, the 'bourgeoisie coalitions' dare to attack welfare much less than the left-wing in the aforementioned countries, and where, with respect to the defence of welfare, there is strong approval of public opinion.
7. We do not want to deny that an 'artisan' form of prostitution exists, managed by women. Nevertheless, it seems to be a marginal phenomenon with respect to a sex industry which is managed by enterprises which for the most part are connected with crime. As we will see later, in the cases of countries where the sex industry is more evident, that no self-management for women exists; this does not mean, however, that some women do not claim that they voluntarily chose to become prostitutes in hotels, massage parlours, etc... whose operation and rules women have never had any chance whatsoever to influence.
8. A partial exception is represented by India, where trafficking, forced prostitution and exploitation in the red light districts exist in various cities, but where the clientele is local for the most part, 'tourism for prostitution, which has become an accepted source of foreign exchange in some countries of Southeast Asia does not exist in India (...) Certainly a certain kind of sexual tourism exists, but it is not organized on a large scale. It is limited to the 'Gulf Connection' and to some call houses which serve the foreign clientele in the big hotels of Dehli or Bombay.'
9. Let us remember that numerous studies on the history of prostitution in connection with immigration and the formation of the nation exist in Argentina. See J. Donna Guy, *Sex and Danger in Buenos Aires: Prostitution, Family and Nation in Argentina*, Lincoln, 1991.
10. In 1990 there were about 20,000 female Philippine residents in Germany. The majority were mail-order brides who came into the country illegally but who then legalized their status through marriage (Council of Europe 1991). Completely dependent on their husbands, they had to bear any abuses through fear of repatriation.
11. Trafficking, states Seabrook, follows the paths of sex tourism. There are numerous cases of Western men who have gone to Thailand as sex tourists and have taken women as 'wives,' subsequently bringing them to Europe to force them to work in prostitution. Seabrook got the confession of a German who practised this kind of trafficking with two Thai 'wives', and of a young Thai woman married to a Swiss man who had brought her to Europe to live off of her earnings as a prostitute.

12. After all, even in the past, at the time of regulation and brothels, autonomous prostitution practices always pertained to a small number of prostitutes. This does not mean that it does not exist. In Brazil, for example, Jeferson Afonso Bacelar's study, *Familia da prostituta*, Editora Atica, São Paolo, 1982, shows how this type of prostitution is very common in poor districts and shanty towns.
13. Thailand, in any case, represents a separate case, precisely because of the choice made by the government in the 1960s to promote the sex industry for the American soldiers stationed in Vietnam. The 'entertainment' sector or, sex industry, made a significant contribution to the rapid industrialization of the country in the 1970s. And even though the majority of the prostitutes' clients are Thai men, sex tourism was strongly encouraged at least up until a few years ago.
14. The conditions of Western prostitution, having reached an autonomous state, seem desirable to some Asian NGOs. The development of the sex industry in Thailand has taken advantage of the subordinate status of women, of a different idea of male and female sexuality, and at the same time, of a system of female responsibilities (for example, the responsibility which daughters have to their families, in terms of the financial support of the parents) (Boonchalanski, Guest, 1994). Because of this, in Thailand, the associations for prostitute support that try to help them through the practice of 'empowerment,' augur the autonomous state of the Western prostitutes for the women of these countries.
15. The issue of the break-up of the family structure and its consequences in terms of social inconvenience is complex. Professor Kua of the University of Bangkok, cited by Seabrook (1996), illustrates how, thanks to the work of the prostitutes in Bangkok, it is possible to support the elderly who care for the children in the villages – a type of extended family. We have found few studies on this topic. The break-up of the family structure seems to be at the root of trafficking (the sale of sons and daughters) and the prostitution of women; only in certain contexts is it a consequence. Elements of traditional culture or community values seem to, in some cases, be combined with a consumeristic push to promote the entry of young women into the sex industry (such is the case, according to the study, of the community cultures of Northern Thailand, where money – and possibly a costly dowry – are more important than a woman's honour). We have not found studies on families of grandparents and children in villages supported by the prostitute daughters nor on the future of the new generations who grow up in this kind of family.

REFERENCES

Alberoni, F., and C. Baglioni (1961): *L'immigrato nella società industriale*, Bologna: Il Mulino.

Appleyard, R., T. Nagayama and C. Stahl (1993): *Conference on International Manpower Flows and Foreign Investment in the Asian Region*, Bangkok: IOM and ILO, no. 1035.

Becelar, J. (1982): *A Familia da prostituta*, Sao Paolo: Editore Atica.

Boonchalanski, W. and P. Guest (1994): 'Prostitution in Thailand', Institute of Population and Social Research. Mahidol University, Salaya, mimeo.

Caldwell, G., S. Galster and N. Steinzor (1997): 'Crime and Servitude. Global Survival Network'. Presentation at conference on The Trafficking of NIS Women Abroad, Moscow, Nov. 3–5, 1997.

Campani, G. (1989): 'Du Tiers Monde à l'Italie: une nouvelle migration féminine', *Revue Européenne des Migrations Inernationales*, 5/2, pp.29–47.

Campani, G. (1991): 'Donne immigrate' [immigrant women], in C. Cocchi (ed): *Stranieri in Italia*, Bologna: Istituto Cattaneo.

Carpentier, A. (1953): *Los pasos perdidos*, La Habana: Editorial Letras Cubana.

Castles, S. and M. Miller (1993): *The Age of Migration*, London: Macmillan
Castoriadis, C. (1998): 'Interview with Cornelius Castoriadis', *Le Monde Diplomatique*, Aug. 1998.
Cazals, A. (1995): 'Prostitution et proxenetisme en Europe', *La Documentation française, Paris*
CEC (1996):
Coria, C. and S. Torres (1986): 'La prostituciòn femenina: indagacion sobre determinantes no-economicas a partir de entrevistas testimoniales en mujeres que ejercen la prostitucion', International Meeting of Experts on the Social and Cultural Causes of Prostitution and Strategies against Procuring and Sexual Expoitation of Women, Madrid, mimeo.
Economist, 14–20 Feb. 1998.
ESCAP Group (1991): Promotion of Community Awareness for the Prevention of Prostitution, Bangkok, mimeo.
Gaidzanwa, R. (1985): *Rural Migration and Prostitution*, Madrid.
Garcia, C. (1994): 'Sex Trade: a multinational industry', paper presented to the conference Stopping Violence against Filipino Women: A Government and Community Responsibility, Melbourne, 6–7 October, mimeo.
'Informe sobre la Comunicacion de la Comision al Consejo y al Parlamento Europeo sobre la trata de mujeres con fines de explotacion sexual', 27 Nov. 1997.
IOM: 'Trafficking in Women for Sexual Exploitation'. National reports for Italy and Austria, mimeo.
Jeffreys, S. (1997): *The Idea of Prostitution*, North Melbourne: Spinifex.
Lim, L. (1989): 'The Status of Women in International Migration', background paper for meeting on International Migration Policies and the Status of Female Migrants, United Nations, mimeo.
Knuttson, K. (1996): 'Social Fields and Cultural Constraints: Reflections on Some Aspects of Globalization', in L. Arizpe (ed): *The Cultural Dimension of Global Change, an Anthropological Approach*, Paris: UNESCO.
Kyle, D. (1998): 'Transparent Economies and Invisible Workers: Human Smuggling under Global Economic Liberalism', presentation at a conference Dilemmas of Immigration Control in a Globalizing World, European University Institute, Florence, 11–12 June 1998.
Penn State Report (1992): international meeting of experts on sexual exploitation, violence and prostitution, Pennsylvania State University, UNESCO and Coalition Against Trafficking in Women.
Perpinan, M. Soledad (1986): 'Annotated Bibliography on prostitution in Asia and South East Asia', International Meeting of Experts on the Social and Cultural Causes of Prostitution and Strategies against Procuring and Sexual Exploitation of Women, Madrid, mimeo.
Pouillon, D (1986): 'Règlement et abolitionnisme: leurs effets sur l'exploitation sexuelle des femmes', Madrid, mimeo.
Quynh Hoa, D. (1993): 'Affaiblissement des ideaux, changement des valeurs: commercialisation du sexe dans le contexte mouvant de l'ouverture, au Vietnam', paper in conference 'Commerce du sexe et droits humains', Brussels, mimeo.
Ruggiero, V. (1997): 'Trafficking in Human Beings: Slaves in Contemporary Europe', *International Journal of the Sociology of Law* 25, pp.231–244.
Saffioti, H. (1986): 'Violence sexuelle et prostitution au Brésil contemporain', International Meeting of Experts on the Social and Cultural Causes of Prostitution and Strategies against Procuring and Sexual Exploitation of Women, Madrid, mimeo.
Salt, J. (1997): 'Reconceptualising Migration Space and Migratory Phenomena', paper presented at conference 'Central and Eastern Europe: New Migration Space', Pultusk, Poland, 11–13 December 1997, mimeo.

Santos, A. (1992): 'Gathering the Dust: The Bases Issue in the Philippines', in Sturdevant and Stoizfus (1992).

Santos, A. (1992a): 'Picking up the pieces of women's lives: prostitution and sexual exploitation in Asia-Pacific', paper submitted to World Health Organization, May 1992, mimeo.

Seabrook, J. (1996): *Travels in the Skin Trade*, London and Chicago: Pluto Press.

Sturdevant, S. and B. Stoltzfus (1992): *Let the Good Times Roll: Prostitution and the U.S. Military in Asia*, New York: New Press.

Tamzali, W (1992): 'The Madrid Report: International Meeting of Experts on the Social and Cultural Causes of Prostitution and Sexual Exploitation of Women (UNESCO 1986), in Penn State Report (1992).

Tamzali, W. (1997): 'La criminalité organisée et les trafics d'êtres humains', in *Actes de la Conférence de Bruxelles: Commerce du sexe et droits humains*, 6 March 1993.

Torres, S. (1986): 'Abordaje a la compresion de la prostituciòn feminine desde una perspectiva feminista', Madrid, mimeo.

Ziegler, J. (1998): *Les Seigneurs du Crime*, Paris: Seuil.

ABSTRACTS

Where Free Markets Reign: Aliens in the Twilight Zone
Martin Baldwin-Edwards

Immigrants arrived almost unnoticed in southern European countries in the 1980s, and found its governments ill-prepared. Weak entry controls and large informal sectors, alongside a virtual impossibility of legal employment, led to expanding informal economies and immigrant niches within them. Policy responses have been directed exclusively at the immigrants themselves – border controls, legalization programmes, deportations – whilst ignoring the structural context, which continues to encourage further illegal immigration. Conformity with Europe-wide measures has done little to address fundamental issues and, through an exclusionary mentality, has probably created more illegality. It is concluded that although the 'problem' of unwanted immigration has been contained, the reactive nature of most policy-making has led to denial of longer-term issues. Thus the location of immigrant communities in southern European societies has yet to be determined: its contestation may, or may not, prove problematic.

A Survey of the Economics of Illegal Migration
Andreas Jahn and Thomas Straubhaar

This contribution gives a short survey of the economic discussions on illegal migration. It starts with two major statements. First, illegal migration is itself determined by migration legislation defining who may enter, stay and/or work legally and therefore who is illegal. If there were no legal barriers to entry, residence or work – as pertains within nation states, or for EU nationals within the European Union – illegal migration would be a non-issue. Secondly, there is a demand for illegal immigrants by certain vested interest groups. They influence the political/economic process in such a way that migration laws are not enforced strictly. Next we discuss several policy options to deal with illegal migration – external border controls, internal controls, employer sanctions and amnesty programmes. We conclude that as a short-term policy, employer sanctions are the most effective instrument to reduce incentives for the illegal employment of aliens. However, illegal employment of both natives and foreigners is the result of inefficiencies in the labour market. Finding and eliminating the causes and nature of these inefficiencies provides the only possible long-term strategy to reduce economic incentives for illegal immigration. A good labour market policy is the only valid option for combating illegal employment.

Illegality, Enlightenment and Ambiguity: A Hot Italian Recipe
Giovanna Zincone

Studying Italian immigration policy gives the author a chance to reconsider public policy making patterns, particularly ones concerning social issues. Innovative measures addressed to low social strata – at least in Italy – often originate in benevolent illegal practices introduced by sympathetic civil servants and social workers, pressed and supported by voluntary sector associations, charities and unions. Practices promoted by lobbying are, step by step, embodied in local administration and social services directives and circulars, and then diffused and standardized over the national territory by central government circulars. Senior public administrators and expert committees eventually filter and integrate these practices in the light of comparative policy studies and with a view to possible political outcomes; also they polish, adapt, and correct the practices to translate them into bills of law. Parliament will discuss and amend them according to party and intra-party alignments. The actual legislation will be the outcome of fights and compromises; even so, a good share of enlightment (expert committees) and benevolence (low strata lobbying) will still be present in the final product. Legislation originating from benevolent illegal practice will in turn be partially eroded by *malevolent* illegal practice, by circulars and decrees illegally used in fields constitutionally protected by law. A remarkable share of the decision making process takes place sheltered from party conflicts, from parliamentary action or from public opinion. This sort of 'extra-political' policy tends to greater significance when new party elites come to power, and to lesser when the new elite becomes established.

The Mass Legalization of Migrants in Italy: Permanent or Temporary Emergence from the Underground Economy?
Emilio Reyneri

Most migrants entered Italy without a residence permit and were legalized afterwards. The three legalization campaigns over ten years were the largest in Europe. However, even when migrants became entitled to regular employment, a large proportion of them went on taking unregistered jobs, thereby running the risk of failing to renew their permits. Measures aimed at making migrant workers emerge from their illegal status as well as from the underground economy had only partial and temporary success because of the large domestic underground economy, which is able to attract those migrants who are prone to accept illegal stay and irregular working conditions. The article shows in particular the outcomes of the last legalization in 1996, analyzing the administrative data and also focusing on fieldwork in the metropolitan area of Milan.

Immigrants in the Spanish Labour Market
Ubaldo Martínez Veiga

Data from a 1994 survey of immigrants show poor correlation of previous professions with current employment in Spain, along with a much-reduced range of semi-skilled occupations – the 'disqualification' phenomenon. Apparent ethnic specialization also is noted, and analyzed as networked or chain migration. The dual labour market hypothesis is examined, and tested in three areas – construction, domestic service and agriculture. It is concluded that the first two are clearly segmented, with immigrants confined to the secondary sector; in the case of agriculture, natives are competing with immigrant workers. This is the only area found where wage and other forms of discrimination are evident.

Italian and Spanish Labour Leaders' Unconventional Immigration Policy Preferences
Julie R. Watts

The expanding global market challenges state capacity to control immigration, the competitiveness of highly regulated labour markets and traditional union organization, and in turn helps to shape the immigration policy preferences of Italian and Spanish labour leaders. Most labour leaders believe that restrictive immigration policies marginalize immigrant workers, undermining the wages and working conditions of natives. Therefore – contrary to the conventional wisdom that unions favour restrictive policies to protect native workers from cheap immigrant labour – most Spanish and Italian labour leaders reason that moderate immigration policies improve the stability of immigrants, which ultimately benefits both native and immigrant workers.

Multicultural Insertions in a Small Economy: Portugal's Immigrant Communities
David Corkill and Martin Eaton

This article presents an overview of the immigrant communities in Portugal, a country with a long tradition of emigration which has now become an entry point into the EU and a net importer of labour. It examines the integration process into Portuguese society with particular reference to the labour market. The question of racist attitudes and tolerance to foreigners is discussed, and an assessment made of immigration legislation, including the asylum laws. It is argued that as Portugal's immigrant policy has been 'Europeanized' (in line with EU arrangements), so it has posed awkward questions concerning the country's handling of its immigrant communities.

Immigration, Clandestine Work and Labour Market Strategies: The Construction Sector in the Metropolitan Region of Lisbon
Jorge Macaísta Malheiros

This article discusses the role of foreign workers in the Portuguese labour market, relating the recent changes in the labour market with the need for foreign workers to satisfy the demand in some sectors. Focusing on the secondary labour market, namely in the sectors that require temporary and flexible work (such as construction and public works), an overview is presented of the strategies supporting clandestine work. Using the example of the construction sector in the Metropolitan Area of Lisbon, the role of diverse agents (firms, sub-contractors, workers, state institutions and trade unions) in this network of informal labour is discussed – as well as the different forms of vulnerability to which the foreign clandestine workers are exposed.

Greece: The Contours of a Fragmented Policy Response
Martin Baldwin-Edwards and Rossetos Fakiolas

Greece has experienced sudden massive inflows of immigration in the 1990s, predominantly from Albania. Lurching between exclusionary ideology and practical permissiveness, policy has been incoherent. A delayed regularization programme is now in operation, but proceeding slowly and potentially problematically. Police and bureaucrats' complicity in the trafficking and forced prostitution of migrants has emerged as an extensive phenomenon. Using a tripartite analytic framework, it is argued that different state agencies and actors have pushed different policies for different reasons. Overall, state capacity to react has been weak and defective.

Socio-Spatial Dynamics and Exclusion of Three Immigrant Groups in the Athens Conurbation
Theodoros Iosifides and Russell King

Based on 135 interviews with three of the main immigrant nationalities in Athens, including Albanians, Egyptians and Filipinos, this article explores immigrants' 'place' in the city. After brief sections on the new trends of immigration to Greece, the nature of Athens as a southern European city and the methodology of the research, the empirical material of the paper is presented in three main parts: immigrants' experiences of work and the labour market in Athens; the significance of space and place for the immigrants; and their living and housing arrangements. Each of these dimensions of work, space and housing acts to confirm immigrants' social exclusion in the city, reinforced by their undocumented or 'illegal' status. The concluding section of the paper attempts to situate migrants in the economy and society of Athens at a more theoretical level.

Trafficking For Sexual Exploitation and the Sex Business in the New Context of International Migration: The Case of Italy
Giovanna Campani

Female migration and related prostitution are not a new phenomenon; however, transnational trafficking of migrants for the sex industry is specifically a feature of the 1990s. Its cause appears to be the globalization of the sex industry, in the context of open borders for capital and trade movements but closed borders for people and labour. Looking at a case study of Italy, an ambiguity of policy is identified: opposition to trafficking on human rights and public health grounds, alongside government reluctance to target profitable industries. It is concluded that there is a need to oppose raw neoliberalism with cultural values common to both sending and receiving countries, in order to attack the roots of the problem.

BIOGRAPHICAL NOTES

Martin Baldwin-Edwards is a graduate of The University of Manchester where subsequently he lectured, as well as at the University of Hull and Manchester Metropolitan University. He was Jean Monnet Fellow in International Migration at the European University Institute, Italy for the academic year 1997/8 and is Editor of *South European Society & Politics*. Publications include *The Politics of Immigration in Western Europe* (ed., with Martin Schain, 1994), 'The Emerging European Immigration Regime', *Journal of Common Market Studies* 35/4 (1997) and two recent papers on the Greek legalization (*Greek Labour Yearbook 1997* and University of Reading Working Papers). Forthcoming are 'Immigrants and the Welfare State in Europe', in D. Massey and J. Arango (eds): *Migration at Century's End* (Oxford University Press) and (with C. Safilios-Rothschild) 'Immigration and Unemployment in Greece: Attitudes, Perceptions and Realities'. He is currently preparing a monograph entitled 'European Immigration Regimes' (Macmillan, forthcoming).
Email: <baldwin-edwards@usa.net>

Giovanna Campani is Professor of Education at the University of Florence.
Email: <campani@CESIT1.UNIFI.IT>

David Corkill is Reader in Iberian Studies at Manchester Metropolitan University. He has written widely on Portugal's economy and politics. He published *The Portuguese Economy Since 1974* (Edinburgh University Press, 1993) and numerous articles, including 'Multiple identities, racism and immigration in Spain and Portugal' in B. Jenkins and S. Sofos (eds.), *Nation and Identity in Contemporary Europe* (Routledge, 1996) and 'The Iberian Economies: Divergence to Convergence?' in B. Foley (ed.), *European Economies since the Second World War* (Macmillan, 1998). His new book 'The Development of the Portuguese Economy: a Case of Europeanization' will be published by Routledge in 1999.
Email: <D.Corkill@mmu.ac.uk>

Martin Eaton is Lecturer in European Regional Development with research interests in economic and industrial geography. He focuses on labour market issues, migration and development funding. His recent collaborative work with the *Universidade Nova* in Lisbon has resulted in publications such as 'Portuguese Child labour: Manufacturing for Change or Continuing Exploitation in the Textiles Industry', *Childhood, a Global Journal of Child Research* (1998, with C. P. Silva) and 'Foreign Residents and Illegal Immigrants in Portugal', *International Journal of Intercultural Relations* (1998).

Rossetos Fakiolas is Emeritus Professor of Economics at the National Technical University, Athens. He was the Greek OECD-SOPEMI correspondent 1991–95 and has been a member or chairman of many Greek government and trade union

committees and employer associations. In 1995/96 he was resident in the Russian Federation managing an EU-TACIS Project on 'How to Address the Social Consequences of the Newly-Established Market Economy' and has participated in several OECD and EU research projects on the Soviet Union. His publications include books and articles on Soviet economics, the application of new technology, migration, trade unions, industrial relations and social security.
Email: <fakiolas@netor.gr>

Theodoros Iosifides has recently finished a D.Phil at the Sussex European Institute, University of Sussex, on recent labour migration to Athens. He is currently doing his military service in Greece.

Andreas Jahn has a PhD from the College of Europe in Hamburg and is now working with the Urlaubs- und Lohnausgleichskasse in Wiesbaden. He has presented papers on illegal migration at several international meetings, among them the CEPR Workshops in Halkidiki (1995) and Athens (1997).

Russell King is Professor of Geography, Dean of the School of European Studies and Director of the Sussex Centre for Migration Research, all at the University of Sussex. Recently he has edited, with Richard Black, *Southern Europe and the New Migrations* (Sussex Academic Press, 1997). He also edited *Mass Migrations in Europe* (Wiley, 1995) and *The New Geography of European Migrations* (Belhaven, 1993).
Email: <r.king@sussex.ac.uk>

Jorge Macaísta Malheiros is Lecturer in the Department of Geography of the Faculdade de Letras, University of Lisbon, where he is researching South Asian immigrants and the problems of immigrant groups in Portuguese cities at the Centro de Estudos Geográficos. His previous published works include *Imigrantes na Região de Lisboa: os anos da mudança* (Lisbon: Colibri, 1996), 'Indians in Lisbon: Ethnic Entrepreneurship and the Migration Process', in R. King and R. Black (eds.), *Southern Europe and the New Immigrations*, (Sussex UP, 1997) and 'Communautés Indiennes de Lisbonne', *Revue Européenne des Migrations Internationales* 12/1, 1996.
Email: <jmalheiros@hotmail.com>

Emilio Reyneri is Professor of Sociology at the Faculty of Sociology, University of Milan Bicocca. He also teaches Economic Sociology at the Faculty of Economics, University of Parma. He is a member of the Italian Government Committee to monitor migrants' integration policies. He has written extensively on Italian and comparative labour market and labour policy. His last publications include *Sociologia del mercato del lavoro* (Bologna: Il Mulino 1996) and *Occupati e disoccupati in Italia*, Bologna: Il Mulino 1997). In English he has recently published 'The Role of the Underground Economy in Irregular Migration to Italy: Cause or Effect?', *Journal of Ethnic and Migration Studies* 2, 1998.
Email: <emilio.reyneri@sociologia.unimi.it>

Thomas Straubhaar is a full time Professor of Economics of the University of the Bundeswehr Hamburg and a Director of the Europa-Kolleg Hamburg. He is also

a Research Fellow of the Centre for Economic Policy Research (CEPR), London. He has written several articles about migration in professional journals, including *International Migration Review*, *International Migration* and *Weltwirtschaftliches Archiv*. He has published *On the Economics of International Labor Migration*, (Bern/Stuttgart/Wien: Paul Haupt 1988) and (with Peter A. Fischer) *Migration and Economic Integration in the Nordic Common Labour Market*, (Copenhagen: Nordic Council of Ministers, 1996). Most recently he has acted as a guest editor of a Special Issue 'Illegal Migration', *Journal of Population Economics* 12/1 (1999).
Email: <Thomas.Straubhaar@unibw-hamburg.de>

Ubaldo Martínez Veiga is Professor of Anthropology at the Universidad Autónoma de Madrid. His most recent publications are *La integración social de los Inmigrantes Extranjeros en España* (Madrid: Trotta, 1997) and *Pobreza, segregación espacial y exclusión social. La vivienda de los inmigrantes extrajeros en España* (Barcelona: Icaria, 1999).
Email: <ubaldo.martinez@uam.es>

Julie R. Watts is Post-Doctoral Fellow at the European Union Center in California. This article is adapted from her dissertation, which compares the immigration policy preferences of labour unions and employers in Spain, Italy and France. Other publications include 'Strange Bedfellows: How Spanish Labor Union Leaders and Employers Find Common Ground on Immigration' (*Policy Studies Journal*, Winter 1998/99).
Email: <jrw1723@is.nyu.edu>

Giovanna Zincone is Professor of Political Sociology at the University of Turin and President of the Committee for the integration of immigrants in Italy (attached to the Presidency of the Council, Department of Social Affairs. She was a member of the two Committees that prepared the present law (March 1998) on the legal status of immigrants in Italy. Recent essays in English include 'The Powerful Consequences of Being too Weak. The Impact of Immigration on Democratic Regimes', *Archives Européennes de Sociologie* (1997) no. 1; 'Multiculturalism from Above: Italian Variation on a European theme' in R. Baubock and J. Rundell (eds.), *Blurred Boundaries: Migration, Ethnicity, Citizenship* (Ashgate, 1998); 'Citizenship Between State and Society', open distance learning course "European Comparative Gender and Politics". Her latest books are *Uno schermo contro il razzismo* (Donzelli, 1994) and *USA con cautela* (Donzelli, 1995).
Email: <zincone@cisi.unito.it>

INDEX